DATE DUE

D0072589

Pretty in Punk

Pretty in Punk

Girls' Gender Resistance in a Boys' Subculture

Lauraine Leblanc

Rutgers University Press

New Brunswick, New Jersey, and London

Library of Congress Cataloging-in-Publication Data

Leblanc, Lauraine, 1968–
    Pretty in punk : girls' gender resistance in a boys' subculture /
Lauraine Leblanc.
      p. cm.
    Includes bibliographical references and index.
    ISBN 0–8135–2650–7 (cloth : alk. paper). — ISBN 0–8135–2651–5
(pbk. : alk. paper)
    1. Teenage girls—Psychology.   2. Teenage girls—Attitudes.
3. Punk culture. 4. Sex role. 5. Sex differences (Psychology).
6. Gender identity. I. Title.
HQ798.L43   1999
305.235—dc21   98–51532
                                                      CIP

British Cataloging-in-Publication data for this book is available from the British
Library

Manufactured in the United States of America

Dedication

*I have, since the very start of this project, always kept in mind
fourteen young women whose voices, dreams, and chances were
ripped from them in Montreal on December 6, 1989:*

Geneviève Bergeron
Hélène Colgan
Nathalie Croteau
Barbara Daigneault
Anne-Marie Edward
Maud Haviernick
Barbara Maria Klucznik
Maryse Laganière
Maryse Leclair
Anne-Marie Lemay
Sonia Pelletier
Michèle Richard
Annie St-Arneault
Annie Turcotte

Still, we mourn you. Still, we work for change.

Contents

List of Illustrations and Table

Acknowledgments

I'll start by presenting my undying gratitude to my mentors, Irene Browne, Robert Agnew, Tim Dowd, Alex Hicks, Mary Odem, and Wendy Simonds. Thank you all for your patience, wisdom, encouragement, support, comments, critiques, and occasional levity (your April Fool's Day prank will not be forgotten soon). Thanks as well to the faculty, staff, and graduate students of the Sociology Department and the Institute for Women's Studies of Emory University.

Field research was funded by a summer grant from the Graduate School of Arts and Sciences of Emory (Montreal research) and by a 1994–1995 Abigail Associates Grant for the study of girls and self-esteem from the Abigail Quigley McCarthy Center for Women's Research, Resources, and Scholarship at the College of St. Catherine in St. Paul, Minnesota (New Orleans and San Francisco sites). Writing was supported by a 1996–1997 American Dissertation Fellowship from the American Association of University Women, who continue the vital work of bringing much-needed attention to the development of girls.

On that note, I want also to acknowledge the contribution made, unbeknownst to them, by two authors to my sanity as this project progressed: Lorrie Sprecher and Francesca Lia Block, thank you both so much for understanding and writing about punk girls with such cool love.

Thank you, Carol Stack, for helping me order my chapters and pull things together. Thank you, Kathleen Blee, for your excellent comments and suggestions for revision. Thank you (again), Wendy Simonds and Randy Malamud, for your excellent advice on publishing and for feeding me a nutritious and delicious meal every week. Finally, thank you, Martha Heller, for your excellent guidance, for believing in my work, and for valuing the integrity of these girls' lives. Thank you, Susannah Driver-Barstow and Marilyn Campbell, for your meticulous editing.

To Thérèse Caouette Leblanc, my mom, and my dad, Ludovic Leblanc, thank you for loving me. To my dogs, Floyd (who was there at the start and stuck around long enough to see me through), Lucky, Karma, Chance, and Buddy, thanks for not chewing up too much of the manuscript. To Christina Jams, Jan Doehring, and Don Wentworth, thank you for giving me shelter during my field research. Thanks especially to you, Tommy Ross, director of the Project Home drop-in center for homeless youths in New Orleans, for the assistance you provided to me in my research and to the kids always.

Thank you, Danielle Rabel, for allowing me to use your photographs and for always being unfailingly encouraging as I described what I was trying to do. Thank you, Lorraine "I Spell My Name Wrong" Muller and 'Becca Cragin, for letting me use your pictures as well.

Finally, I extend my extreme gratitude to all the punks, and especially the punk girls who welcomed me into their world and encouraged me in my efforts to represent your lives. Alexea, Allie, Amalia, Andie, Anna, Arizona, Ava, Basilisk, Camille, Candace, Carina, Carnie, Cathy, Chloe, Clara, Connie, Cora, Courtney, Denise, Elle, Emily, Hallie, Jennie, Jessie, Joanie, Justine, Lisa, Lola, Lydia, Mina, Nikita, Rosie, Rudie, Sheila, Sloopy, Sophie, Stone, Sue, Tori, and Wanda (you know who you are) thank you for trusting me, for telling me your stories, and especially for having the courage to fight to remain true to yourselves. Be strong and resist always.

Pretty in Punk

"Not My Alma Mater"
A Vitriolic Prologue

Montreal, May 1984

I got kicked out of high school today. I can't fucking believe it. I have an A average and I've never gotten a detention or even so much as a demerit point and those fuckers go and kick me out. Fucking assholes.

It's not like I was doing anything that I don't usually do. I was hanging out at my locker wearing my spraypainted "Eat Dirt and Die" shirt that I made and the vice principal walks by and tells me not to wear That Shirt anymore. Totally out of the blue. I've been wearing this shirt two, maybe three times a week for the past six months, and today he decides I can't wear it anymore. Dickwad.

Then later I'm in technical drawing and he comes back and takes me out of class. He makes me go to the principal's office and they tell me not to come to school anymore looking like this. I tell them to call my mom and she shows up and totally supports them. I mean, I know she hates the way I look, but this has BULLSHIT written all over it in mile-high letters and everyone's acting like it's totally my fault.

The v. p. tells me that I'm distracting the other students. Sure, when I got my mohawk, the lady who runs the cosmetology department asked me not to hang around there because I scare the old ladies who come in to get their hair dyed blue (now, that's a joke) by the girly-girls. So I try, but it's kind of hard to do with my locker right down the hall and my technical drawing class right across from cosmetology. Still. I sit in the back of the class all the time, so

1

there's no reason why they should say I'm distracting everybody. Besides which, my hair's been like this for six, seven months now. Get over it already.

Then the v. p. says that I'm just trying to be like this girl whose picture's in my locker. What the fuck? The only reason Ms. Wendy O Williams of the Plasmatics graces my locker door is because she looks like me, not the other way around. I had a big, blonde fin way before I'd ever seen one on anybody else. And when's the last time they saw me standing on a tank wearing nothing but leather underwear? Please. "Besides," I tell them, "if anyone's going to be like anyone else, you should want your other students to be like me. I'm the one that gets straight A's and has never got a detention." Right, assholes?

Okay. That didn't go over so well. The principal says that the way I dress is indecent. Like, the first time I came to school in ripped-up fishnets, spike heels, thigh-high red mini, spiked belt, ripped-up T-shirt (no skin, though), lace gloves, full geisha make-up and full-up fin, I brought a pair of jeans. I knew I was pushing it. Did they say anything then? No. But everyone else did. For some reason, the little peckerhead boys in this school thought I was trying to be sexy, just like these asswipes are thinking now. Guess again. I'm just taking what they and their society thinks is sexy and I'm making it ugly, because that's what it is. Get it? Guess not.

So I'm outta here. I got one year of high school left and they've just kicked their smartest student out of their ugly dumb-ass building. They just don't get it. Well, fuck 'em if they can't take a joke.

Atlanta, March 1998

Although these events occurred half a lifetime ago, their effects of linger in my life, their repercussions defining my present and shaping my future. Had I not been expelled from Rosemere High School, I would probably be a draftsperson, maybe even an architect or civil engineer, today. This particular episode remains a fresh and vivid memory. I can still recall the precise shade of the brown carpet in the principal's office, the placement of the cheap office furniture. Even more distinctly, I remember how I felt: bewildered, frustrated, angry, powerless. It was like a bad anxiety dream, the kind where you talk or scream but no sound comes out. Of course, in reality, I was talking out loud. But still no one heard me.

If you had asked me, then, who I was, what I was doing, and what I had to say, I would have told you that I was protesting The Injustice of The System. I would have told you that I was not trying to anger people, but to scare them, to wake them up. I would have told you, perhaps not in these words, that I

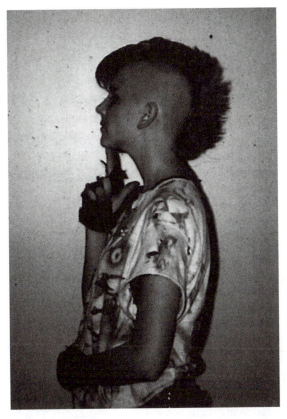

_____ *Illustration 1* _____
The hairstyle and shirt that precipitated these events
(*Photo: T. Leblanc*)

was not trying to be sexual or indecent, but that, although still a virgin, I was mocking female sexuality through parody. I would have told you how becoming a punk was, for me, the ultimate in self-empowerment—that I had moved from a position of victimization, as the smartest, dorkyest, most persecuted girl in school, to one of agency, as a person in control of my self-presentation. I would have told you how I had gone from being a social outcast to being a core member of a marginal group, that it was no longer the case that the world was against me, but rather that I was against the world.

I would have told you how punk saved my life. I recall, ever since elementary school, being told by boys—often, and to my face—that I was ugly. A smart, myopic, francophone, working-class girl, I was all the wrong things in my school's social circles. Not only did I wear large glasses, but my parents could not afford to dress me in the latest designer jeans and Lacoste shirts that denoted mid-eighties preppie cool. Before I became a punk, my "ugliness" humiliated me. I walked hunched over, staring at the floor, so ashamed of my appearance that I did not dare look anyone in the face. The tough, older kids in the back of the school bus taunted me, threatened me, and threw rotten lunch remains at me as I got off the bus in the afternoon. This was in part what precipitated my rejection of social norms and my entry into the world of punk. Of course, none of these objective circumstances changed when I became a punk; I stopped wearing my glasses and shaved my head, but, in fact, my persecution only increased. What did change was how I felt about myself. After I became a punk, when I was confronted with negative evaluations of my supposed ugliness, I had the strength to turn the tables on these assailants, to reply, "Yeah, but at least *I'm* ugly on purpose."

My peers, the other punks in my high school, understood this, and didn't have to ask what I was doing, or what I had to say. With ease and simplicity, they adopted me as one of their own, just another rebel in the ranks of the high school rejects. As a matter of fact, no one ever asked me, not even the administrators of my high school on the day they expelled me for transgressing their (gender?) norms. I distinctly recall sitting in the principal's office that day, listening to their declarations that my hairstyle was disrupting class and that I was a bad influence on the other students. As much as I tried to defend my appearance and my actions, they tried to force their interpretation on me. It made no sense to me then, and it doesn't to this day. To tell you the truth, it *still* pisses me off.

It seemed at the time that everyone had a theory about who I was, what I was doing, and what I was declaring, and people often "shared" these with me, in a most unpleasant and confrontational manner. No one ever asked me, or really listened to what I was saying. I was dying (dyeing?) to tell people what was on my mind. My adoption of the punk style was an attempt at communicating what I thought and felt about nuclear war, sex, religion, language, politics, racism, classism, or any other topic, but no one wanted to hear it. I was a fifteen-year-old girl challenging the entire world on a number of fronts, but no one cared to listen.

When I became an academic, my interest in feminist theory, cultural studies, and social science methodology led me to investigate the literature on punks and on girls in general. Today, having read numerous ethnographies, histories, theories, and reports, it seems to me that no one really knows what punk girls, or any girls, have to say, because few adults care to ask. I found the same misinformation and lack of understanding in many of these texts as I had found in the administrators of my high school, not to mention my former schoolmates. So, over a decade after being expelled from high school, now a feminist and a researcher, it occurred to me: why not tell not only my story, but that of other punk girls as well? I knew these girls had plenty to say about their positioning in society; why not just ask them? And so, I did.

One

"The Punk Girl Thing"

Introductions

"The punk guys will really overpower what the punk girls have to say. I think the punk girl thing is a very aggressive scene, and very assertive and aggressive girls tend to get into it. I don't know many passive, timid little girls who are going to shave their heads and look like a freak, take harassment from everybody all the time, and then fight off the guys in the scene."

"Then why do it?" I thought, as Sue made this statement. Sue, a petite self-described former "little pixie model" with a six-inch-long green mohawk, was only the second girl I interviewed during my research.[1] Like me, she felt troubled about the male-dominated gender dynamics in the punk subculture, a subculture that portrays itself as being egalitarian, and even feminist, but is actually far from being either. Yet, like me, she had found that this same subculture gave her a place to be assertive and aggressive, to express herself in less "feminine" ways than other girls. It is this paradox that led me to this research: on the one hand, punk gave us both a place to protest all manner of constraints; on the other, the subculture put many of the same pressures on us as girls as did the mainstream culture we strove to oppose. Punk had been the instrument of my liberation and self-empowerment. When I started this research, I wanted to discover whether this was the case for other girls; I wanted to know how other girls within the punk subculture had negotiated this paradox. It was with considerable pleasure that I found forty girls who agreed to discuss this with me, and it is my privilege to present their stories to you.

With considerable acumen, Sue described herself as "intelligent, but not educated fully." When we met, I was impressed by the aura of assurance she

_____ *Illustration 2* _____
Power pose: A mohawked girl with columns
(Photo: D. K. Rabel)

projected. At a mere fifteen years of age, she spoke at length about her commitment to anarchist politics as well as her plans to go to college and study broadcast communications. Why would such an articulate, thoughtful girl shave off most of her hair, dye the remainder green, and glue it into a mohawk upright on her head? Who are the "assertive and aggressive" girls she described? Why do such girls choose to contravene conventional norms of female beauty so as to "look like a freak," when their only reward is that they must not only "take harassment from everybody all the time," but then be forced to "fight off the guys in the [punk] scene"? What attracts these girls to male-dominated youth subcultures such as punk? What are girls' roles within the subculture? What role does the subculture play in their perceptions of themselves and in their self-esteem? How do punk girls, with their shaved heads and combat boots, view the cultural construction of adolescent femininity, the pretty, boy-crazy girl of teen magazines? How do they construct gender identities in a subculture that demands both masculine toughness and feminine compliance? What does their reconciliation of these contradictory expectations tell us about the construction of gender?

Girls in male-dominated youth subcultures such as punk continually confront ideologies of gender that remain largely invisible, perhaps even tacitly accepted, in many young women's everyday lives. Punk girls struggle to construct their gender within the confines of a highly male-dominated and therefore "masculinist" context. The punk subculture highly valorizes the norms of adolescent masculinity, celebrating displays of toughness, coolness, rebelliousness, and aggressiveness. Girls are present in the subculture, but the masculinity of its norms problematizes their participation. Thus, gender is problematic for punk girls in a way that it is not for punk guys, because punk girls must accommodate female gender within subcultural identities that are deliberately coded as male. How do they negotiate between these seemingly conflicting sets of norms?

As I explored these questions by seeking out explanations in cultural and sociological theories of youth and youth subcultures, I found no answers, as these, for the most part, have focused on male members, failing to address girls' subcultural participation. Turning to feminist theorists, I found that they also often failed to explore girls' active constructions of gender. In foregrounding the social construction of gender, these theorists have focused on girls' socialization, rather than on young women's resistance to and reformulation of these norms. Clearly, what punk girls were seeking to accomplish had remained unrecognized and undocumented. Yet how could their experiences of gender construction enhance our knowledge of female development? What stories could they tell us that would enrich our struggles to create better gender roles for generations of girls? I had begun this research with one question: How do punk girls reconcile a subcultural identity that is deliberately coded as masculine with the demands of femininity? What I found was that they use the punk subculture to construct various strategies of resistance to both mainstream and subcultural norms of femininity, strategies that hold broader implications for our thinking about girls' lives.

Sue's description of the "assertive and aggressive" girls of the punk subculture differs markedly from that of contemporary adolescent girls depicted in current research. Recently, a number of publications apprising us of the dire situation of girls' self-esteem have garnered much attention. As I began writing this chapter, therapist Mary Pipher's *Reviving Ophelia* (1994), based on her accounts of helping adolescent girls resist "lookism" (the tyranny of female beauty norms), was fourth on the *New York Times* bestseller list. Peggy

Orenstein's *Schoolgirls* (1994), a journalistic account of the impact of the "hidden curriculum" of gender roles on girls' self-esteem (and based on the 1991 and 1992 reports of the American Association of University Women), had just relinquished its place there. It was not only Americans who were alarmed by reports of adolescent girls' plummeting self-esteem; the Canadian Advisory Council on the Status of Women (CACSW) had released reports of its own that, like their U.S. counterparts, demonstrated that girls lose a sense of self-reliance as they progress through their adolescent years (1992; Holmes and Silverman 1992). These many reports argued that as girls grow, they fall victim to a socialization process that robs them of the qualities of self-reliance, efficacy, and assurance.[2] The girls Sue described seemed somehow to have circumvented that process. If they had, then their forms of resistance to the pressures of feminine socialization should surely be brought to the attention of those who seek to counter this debilitating process for all girls.

Girlhood to Womanhood: The Drop in Self-Esteem

Constructed as a transitional stage between childhood and adulthood, adolescence is a time of intense socialization into the adult role. This is the period when sexual identities gain salience and when adult gender role expectations come to the fore. Physically, this is the period when the puberty effects profound changes on boys' and girls' bodies. As a result, this time has become socially defined as the beginning of maturation; boys are expected to begin behaving as "men," and girls are often told that they are "women" at the onset of menstruation. This is also the developmental stage in which adolescents undergo profound psychological changes, a stage that is characterized by adolescents' uncertainties about their physical selves as well as intense questioning about their inner selves. Paradoxically, at this time, an adolescent is expected to gain a sense of identity, independence, and responsibility.

The development of autonomy in adolescence has important effects on current and later feelings of self-reliance and self-efficacy. The development of girls' self-images at this time is crucial to their future well-being. The findings of the studies cited above are not new. Studies of girls and self-esteem dating back to the early 1970s (when such research initiatives originated) have consistently demonstrated a gap between girls' development of qualities of self-reliance and autonomy and that of boys. As early as 1973, Janis Bohan's study of middle-class white adolescents showed that girls had lower self-concepts than did their male peers. Previous researchers had found that self-esteem rises throughout adolescence, but Bohan discovered that taking gender into account revealed significant gender differences in self-concept.

Since Bohan's findings, a number of further studies have documented various aspects of this self-esteem gender gap. They have found that girls are more likely than boys to have low self-esteem and high self-consciousness, and that this level of self-consciousness increases sharply in early adolescence. Adolescent girls are overly concerned with being liked, valuing others' opinions of themselves more highly than they do other forms of self-validation. Girls are especially concerned with achieving male approval, and with outward forms of validation through relationships. This can have negative consequences: although girls are trained to value relationships with, and the opinions of, others more highly than they value their own self-assessments, they also learn that the trait of relationality is deemed inferior to those virtues of independence and self-reliance that are reinforced throughout boys' development (see Rosenberg and Simmons 1975; Eder 1985; Feiring and Lewis 1991; Allgood-Merten and Stockard 1991).

This self-esteem gap is also affected by girls' growing consciousness of their physical development; girls' images of their bodies are intimately linked with their feelings of self-worth. The AAUW study (1991) revealed that girls are more likely than boys to point out physical characteristics, rather than skills or talents, as their best features. This focus on the physical becomes especially dangerous when assessments of one's physical features are negative. Girls routinely report that they are less satisfied with their body images than are their male peers; not surprisingly, this may be an important factor in young women's disproportionately high rates of eating disorders. Again, attributes that girls are taught to value, including physical attractiveness, are also the source of the majority of their negative self-evaluations (see Mintz and Betz 1985; Rauste-von Wright 1989).

It is not merely the case that girls have overall lower self-esteem than boys, but also that girls' self-esteem plummets as they progress through adolescence. The ongoing work of psychologist Carol Gilligan and her colleagues (Brown and Gilligan 1992; Gilligan, Ward, and Taylor 1988; Gilligan, Lyons, and Hanmer 1989) demonstrates that girls lose their "voice" as they mature. Girls not only become literally less audible, but their speech is more halting, less certain, their statements, when uttered at all, less assured. These findings are confirmed once again by the studies commissioned by the AAUW and the CACSW. The AAUW report notes: "Girls aged eight and nine are confident, assertive, and feel authoritative about themselves. Yet most emerge from adolescence with a poor self-image, constrained views of their future and their place in society, and much less confidence about themselves and their abilities" (1991:7). Like the AAUW, the CACSW (Holmes and Silverman 1992) discovered that throughout their adolescent years, girls rank themselves lower than males do in terms of their self-esteem and self-efficacy. Thus, as they mature, girls become less assertive, less confident, less vocal, and feel increasingly self-conscious and dependent upon others' approval in developing positive self-concepts.

What can account for girls' dramatic decline in self-esteem? In answering this question, researchers focus once again on girls' development in early adolescence, more specifically, on the process by which the norms of femininity become central in girls' lives. Many attribute girls' declining self-esteem to this process of feminine socialization. Again, over two decades ago, scholars had already begun to speculate that this drop in self-esteem may be due to girls' realization that the gender role that they are internalizing is deemed inferior to the male gender role. Thus, Bohan concludes: "As the adolescent girl comes to recognize that the role she is expected to assume as a female is relatively inferior in status and prestige to the male role, the assumption of her sex-role results in a corresponding decrease in her own evaluation of herself. That is, the adolescent girl accepts and incorporates society's evaluation of her role as inferior, and so values herself less" (1973:383).

As girls enter adolescence, they lose self-esteem in their attempt to conform to the constraints and demands of the female gender role. In her reevaluation of older women's narrative accounts of their youth, Emily Hancock discovered that "[s]elf-confidence yields to self-consciousness as a girl judges herself as others judge her—against an impossible feminine ideal. To match that ideal, she must stash away a great many parts of herself. She gives up being childlike in order to be ladylike. She loses her self-possession; she loses her sense of self as subject; she senses that she is now "other" and becomes an object in the male world" (1989:22).

This echoes Simone de Beauvoir's earlier existentialist account of female development; in becoming women, she argues, girls must first endure the "dementia and neurosis" of negotiating between their former girlish autonomy and the constraints of female sexuality and submissiveness. As early as 1949, de Beauvoir argued that "[t]o be feminine is to appear weak, futile, docile. The young girl is supposed not only to deck herself out, to make herself ready, but also to repress her spontaneity and replace it with the studied grace and charm taught by her elders. Any self-assertion will diminish her femininity and her attractiveness" (1989:336).

Thus, in the attempt to mold themselves to the impossible ideal of femininity, girls are asked to suppress positively valued attributes such as assertiveness, spontaneity, and self-possession in favor of attractiveness, docility, and passivity.

Despite the best efforts of various waves of the women's movements to challenge these damaging gender ideologies, sociocultural expectations of girls have remained constant in the past half-century. Again, sociologists find that adolescents' perceptions of sex roles have changed little since the second wave of feminism in the 1960s. In both 1975 and 1982, separate studies found that girls rated being female less highly than boys rated being male (see Bush, Simmons, Hutchinson, and Blyth 1977/8; Lewin and Tragos 1987). In fact, it may even be the case that girls' levels of self-esteem had actually *declined* since the late 1950s. The gender-role critiques sparked by the women's movements have failed to trickle down into adolescents' lives, and have yet produced a noticeable impact on adolescents' gender role expectations.

The "feminine" norms to which girls are still taught to aspire include an emphasis on appearance and the highlighting of relational skills. In the process of girls' socialization, these are valorized over such "masculine" attributes as competence, strength, and assertiveness. However, in the greater social context, the norms of femininity are construed to be inferior to those of masculinity. Socialization into adult femininity requires girls to abandon all vestiges of socially valorized masculine attributes. In this way, girls develop impoverished self-images, leading to lowered expectations and achievement. This places girls in a perilous situation. Those who achieve the feminine ideal can only come to the "realization" that they are inferior. Those who do not achieve the ideal must suffer the consequences of their "failure" in femininity.

Given that the norms of femininity command such a heavy toll on girls' self-concepts, it is crucial that we examine girls' encounters with these damaging gender ideologies. Feminist scholars have begun to evaluate critically the ways in which girls learn gender as well as the social forces that devalue femininity. Various theories of gender socialization explain the mechanisms of both internalized and external constraints, showing how femininity is imposed both from the outside environment and from internalized pressures (England and Browne 1992). Writing in the feminist journal *Signs,* Greer Litton Fox (1977) argued that the norms of femininity restrict women's lives; the "value constructs" of "good girl," "lady," and "nice girl" function as a form of social control. These norms, internalized throughout childhood and cemented in adolescent development as well as externally constraining through comparisons with the feminine ideals portrayed primarily in the media, are the very factors responsible for the gender gap, and decline, in girls' self-esteem.

Much of the research on girls and self-esteem follows the lead of socialization theories by documenting the ways that girls are traumatized by their encounters with these constraints. Such research portrays girls as victims of a culture that Pipher (1994) describes as "girl-poisoning"; contemporary film, television, music, and advertisements portray unattainable ideals of feminine beauty, ideals for which some girls would willingly starve to death if only they could approximate them. Pipher concludes: "To totally accept the cultural definitions of femininity and conform to the pressures is to kill the self" (44). To become a girl or a woman, then, is to lose subjectivity and strength, and with them, a strong sense of self.

In describing this process, these researchers depict girls as passive victims of feminine socialization, casting young women as dupes of cultural forces that systematically degrade us. Yet, however well this process of socialization into inferiority has been documented, few researchers adopt the view that girls are also agents in their construction of gender identities. Thus, few document the strategies of resistance that girls create to counter the pressures of socialization.[3] Given that these norms are so debilitating, it is vitally important that we unearth girls' strategies of resistance to these dominant models of femininity. Such accounts of resistance demand that we recognize girls not as passive victims of their gender role socialization, but as active subjects in their construction of gendered identities. The dominant norms of gender act as a set of rules dictating adolescent girls' constructions of selfhood. In the remainder of this work, I argue that, by joining male-dominated youth subcultures, girls construct forms of resistance to the dominant cultural models of femininity, and they do so at a critical time in their development. Although women and girls encounter the norms of the female gender role, in particular, femininity, on a daily basis, punk girls' struggles with these gender norms open their prescriptions to critical examination that they might not otherwise be accorded. What we can all learn from their struggles are the costs and rewards of struggling against femininity.

As I interviewed girls and observed their interactions with punk guys, with other punk girls, and with strangers, I found that they navigated through conflicts between the gender norms of punk and femininity by constructing strategies of resistance to traditional gender norms. In contrast to research concerning mainstream girls' lack of self-esteem, my research shows that punk girls, by positioning themselves outside of the mainstream culture, engage in active resistance to the prescriptions and proscriptions that overpower many contemporary adolescent girls. In negotiating between the norms of femininity and the masculinity of punk, these girls construct forms of resistance to gender norms in ways that permit them to retain a strong sense of self. Uncovering such strategies of resistance to female socialization is important, for, as Paula England and Irene Browne note in their work on internalization and constraint in women's subordination, "the resistance generated by domination sometimes gives rise to change" (1992:97). It is in resisting these gender norms that girls both subvert and challenge femininity, engaging in a reconstruction of its norms. Such reconstructions have important effects on our conceptualizations of gender and gender role socialization, as well as on girls' own self-assessments. Such reconstructions can also have important implications for the ways we view and react to adolescents' forms of gender resistance.

Re(de)fining Resistance

For such an important aspect in the daily lives of the subordinated (adolescents, women, people of color), "resistance" is a rather loose concept, one open to many interpretations. It is a central concept in feminist theorizing and politics; identifying strategies of resistance informs much of the research in feminist cultural studies. Importantly, in the context of this research, resistance is also central to theorizing and research on youth subcultures. By drawing from a Marxist cultural perspective, British theorists of the Birmingham school have identified resistance as the central factor in the formation of, and adolescents' participation in, a number of oppositional subcultures. Resistance has thus been broadly defined: in subculture theory, it can be found in working-class youths' construction of sartorial style, whereas in feminist cultural studies it often emerges in reports of women readers' subversive interpretations of texts. Resistance has thus been conceptualized in many ways. Yet, what is resistance? How can we reliably recognize and identify instances of resistance? In this section, I draw on subcultural and feminist conceptualizations, as well as on critical theories, in order to elaborate a more analytically and theoretically adequate definition of resistance.

Subculture Theory and Resistance

A number of U.S. and British theorists of youth subcultures have argued that engaging in subcultural deviance, that is, becoming a gang member, a skinhead, a punk, or a Mod, is a youthful way of constructing resistance to many of the strictures of everyday life. Most often, researchers define these constraints as inequalities attributed to class, less often to race, and almost never to gender. Sociologists have argued that, in entering a subculture, a (working-class) (white) (male) youth actively constructs a subject position that puts him at odds with the mainstream, dominant culture, thereby individually resisting the structural oppression *he* faces. Cultural theorists of the Birmingham Centre for Contemporary Cultural Studies (BCCCS) argued, in the early 1970s, that due to the specific class structures of British society, subcultures are best understood through the lens of Marxian cultural theory. This led the Birmingham school to focus on working-class youth subcultures, and especially on the forms of resistance exhibited by white working-class youths.

The Birmingham school's primary methodological approach to the study of youth subcultures was strongly influenced by emerging French theories of structuralism and semiotics, methods of analysis that examine large-scale systems by investigating the relations and functions of their smaller constituent parts. British researchers focused on symbolic cultural aspects of youth subcultures, such as music, language, and especially dress. In doing so, they constructed semiotic readings of the cultural artifacts of youth subcultures, analyzing these as sign systems, codes, and conventions, and focusing especially on the homology, or symbolic fit, between these elements. Birmingham school theorists posited that resistance to cultural norms is primarily conducted through the construction of such distinctive styles. These styles, they held, constitute resistances to the dominant culture, with Dick Hebdige (1979) arguing that subcultural adolescents engage in "semiotic guerrilla warfare" through their construction of style. Examining a variety of spectacular postwar subcultures such as Teddy boys, Mods, punks, and skinheads allowed such theorists to elaborate how such varied clothing styles constituted challenges to the dominant order.

Critic Lawrence Leong (1992) raises a series of important questions pertaining to this construction of stylistic resistance. The most pertinent to this discussion is a methodological critique: Leong points out that semioticians imputed resistance to sartorial acts without this being expressly articulated in subcultural members' own words. In these semiotic readings, resistance was attributed wholesale to parodies of both upper-class and working-class style—any mode of dress was resistant, it seemed, when worn by the right (or rather, the wrong) person. And yet, none of these researchers mention any explicit articulation on the part of any subcultural member explaining how any particular garb was designed to affront the dominant culture. At no point do these researchers record asking adolescents whether they use a certain type of shoe or an outlandish hairstyle in order to counter any specific political ideology or class oppression, or being told by them that they do. Indeed, Hebdige, the primary theorist of style, claimed that such resistance "may be conducted at a level beneath the consciousness of the individual members of a spectacular subculture" (1979:105). He argued that such resistance is clearly articulated to the researcher in the subculture's symbols, even though the subculture's members may not be aware of it, and thus unable to articulate their dissatisfaction. Yet, despite their lack of first-person accounts of resistance, semioticians argued that subcultural adolescents were engaged in constructing highly nuanced and subtle forms of resistance. For such an important concept in their theorizing (the main text of the Birmingham school is titled *Resistance through Rituals*), these scholars did remarkably little to define, rather than assume, attributions of resistance.

This reading of resistance highlights a methodological failing of the semiotic approach. Although the Birmingham school strongly advocated the use of ethnographic methods, its adherents seem largely to have constrained themselves within observational methods of data collection, rather than including the interview components that are such an important facet of this type of research.[4] Thus, they gathered no support from first-person, subjective accounts for this attribution of resistance. Although such semiotic readings are important and interesting, their failure to present accounts of intent in the construction of resistance seriously impugns their validity.

Feminist Accounts of Resistance

Feminist cultural studies also center around the construction of resistance. Whereas British subculture theorists retained a Marxian focus on class issues, feminist theorists view patriarchy (in its broad sense as male domination) as the primary oppressive order that women resist. Unlike subculture theorists, feminist cultural theorists foreground the subjectivity of the women we study. Using in-depth interviews, feminist researchers have probed and documented women's relations to texts and to other consumers of these texts. With methods derived from both the interpretivist (qualitative) perspective in sociology and the literary method of reader-response theory (see Fish 1980), feminist researchers have described women's constructions of resistant readings to texts as diverse as romance novels (Radway 1984), self-help literature (Simonds 1992), and television programs (Brown 1994; Press 1991). Feminist cultural researchers argue that in their consumption of mainstream texts, women create "resistant readings" (Fetterley 1978). That is, these women do not simply consume the surface meanings of texts, but instead construct their own meanings of even egregiously condescending (i.e., self-help) or sexist (i.e., romance) texts. Through the use of interview data, these researchers have argued that women readers create resistant interpretations of these texts. Janice Radway (1984), for example, found that a community of middle-class white women readers of romance novels not only drew from these the meaning of the surface text (erotic tension and resolution), but used their reading to resist traditional masculinity (the feminized man wins the woman), to claim time and space away from their domestic chores (resisting their role in the domestic economy), and to construct a community of women (other readers of romance novels).

The strength of these conceptualizations is that they emerge from a methodological perspective—interviewing—that is based on and values subjective accounts of the construction of resistance. However, like semiotic readings, these are overly dependent upon researchers' presentations of a still-underdefined resistance. Although studies such as these offer important insights into women's forms of opposition to mainstream cultural discourses, they often do not focus explicitly on the effects of such resistance in their lives. They fail to document whether these women feel that their resistant readings have any impact on their self-concepts or on the world around them.

Both subcultural and feminist concepts of resistance offer important insights into how resistance is constructed and how it can be discovered through research. Feminist cultural researchers point out that such resistance is not pure, but rather mediated between conflicting issues of accommodation to the dominant order and opposition to it—resisters, after all, remain within the social system they contest. The BCCCS theorists argue that style can be resistant, although they do not sufficiently account for the intent behind such resistances. Feminist cultural researchers, on the other hand, demonstrate that resistance can be constructed discursively, and that it is found in women's descriptions of their thoughts and actions. Although both offer valuable insights into both the construction of resistance and methodological strategies to uncover it, neither has produced a well-defined concept of resistance, its markers, and its effects.

Reconceptualizing Resistance

Whereas subculture theorists conceptualize resistance as stylistic, and feminist theorists consider discursive accounts, recent critics of resistance theorizing have begun to examine the behavioral forms of resistance constructed by oppressed individuals in their everyday lives. Anthropologist James Scott (1985) argues that the concept of resistance must include individual opposition to domination; he describes acts of resistance such as "slacking off" and sabotage among peasant workers as "weapons of the weak." Within the context of critical pedagogy, Henry Giroux (1983) further elaborates the meaning of such small acts of resistance. Youths engaging in oppositional behaviors that counter adult authority are often deemed deviant or in need of discipline. Giroux asserts that such behaviors have important political implications: "Resistance in this case redefines the causes and meaning of oppositional behavior by arguing that it has little to do with the logic of deviance, individual pathology, learned helplessness (and, of course, genetic implications), and a great deal to do, though not exhaustively, with the logic of moral and political indignation" (107). Whether conducted as individual acts or as part of a larger constellation (i.e., subculture) of resistance, such oppositional acts cannot be viewed simply as deviant, but should be recognized as political protests by members of disenfranchised groups.

This conceptualization of resistance highlights human agency in the struggle against domination, rather than presenting the dominated as passive victims oppression. Resistance implies action and a critique of domination. Attributions of resistance must be carefully evaluated, rather than ascribed wholesale to any manner of "oppositional behaviors." Giroux states, "resistance needs to be viewed from a very different theoretical starting point, one that links the display of behavior to the interest it embodies" (110). This is the basic definition of resistance I employ in this text: resistance is primarily, although not exclusively, a form of political behavior. Along with Giroux, I argue that accounts of resistance must detail not only resistant acts, but the subjective intent motivating these as well. Drawing from subculture theory and feminist research, I add to this that such resistance includes not only behaviors, but discursive and symbolic acts as well. This perspective supports Howard Becker's (1963) argument that deviance occurs within a political context; in rejecting gender norms, I argue, punk girls are not just deviant, but resistant as well.

In order to reconceptualize resistance in a politically and theoretically adequate manner, we must consider both subjective and objective accounts of resistance. This reconceptualization combines the strengths of semiotic readings with those of interpretivist accounts, and allows the strengths of each methodology to address the weaknesses of the other. In this conceptualization of resistance, an attribution of any type requires three distinct moments: a subjective account of oppression (real or imagined), an express desire to counter that oppression, and an action (broadly defined as word, thought, or deed) intended specifically to counter that oppression. The first two aspects of such an attribution of resistance require access to a person's subjective state, while the last account can be constructed either through observation or again through subjective narrative. It is crucial that the first two conditions hold before any observational account can be deemed resistant. That is, the person engaging in resistant acts must do so consciously and be able to relate that consciousness and intent. Such accounts, because they combine intention with action, may fail to capture some instances of resistance, but they do present criteria for making the strongest possible case for attributions of resistance. Such accounts are also important because the subjectivity of women, of adolescents, and especially of girls, remains an unexplored area in contemporary sociological research. Further, examining girls' subjective accounts of resistance thus casts a new light on our knowledge of adolescent female development. How can we go about finding such constructions of resistance in the lives of young women?

Once I had arrived, safe and sound—in one piece—in Atlanta for graduate school, my mother's relief was palpable. I imagine that she was anxious about our separation—we would now live 1,240 miles (more or less) from one another—but I also think that she was relieved and a little incredulous. You know, by now, that this research arose not only from an academic interest in youth, subcultures, and punk, but from my own extended participation in the subculture as well. From being expelled from high school, through repeated running away, to staying out until all hours of the night, I had put my parents through the wringer. When I was expelled from high school, I felt that my mother betrayed me. When I repeatedly ran away, she once hoped (as she later confessed to me) that I would not come home, and yet she came looking for me anyway. When I was fifteen and stayed out all night in bars with older kids, she waited up for me once, and then gave up. She told me that I should not count on her to raise any babies I might have as a teenager, nor to call her to get bailed out of jail. She took me to the doctor for birth control pills. She stipulated that my freedom was contingent upon my keeping up my grades. Then she let me go.

So when I graduated from M.I.N.D. (an alternative high school), and then from Dawson College, and then from McGill University, I could almost see the burden lifting from her shoulders. When I decided to pursue a doctorate, I could sense her incredulity, her realization that by letting me go to pursue my own ends, she had actually salvaged our relationship, which grew stronger as we both grew older. When I decided to write about punk, and specifically to conduct ethnographic and interview research on punk girls, I called her: "Hey, Mom," I declared, "Guess what? My youth wasn't wasted—it was just extended preparation for my field research!" She made soothing sounds about how she had never felt that my youth was wasted, but that was really *not* the feeling I got back then.

I realize today that we both have revisionist accounts of my past—I tend to believe that I was tougher, more political, and more assured than I really was, and she tends to believe that she was more supportive and accepting than I recall. We have both been told tales of my punk misbehavior, about how I beat up neighborhood kids and roughed up other punks, events of which I have absolutely no recollection (and assert plausible denial of any knowledge). As my cousin Martine, who once interviewed the fifteen-year-old punk me for a paper for her college psychology class, said to me: "*La memoire est une faculté qui oublie*" (Memory is a faculty which forgets). What I do know is that I emerged from a decade of punk with a good deal of assertiveness, a wide vocabulary of profanities, a penchant for looking out of place, a political stance at odds with that of most people I meet, and the perfect preparation for my field research. As my mom said in a recent conversation, "It paid off." I, of course, always knew it would. Right.

Thus far, I have claimed that by joining the punk subculture, punk girls seek refuge from mainstream gender norms. I have said that within the context of this male-dominated subculture, they must negotiate between their own femininity and the masculinity of punk. I have noted that punk girls do this in a situation in which they are pressured by male punks and by non-punks to conform to conflicting sets of expectations. I have argued that in constructing their gender, punk girls actively resist both the norms of femininity and those of punk. Following this, I have offered a definition of resistance that encompasses both objective and subjective accounts, and have stated that I would demonstrate (and celebrate) the ways in which punk girls construct and express such resistance in the face of ongoing oppressions. This argument sounds plausible to me, and given my liking for punk and its adherents, I would be inclined to believe it. You, however, can, and indeed, should require more proof than my word (although it really is my bond—trust me). In the remainder of this chapter, I describe how I arrived at such conclusions by presenting the epistemological and methodological underpinnings of my research, which I describe as belonging to the constellation of feminist research. Having found accounts of resistance in the words and deeds of punk girls, I have retroactively called this "an ethnography of resistance."

Ethnography of Resistance

The best methodological strategy to discover acts and accounts of resistance as I have defined it is ethnography. Otherwise known as "participant observation" or "field research," ethnography is a method of data collection and interpretation used by both anthropologists and sociologists. Ethnography immerses the researcher in the research, allowing, even requiring her to experience the world in some of the ways that its natives do. By combining observational and interview methods, ethnography presents researchers with a multi-methodological and thus highly reliable means to study people's lives. In ethnographic research, observations or interviews can serve to verify aspects of self-presentation observed by the researcher. As well, this leads to a richer source of findings, in allowing researchers to access both the "objective" and "subjective" aspects of lives, which provide the only types of accounts that can satisfy both the objective and subjective determinants of accounts of resistance. Thus, ethnography is one of the best tools that a researcher of resistance can use.

Ethnography as a methodology is not, however, without its weaknesses. As a research method, ethnography is subjective and ungeneralizable. As a "partial perspective,"[5] ethnography both offers a limited view of social phenomena ("partial" in the sense of incomplete) and asserts the validity of the perspectives of its participants ("partial" in the sense of favoring or biased). Feminist critic Judith Stacey (1988) also argues that ethnography is ethically dangerous, as it relies upon exploiting interpersonal relationships. However, ethnography has been the preferred method of feminists because of its many advantages: it can also give voice to the voiceless, bring critical attention to the disenfranchised, and offer fresh perspectives to sociologists and feminists alike.

My primary means in discovering punk girls' constructions of resistance to femininity is the phenomenology, or experiential account, of punk girls' everyday lives. Phenomenological research is a prime example of what Canadian sociologist Dorothy Smith (1979) calls "a sociology for women"; it starts from, focuses on, and validates women's experiences. This method shares two assumptions with feminist research: first, that no truly objective account can exist, and second, that lived experience requires attention and interpretation (Langellier and Hall 1989). This approach begins from the standpoints of women, and seeks to discover the meanings that women create in our everyday lives.

Phenomenology also privileges the subjectivity of participants in the research—those of the researcher and of the researched. The face-to-face interview is the prime means of conducting such research because it provides the clearest practical instantiation of the feminist research principle of intersubjectivity (Nelson 1989), as it relies upon interaction between the researcher and the researched. Thus, although my research does include the more traditional participant observation of ethnographic research, my primary source of data in this project is the phenomenological interviews that I conducted with punk girls.

Research Sites

From 1993 to 1995 I interviewed forty punk girls in four North American cities. I began by interviewing ten punk girls in Atlanta in 1993 and then spent my summers traveling throughout North America, interviewing girls in Montreal in the summer of 1994 and in New Orleans and San Francisco in the long, hot summer of 1995. My travels into these various punk scenes allowed me to meet more, and a greater diversity of, punk girls than I could have had I stayed in one place. My choice of cities was influenced by both pragmatic and research-based considerations: I was already familiar with both the Atlanta and Montreal scenes, and, with free accommodations in San Francisco and New Orleans, was able to conduct research in these areas very cheaply. These cities also host very different punk scenes. Atlanta and Montreal host smallish scenes with fairly stable local populations of "punk rockers" while New Orleans and San Francisco are temporary homes for a larger number of itinerant "gutter punks." It occurred to me, towards the end of my research, that I had constructed a strange parallel between my research on punks and the arrival of British punk in the United States; in 1978, the Sex Pistols began their U.S. tour in Atlanta, and ended it with the break-up of the band in San Francisco. Of course, my North American tour was considerably longer and took a different route, but at that point in my research, everything seemed to be highly significant. . . .

When meeting punks, I always identified myself primarily as a researcher, or, as I became known in San Francisco, "the lady that does the interviews." Throughout this period, my appearance retained elements of my past involvement with the subculture, including dyed hair, punk clothes, and tattoos (one of which is on my wrist and therefore often visible even in the coldest weather). When I began my research, I still had a punk haircut (long on top, shaved on the sides and back), but as I allowed this to grow out (my mother was right, it was a phase, albeit one a decade long), I sought out more dramatic hair coloring, finally settling on a cranberry shade achieved with considerable chemical effort. I was often acknowledged, in the words of one Montrealer, as an "old punk" (sigh). This eased my establishment of rapport with punks. One of the first girls I interviewed reported the following incident to me: I had approached Jessie for an interview, and she agreed to meet me the next day at a local eatery. That evening, while she was at a punk show, she told a male punk, with whom I was not acquainted, that she was going to be interviewed. He reacted rather negatively to this, "explaining" to her that I was going to distort her words and "make her look bad." He then offered to give her twenty dollars to refuse the interview. The next day, as I finished interviewing her, I asked her what had prompted her to decline his offer, to which she replied, "You seemed cool." I then asked her why she had not taken the male punk's twenty dollars and come to the interview anyway. Contrary to the popular media depiction of punks as corrupt and contemptible, she expressed considerable moral outrage at the very idea.

In the first phase of my research, just a little over half the girls I approached agreed to be interviewed; as I incorporated more participant observation, this improved steadily until, at the last research site, I had a positive response rate of 100 percent, and even had to begin refusing interviews. In eliciting and conducting interviews, I offered remuneration of ten to fifteen dollars for interviews that lasted from twenty minutes to one and a half hours. I found that financial compensation encouraged positive responses (and how!), offered an incentive to take time away from other potentially profitable activities (such as panhandling), and assured respondents that their narratives and accounts

_____ *Illustration 3* _____
The author at the beginning of field research
(Photo: 'B. Cragin)

are of value. I must admit to some conflict between my (and other punks') anti-capitalist ideological stance and the mercantile nature of such transactions. However, within the subculture, money is scarce and often required for the acquisition of such necessities as food (or for establishing telephone service, in one case). I was always concerned that interviewees might use this money for illegal purposes (for example, that they might use it to buy drugs), but did not encounter any such occurrences; one girl used it to attend a Native American powwow and another bought a bus ticket to visit her mother, who lived out of town. Financial remuneration of this type and in this setting does not differ substantially from that offered by psychologists or scientific researchers for participation in experimental research. In Montreal, punks had been paid to participate in HIV research, and in San Francisco, they were often approached to participate in research on illicit drug use—both of those research projects offered remuneration as well. Finally, this also served to redistribute some of the financial proceeds of the research process.

In addition to conducting interviews, I also spent time hanging out with, talking to, and observing the punks in their respective scenes. Cognizant of the possibility of exploitation of participants in ethnographic research, I did not conduct interviews or observations without the full consent of the participants in the subculture, both the girls I interviewed and the other punks I observed. As some punks are homeless and privatize public areas (using the street as a living room), I was careful to respect their boundaries and to refrain from intruding on their privacy. I sometimes had to negotiate between my responsibilities as a researcher and my role as a fellow punk, but no major conflicts between these dual identities arose, and no lasting damage was done. I was always conscious to keep my respect for these kids and their lifestyles and choices in the forefront in my interactions with them, even when their actions ran counter to my own beliefs. For example, on the rare occasions when I did observe or was made privy to minor crimes and delinquencies, I kept my counsel and prized their confidences. It is only in cases where requests for my assistance countered my personal beliefs (e.g., being asked to buy beer for minors) that I felt free to express my disapproval. When I was asked for assistance in other matters (e.g., for food, rides to shows, etc.), I was more than pleased to acquiesce. It is not unusual for ethnographers to maintain confidences or to accede to requests for favors. I did so not only for the usual ethnographer's disclaimer of preserving one's position in the group, but because I was genuinely sympathetic to and often supportive of their myriad small rebellions against mainstream society.

My field research, although generally trying (it required about a week of decompression at the end of each phase for me to shed my punk mannerisms, such as swearing at least once in every sentence), also had its high points. In Atlanta, I attended several punk shows (well, I would have anyway) and realized that this was not the best way to meet punks; they could never hear my requests for interviews, and, in many cases, they lived outside the city. I resorted at one point to advertising, passing out handbills and running an ad in the classifieds of the local alternative publication. Not only was this an unsuccessful tactic, but I then became the target of some very bizarre telephone calls. In New Orleans, I volunteered at the drop-in center that the punks frequented and hung out with them by the Mississippi river; I was invited to visit their squat and drove them on errands and, once, crammed eleven of them into my VW bus (dubbed "the punk bus") and took them out to the only punk show that occurred during my stay. I nearly "went native" and was inducted into their

"Born Again$☩" tribe. As five of the gutter punks were on their way to Toronto for the 1995 Punkfest, I also drove them to Atlanta on my way back from New Orleans; surprisingly, the sight of six punks driving a Volkswagen van through rural Mississippi and Alabama did not seem to perturb anyone, except for the Deadhead hitchhiker we picked up and who remained with us only a brief time (although the gas station attendant in Mississippi was a little taken aback by the pet rats). In San Francisco, I was hustled off the stairs of the Haight-Ashbury McDonald's, along with the other punks, by security guards who appeared to have been hired solely for that purpose. I hung out in Golden Gate Park with the squatter punks, discussing tattooing as a career option with one girl on her eighteenth birthday. In Montreal, as I sat on a concrete block bordering a vacant lot, observing one girl, Justine, panhandle, two well-dressed passers-by, a man and a woman in their late twenties, yelled at me to "Get a job!" Little did they know, that *was* my job.

Sampling

Deciding who to interview, in theory, was easy: punk girls. Doing so in practice was somewhat more problematic. Sampling is perhaps the most difficult issue in ethnographic field research, and obtaining a random sample is impossible. Field researchers must therefore rely chiefly upon methods of nonprobability sampling. In order to access punk girls, I resorted to two such sampling strategies that offered me a convenience sample. The first is snowball sampling, which begins with a single subject identifying other possible candidates for participation in the research. In some punk scenes, such as Atlanta and Montreal, I had only limited success with this method, as many of the punk girls knew few, if any, other punk girls. I therefore resorted to the use of a broader purposive, or judgmental, sample; a judgmental sample is selected on the basis of the researcher's own knowledge of the population and the purpose of the study (Babbie 1989:204). I began referring to this as "ambush sampling"; I would hang out in locales frequented by punks, on the lookout for likely subjects, pounce on any punk girl, and through fast talking, usually wind up interviewing her. I add as a note to future ethnographers that the presence of my dog Lucky, then a puppy, greatly facilitated interaction with strangers. As I increased my participant observation in the punk scenes of Montreal, New Orleans and San Francisco (where I could no longer rely on Lucky), I relied less upon such ambushes and more upon snowball samples. These sampling strategies were not meant to produce a representative sample, but rather to present a good coverage of the diversity of the subculture's membership, a goal that I feel I achieved.

Within the field, I sought out self-identified punk girls. In many cases, I resorted to my own initial judgments of subcultural participation through observation of possible interviewees' clothing and demeanor; this is consistent with other researchers' methods (Burr 1984) and is supported by Kathryn Fox's (1987) argument that the extremes of punk style (such as permanent or semipermanent body modifications) are indicative of subcultural commitment. In my initial approach, I asked interviewees to self-identify as members of the subculture prior to conducting interviews. As I began to use more snowball sampling, and as people began to approach me upon hearing of my research, this became easier. However, I always made sure that interviewees self-identified as members of the subculture prior to conducting interviews. Wariness concerning labels is a part of the punk ideology, so this was sometimes more difficult than was absolutely necessary, but it did come out all right with some negotiation (to the tune of: "Well okay, but if you *had* to label yourself . . . "). Because there is so much diversity in the punk subculture, and such contention as to what a "real punk" is, this was the most inclusive method of sample selection and did not require me to act as an arbiter of all things punk.

The group of forty young women I interviewed was fairly representative of the female membership of punk subculture as a whole. The group was predominantly white, with only one Vietnamese-American, one Hispanic-American, and one African-American participant; this is fairly typical of the racial composition of the entire punk subculture. Their ages at the time of the interview ranged from 14 to 37, with 19 the median. All participants were actively involved in the punk subculture, although the extent and nature of their involvement varied. Seventeen were locally-based "punk rockers" who had strong ties to the local scene, including "old school" or "Spirit of '77" punks. The other twenty-three were involved as "gutter punks" or "street punks," including "crusty punks."[6] Table 1 offers the breakdown of the pertinent characteristics of the sample of girls who participated in this research.

Although the sample was not randomly selected, it did include girls representing a wide variety of punk types, ages, and years of experience with the subculture, and is, from both my own knowledge of the subculture and existing sociological literature, fairly representative of the girls who participate in the scene. This numeric account, however, fails to present the wide array of individual personalities and family histories of these girls. I invite you at this point to turn to appendix B and peruse the brief biographies that must perforce serve to introduce them to you.

Interviews

Formal interviews usually took place after I had spent time with the punks of the city and thus had established some rapport. In conducting these

_____ *Table 1* _____
Sample Characteristics
(N=40)

Characteristic		N	%
Age	14–15	5	12.5
	16–17	6	15.0
	18–19	11	27.5
	20–21	11	27.5
	22–23	2	5.0
	24–25	2	5.0
	26–37	3	7.5
	Median: 19		
Ethnicity	African American	1	2.5
	Asian American	1	2.5
	Caucasian	37	92.5
	Latina	1	2.5
Class[a]	poor	5	12.5
	working	10	25.0
	middle	14	35.0
	upper-middle	8	20.0
	unknown	3	7.5
Sexual Orientation[b]	bisexual	7	17.5
	heterosexual	33	82.5
Education	high school dropout/expelled	18	45.0
	in high school	3	7.5
	high school graduate/GED	9	22.5
	some college/technical school	8	20.0
	completed college degree	2	5.0
Currently in school	Yes	6	15.0
	No	34	85.0

(continued)

semistructured interviews, I drew on an interview guide (see appendix C) comprised of main questions and follow-up probes. I began each interview with an explicit agreement to allow tape-recording. I assured confidentiality and explained that I would be using pseudonyms to identify speakers. I also agreed to full reciprocity and offered to answer any questions that they want to ask me (although questions directly concerning the findings of the research were postponed until we concluded the interview). I also assured the girls that they were free to volunteer any additional information or to refuse to answer any question. Using this pre-scripted interview guide, we discussed a variety of topics, including family and peer relationships, entry into the punk subculture, relations with males in the subculture, interactions with strangers, future plans, and perceptions of gender identity. Throughout, girls were invited to elaborate

_____ Table 1 _____
Sample Characteristics (continued)
(N=40)

Characteristic		N	%
Currently employed	Yes	10	25.0
	No	30	75.0
Situation in which raised	both biological parents	9	22.5
	foster care	13	27.5
	single parent[c]	18	45.0
Region of origin	Canada—East	9	22.5
	Canada—West	2	5
	England	1	2.5
	U.S.A.—Northeast	5	12.5
	U.S.A.—Northwest	6	15.0
	U.S.A.—Southeast	10	25.0
	U.S.A.—Southwest	6	15.0
	Unknown	1	2.5
Age when entered subculture[d]	10 or under	5	12.5
	11-12	13	27.5
	13-14	9	22.5
	15-16	8	20.0
	17-18	2	5.0
	unknown	3	7.5
	Median: 13		
Type of punk affiliation	gutter punk	23	57.5
	punk rocker	17	42.5

Notes
[a] Based on parents' occupation and educational attainment.
[b] Based on unsolicited self-report.
[c] Due to divorce, abandonment, or death of parent.
[d] Youngest age mentioned.

on their responses, and we sometimes departed significantly from the planned interview. The interview guide merely represented a set of topics and questions that I intended to address. The girls I interviewed often offered interesting tangents and ideas that I then pursued in that and subsequent interviews. Therefore, I constantly included new questions and topics in the interview guide.

Formal interviews took place wherever I could find quiet and privacy: in coffee shops and restaurants, on park benches, and in the back office of a youth center. I interviewed most punk girls individually; my one attempt to interview two girls together (Cora and Clara) yielded interesting results, as the girls talked to each other about their experiences. However, this technique proved impractical in most cases, as well as nearly impossible to transcribe. Formal interviews lasted anywhere from twenty minutes (for one particularly mono-syllabic girl) to almost two hours. They tended to started off rather stiltedly and then turn into conversations. I always ended by asking each girl whether she had anything to add, and this often led us into further discussions about life, punk, politics, and society.

Although I did not conduct inquiries concerning sensitive topics, some girls occasionally discussed such issues spontaneously. When I discovered that some of these girls had experienced sexual abuse, I underwent training as a rape crisis counselor, and twice turned off the tape recorder to discuss personal issues with these girls, offering them references to local resources. I was very aware that some of the punk girls were minors and that obtaining parental permission for interviews was impossible. At the suggestion of Emory University's Human Subjects Committee of the Institutional Review Board, I asked no questions concerning sex, drugs, alcohol, or anything illegal and assured the participants of that, nor did I record observations of such activities. This may have detracted from my accounts of resistance (for example, the use of delinquency as a tool of resistance), but I assert that it was a necessary limitation. In keeping with the ethical code of the American Sociological Association, I offered confidentiality and destroyed all audiotapes following full transcription. In order to protect the identities of the girls I interviewed, I used pseudonyms on all notes and transcripts, obscured some references to geographical locations, and changed descriptions of some physical characteristics.

Upon completion of the interviews, I fully transcribed all tapes. I did not transcribe with the rigor of conversational analysis, that notes all pauses and overlaps, but did transcribe every word of every tape. At that point, I translated the six French interviews into English. I quickly learned that transcribing tapes between interviews was, for me, a very bad idea. I hated the transcription process so much that I once found myself trying to curtail someone's lengthy answer during an interview so as to decrease transcription time. I then decided to wait until the end of each segment of my field research to begin my transcription; this did little to facilitate the transcription process, but did have beneficial psychological effects on the researcher. I also maintained notes and issued research reports on a regular basis while in the field.

Analysis and Writing

Although the interpretation of qualitative data is, ultimately, a craft rather than a science, there are certain guidelines that other researchers have employed in approaching what originally appears to be a largely undifferentiated mass of data. In analyzing the data, as in designing my field research, I drew heavily on the guidance of John Lofland and Lyn Lofland's *Analyzing*

Social Settings (1995). I had begun this research with one central question: How do punk girls reconcile a subcultural identity that is deliberately coded as "masculine" with the demands of femininity? In addressing this and the questions that arose subsequently, I drew on three main sources to derive concepts and categories. Temporally, the first source was my own experience with the punk subculture from 1984 to 1992; this was the origin of many of the questions that led me into my initial fieldwork. Thus, my own experiences with parental conflict over my punk lifestyle led me to include questions on parental pressures toward conformity; likewise, my experience of being expelled from high school led me to seek out conflicts between these girls and school authorities. The second source of concepts and categories I explored emerged from my discussions with punk girls in the course of my fieldwork. For example, my own experiences with being harassed by strangers because of my appearance led me to ask whether girls were ever hassled. To my surprise, many reported being subjected to a good deal of what I define as "public sexual harassment," such as being solicited by strangers for the purposes of prostitution; this led me to add questions specifically addressing the issue of sexual harassment. Throughout the transcription process, I began to jot down ideas and to create files of miscellaneous ideas and quotes as topics emerged; before I had completed my field research, these sometimes led me to add questions to the interview guide. The third source of questions underlying this research was sociological literature on various topics such as gender, harassment, sexual harassment, and subcultures (on the punk subculture in particular). All of these categories then dictated chapter divisions.

Chapter Breakdown

Before I can discuss the intricacies of gender resistance and punk participation, I must begin by introducing the subculture and its members. In chapter 2, "'Punk's Not Dead—It Just Smells That Way': Punk to Hardcore, with Girls on the Side," I examine the origins and development of the punk subculture, from its inceptions in the United States and Britain to its current forms in North America. I discuss variants of the subculture, such as Spirit of '77 punks, gutter punks, crusty punks, softcore and hardcore punks, and British and North American punks. In doing so, I focus especially on the roles that women and girls have had in the formation and perpetuation of the subculture.

Following this, I turn to the girls I interviewed, examining how and why young women join a male-dominated youth subculture such as punk. In chapter 3, "'I Grew Up and I Was a Punk': Subcultural Stories," I draw on two girls' very different narratives of entry into the punk subculture in order to frame my analysis of girls' attractions to and experiences of subcultural affiliation. I discuss the girls' backgrounds, their various definitions of the subculture, their narratives of entry into the subculture, the effects of media and of peers, and the ways in which punk has changed their lives. These narratives illustrate themes as diverse as rebelling against parents, finding political affiliations, rejecting mainstream cultural roles, being a runaway/pushout, and using the subculture as a survival network.

In the remaining chapters, I discuss in greater detail the ways punk girls construct resistance within the punk subculture. In some ways, these build on the quote with which I opened this introductory chapter. Sue began by saying that "the punk guys will really overpower what the punk girls have to say"; I used this quote as the title of chapter 4, in which I discuss punk as a discourse of masculinity by exploring present-day gender relations between punks, both as friends and in intimate relationships. I argue that punk was originally constructed as a masculine subculture and continues to be so as the males in the subculture reinforce these norms through their interactions with punk girls. Drawing on interviews and observations, I explode the myth of punk as an egalitarian or, ironically, feminist youth subculture. In chapter 4, I turn to accommodation rather than to resistance, exploring how punk girls experience, and why they tolerate, these forms of male domination.

Sue then remarked that "the punk girl thing is a very aggressive scene, and very assertive and aggressive girls tend to get into it." In chapter 5, "'I'll Slap on My Lipstick and Then Kick Their Ass': Constructing Femininity," I directly address the main question of the book: How do punk girls accommodate female gender norms within subcultural identities that are deliberately coded as "masculine"? I explore how these "assertive and aggressive" punk girls actively construct gender, beginning with their outright rejections of conventional adolescent female gender norms. Drawing on both interviews and observations, I discuss punk girls' behavioral, discursive, and stylistic reconstructions of gender within the context of the punk subculture. These reconstructions range from punk girls' adoption of male garb to their juxtaposition of stereotyped feminine and masculine attributes, and, finally, to their discursive reconstructions of femininity.

Sue also noted: "I don't know many passive, timid little girls who are going to shave their heads and look like a freak, take harassment from everybody all the time. . . . " In chapter 6, "'Oh, I Hope I Don't Catch Anything': Punk Deviance and Public Harassment," I move out of the insular confines of the subculture to examine punk girls' interactions with the mainstream public. I explore public reactions to punk girls' self-presentation, primarily through the lens of "public harassment," in order to explore how this is a form of social control of punk "deviance." I conclude this chapter by examining the ways punk girls react to these representations of themselves and how they resist these representations by discursively reversing these imputations of deviance.

Punk girls also experience harassment that is based not only on their presentation as punks, but by virtue of their gender as well; not only do they have to "fight off the guys in the scene," but they have to fend off a good deal of public sexual harassment. I argue in chapter 7, "'I Bet a Steel-Capped Boot Could Shut You Up': Resistance to Public Sexual Harassment," that punk girls experience a good deal of what I call "public sexual harassment." In chapter 7, I define this term more narrowly and explore the types of sexual harassment that punk girls experience. As in the previous chapter, I conclude by detailing their strategies of resistance to these sexual threats, and argue that these offer strategies that can be of greater use to all women.

I conclude in chapter 8, "'Girls Kick Ass': Nonacademic Conclusions," by drawing on girls' own accounts of personal empowerment in the subculture in order to suggest ways in which other theorists and researchers might reconceptualize girls' subcultural participation. I address both U.S. and British theorists and researchers, who have either ignored women's participation in male-dominated youth subcultures or replicated the male members' descriptions of women as marginal to the subculture. I conclude by drawing on punk girls' self-perceptions and self-presentations in order to address parents', teachers', and youth authorities' perceptions and (mal)treatment of these marginalized girls.

Welcome to the punk girl thing.

Two

"Punk's Not Dead— It Just Smells That Way"

Punk to Hardcore, with Girls on the Side

Punks and pundits agree that punk started out as a music-based subculture. Beyond that, there is little agreement about its geographic origins, its
ideologies, its membership, and even, as the quotations above demonstrate,
its continued existence. Most published accounts of punk focus on the origins
and flourishing of the punk subculture from the late 1960s to late 1970s. These,
in turn, are subdivided into works about the New York scene of the late sixties and early seventies and those describing the U.K. punks of the mid-to-late
1970s. Most scholarly works on punk take an abstract tack, analyzing the subculture as a specific moment in post-modern political art movements. Accounts
such as Greil Marcus' *Lipstick Traces* (1989), Tricia Henry's *Break All Rules!*
(1989), and Neil Nehring's *Flowers in the* [sic] *Dustbin* (1993) present abstract
"readings" of the punk phenomenon as iterations of avant-garde dadaism, fu-
turism, surrealism, or expressionism. On the other hand, historians and chroni-
clers of the punk subculture tend to focus on band biographies, music criticism,
or specific local punk scenes. These document, in sometimes excruciating detail, the doings of major and minor players in the punk scenes—(mostly male)

band members, (male) promoters, (male) club owners, and (male) record-company executives. In all these texts, women and girls appear only in glimpses, in the margins of the marginal.

In focusing on the roles of major figures of punk, these accounts neglect the punks themselves, the kids who are responsible for the enactment and continuance of the particular cultural manifestations that make up punk. Few punk kids—and much less punk girls—would recognize themselves within these academic-jargon-laden interpretations of punk, or even in the more concrete histories. In essence, these accounts accomplish exactly what punk set out to destroy: they codify and glorify the star system by focusing solely on the innovators who held central positions in early punk. They do not explore the phenomenology of punk: What attracts adolescents to the subculture? What do they experience in it? How do they construct their everyday lives once they have adopted such a spectacularly deviant identity? As a result of this lack, when commentators proclaim the death of punk, they are right in one respect: the original music scene that spawned the subculture is no more. What they forget, however, is that punk was not only, nor even primarily, about punk music, or events, or obscure political and artistic affiliations—punk was, and is, about living out a rebellion against authority. In this sense, punk as a subculture is still alive, with kids all over North America spawning new scenes and constantly adding to its maintenance and development. This history of punk is underground, found only in reprinted 'zines and scene histories. Within this fragmented history lies a subtext, a hidden history of punk girls. In this chapter, I unearth the underground history of the punk subculture, and bring to light some gems of punk girl history.

Generation X: The Spirit of '77

Appropriately for such an oppositional subculture, there is some contention as to the geographic origins of punk. U.S. punk historians locate punk completely within the 1970s United States, only mentioning U.K. punk as a later emulation of the true U.S. punk style. British writers on punk acknowledge its American roots, but argue that punk is a distinctively British subculture, born out of the political turmoil of the United Kingdom in the 1970s. Both are, in a sense, correct.

"The Blank Generation": North American Punk

North American punk began in the late 1960s with a loose underground of Detroit garage rock bands (MC5, Iggy and the Stooges), art house rock (The Velvet Underground) and trash/glam cross-dressing bands (The New York Dolls, Jayne/Wayne County). This scene coalesced in 1973 with the opening of a club, CBGB-OMFUG (Country, Bluegrass, Blues, and Other Music For Uplifting Gourmandizers), on the Bowery in the Lower East Side of New York City. CBGB rapidly became the center of the low-rent underground New York rock scene, and began to flourish in 1974 when Television, a garage band that included style maven Richard Hell, played nearly every Saturday night (Kozak 1988). Other bands such as the Ramones and the Dead Boys soon followed, influenced by Television, MC5, the Stooges, and the New York Dolls. Unversed in the intricacies of their instruments and weary of the posturing virtuosity of the stadium rock bands of the early 1970s, the young men in these bands established a "do-it-yourself" (DIY) garage band atmosphere in the club. This prompted other patrons, such as Debbie Harry (Stilettos/ Blondie), Patti Smith and Lenny Kaye (Patti Smith Group), and David Byrne (Talking Heads) to form their own bands.[1]

The CBGB scene was dubbed "punk" in 1975, when Legs McNeil and John Holstrom used the term to title their new fanzine ('zine), a homemade, hand-lettered, cartoon-filled, photocopied magazine that brought DIY into the realm of publishing. Until then, the label *punk* designated either a young male hustler, a gangster, a hoodlum, or a ruffian. McNeil later explained that he chose the label precisely for its negative connotations: "On TV, if you watched cop shows, *Kojak, Beretta*, when the cops finally catch the mass murderer, they'd say, "you dirty Punk." It was what your teachers would call you. It meant that you were the lowest. All of us drop-outs and fuck-ups got together and started a movement. We'd been told all our lives that we'd never amount to anything. We're the people who fell through the cracks of the educational system" (quoted in Savage 1991:131). His co-editor, John Holstrom, elaborated on this in an editorial in the 'zine: "The key word—to me anyway—in the punk definition was 'a beginner an unexperienced [*sic*] hand.' Punk rock—any kid can pick up a guitar and become a rock 'n' roll star, despite or because of his lack of ability, talent, intelligence, limitations and/or potential, and usually does so out of frustration, hostility, a lot of nerve and a need for ego fulfilment [*sic*]" (Holstrom 1996:18). U.S. punk appealed to white adolescents, predominantly young men, who found little to capture their interest or imagination in the rock and roll scene of the early 1970s, with its prevalence of slick stadium concerts and unattainable rock icons. Richard Hell of Television dubbed these kids "The Blank Generation," a set of disaffected, disgruntled, and apathetic adolescents—in a word, punks. Rather than buying into the commercialized youth culture offered them, they set out to make their own.

Although they were in the minority, this scene of disgruntled adolescents included young women who were as disaffected and rebellious as their male peers. Despite their small numbers, those women in the New York scene played an integral role, and their presence in these new punk bands was (and still is) perceived as a watershed in the involvement of women in rock. Mo Tucker, the androgynous female drummer of The Velvet Underground, opened the underground rock scene to women's presence in other than their traditionally ornamental/sexual roles in mainstream rock: lead or backup singers, groupies, and girlfriends. With the prevailing idea that anyone can play music, women could be, and were, bassists, guitarists, and drummers. In the New York underground, and then punk, scenes, women such as Patti Smith, Debbie Harry, Ivy Rorschach of the Cramps, and Tina Weymouth of the Talking Heads found opportunities to form and participate in bands, perhaps more so than did women in more mainstream rock. Rock journalists Simon Reynolds and Joy Press note that "[i]n the official history of rock, punk is regarded as a liberating time for women, a moment in which the limits of permissible representations of femininity were expanded and exploded. Women were free to uglify themselves, to escape the *chanteuse* role to which they were generally limited and pick up guitars and drumsticks, to shriek rather than coo in dulcet tones, to deal with hitherto taboo topics" (1995:33).

Liberated from their traditional rock roles, the women who participated in the New York punk scene were also free to experiment with other forms of gender transgressions. Stylistically, they embodied the range of options of gender construction open to women in punk. Rail-thin, dressed in torn jeans and ratty T-shirts, Patti Smith constructed an androgynous image. On the other extreme, Debbie Harry, with bleached-blonde hair and microdresses, played upon the sex goddess image in Blondie. For a brief moment, all forms of transgression had free rein, and women in punk took full advantage of this atmosphere of permissiveness and rebellion. Yet, despite the doors that opened for women in the underground New York punk rock scene, the subculture was heavily male dominated, and remained so when exported to the United Kingdom.

Sex, Style, and Pistols: British Punk

Punk as a music scene may have originated in the United States, but punk as a subculture gelled in mid-1970s Britain. Dick Hebdige (1979) situates the origins of British punk in the depression and drought of the summer of 1976. Rioting and mayhem colored the summer, with the Notting Hill Caribbean Carnival erupting into violence. White working-class youth seemingly had no part in the revolution until punk arrived. British adolescents had long created stylish subcultures in order to express all manner of rebellions—from Teddy boys' and Mods' appropriations of upper-class style to skinheads' revival of working-class style. Much of this stylistic innovation drew on black immigrant youth culture, and punk was no different (Hebdige 1979). Punk adopted the apocalyptic undercurrents in the air, transforming the Rastafarian rhetoric of revolt against Babylon stylistically into a nihilistic refusal of British society. Punks deliberately structured their dress, music, and behavior to oppose and confront dominant norms of mainstream politics, propriety, and taste.

By some accounts, punk was originally constructed as a marketing tool for its sartorial style. Tailor and sometime impresario Malcolm McLaren engineered the Sex Pistols phenomenon in order to promote the clothes he and Vivienne Westwood produced at their King's Road shop (Savage 1991). McLaren and Westwood, an art school dropout, owned a clothing shop that had undergone a number of transformations as they kept up with subcultural trends. However, as dabblers in Situationist International politics, Westwood and McLaren found little satisfaction in outfitting Teddy Boys and Rockabillies, whose politics were more reactionary than radical.

Then, during a visit to New York, McLaren spotted Richard Hell of Television wearing a garment of his own construction: a deliberately ripped-up T-shirt held together with safety pins. McLaren, taken with the angry energy of punk rock and liking the paradox of the garment, copied the T-shirt, and McLaren and Westwood reinvented the King's Road shop upon his return. The shop, now called "Sex" (and later "Seditionaries"), marketed clothing that drew on any cultural taboo: sadomasochism, fascism, poverty, pornography—meant as antifashion. Sex sold the Hell-inspired T-shirts, along with shirts featuring Situationist International slogans ("Be Reasonable: Demand the Impossible") and such taboo items as bondage gear (rubber T-shirts, leather miniskirts, fetish items, S/M implements) meant to be worn as street clothes, along with Westwood's "bondage" suits and trousers, which melded leather bondage gear straps to masculine haberdashery. The shop hired Jordan, an androgynous clerk who was the first punk to promote Sex gear by wearing it out in public. Julie Burchill and Tony Parsons noted that the intent of this public display of perversity was not to titillate, but to provoke: "None of these clothes were either designed or worn to make the customer look alluring; on the contrary, the flagrant fashion in which the clothes used sex as an offensive weapon required a certain asexuality on the part of the wearer. They used sex not to entice but to horrify, the perfect expression of which was found in Jordan 'Don't Call Me Pamela' Hook, the *Sex* salesgirl who wore cutaway-buttock plastic leotards with black suspender belt and thigh boots while striving to make her hair, face and body as puke-promptingly repulsive as possible" (1978:16).

Despite his failure in the United States to revive the New York Dolls by outfitting them in red patent leather and communist regalia, McLaren was still taken with the idea of promoting his clothing through outfitting a band. He recruited four youths, including John Lydon (Johnny Rotten) as lead singer, reportedly because he had the right look and attitude for the band—McLaren was impressed by his homemade T-shirt, on which he had penned "I hate" over the band logo on a Pink Floyd shirt. Called the Sex Pistols after the shop, the band began performing in 1975. The look and sound of the Pistols owed much to the New York scene; reportedly, McLaren urged the Pistols to sound like the Ramones, and even the trademark spiky punk haircut sported by Johnny Rotten was copied from a photograph of Richard Hell (Jones 1990). The Sex Pistols played their first gig on November 6, 1975, dressed to kill in Sex shop clothes. Their lack of musical ability may not have made an impression, but their bravado and their style had an important impact on a growing fan base.

The London punk scene quickly took on a life of its own, independent of McLaren's machinations. Immediately following their debut, the Sex Pistols acquired a following of friends, fans, and imitators. The Pistols' main fan base, The Bromley Contingent, a group of fans that included Steve Severin, Sid Vicious, Debbie Juvenile, Sue Catwoman, Steve Havoc, Siouxsie Sioux, and Billy Idol, was a particularly fertile ground for the rooting of punk. In the emergent British punk scene, as in the New York scene, the line between bands and fans was very tenuous. Encouraged by punks' disdain for musical virtuosity, fans quickly formed their own bands. Soon after seeing the Pistols, Billy Idol fronted Generation X, a band that speeded up punk music and cranked up its volume, before moving on to a solo pop career in the 1980s. Sid Vicious, before becoming a Sex Pistol, joined Siouxsie and the Banshees on stage at the Roxy. New bands quickly cropped up from the scene's fans, extending the DIY ethic originally found in the New York scene.

The punk DIY aesthetic deeply influenced the creation, production, and distribution of punk music, as well as the dissemination of information about punk. Although some punk bands courted, received, and (occasionally) honored recording contracts with major record firms, most punk bands either started or signed with independent recording companies. DIY also flourished in textual production. Inspired by the U.S. 'zine *Punk,* London soon had its own punk 'zine, *Sniffin' Glue.* 'Zines and advertisements for punk shows shared a cut-and-paste homemade aesthetic that came from their designers' lack of resources, art school backgrounds, and access to photocopiers. 'Zines promoted local bands by reviewing shows and recordings and by interviewing local musicians, as well as promoting DIY, urging readers to form their own bands. *Sideburns,* a 'zine dedicated to the Stranglers, printed a chart of three guitar chords (A-E-G) with the rubric: "This is a chord . . . This is another . . . This is a third . . . Now form a band" (reprinted in Savage 1991:280). Many adolescents complied, resulting in a cacophony of near-deafening, but politically passionate, punk rock.

It was also at this stage that punk and reggae momentarily meshed, with Don Letts, the Rastafarian DJ at the Roxy, playing reggae for the audience in between bands' sets. Punk and Rastafarianism found common ground in their opposition to the mainstream system ("Babylon" to the Rastas; "the fascist regime" to the punks) and their shared sense of oppression (Cashmore 1984; Dancis 1978; Hebdige 1979). Some punk bands, such as the Clash and the Slits (and protopunks the Police), incorporated reggae rhythms and themes into their music, and the punk/reggae alliance was cemented by common participation in Rock Against Racism concerts and Bob Marley's celebratory anthem, "Punky Reggae Party." This interracial coalition was short-lived, ending in the 1980s with the rise of Nazi punks, but its influence on the progressive politics and musical tastes of many punks remains strong to this day.

The London punk scene achieved a good deal of notoriety and momentum in a two-day punk festival held at the 100 Club on September 20 and 21, 1976. Besides showcasing almost all the current punk bands, the show was a watershed event in punk history. It was at this festival that Sid Vicious, standing at the back of the crowd and unable to see the bands, began jumping up and down, thereby inventing the dance called "the pogo." It was quickly adapted into more symbolically violent forms of dance. When performed in pairs, the pogo eventually became "the strangle," with both partners gripping each others' necks and jumping up and down.

Another incident that made the 100 Club festival notorious was tragic: a girl attending the festival was reportedly blinded in one eye by shards of glass from a thrown beer mug (Marsh 1977). This incident was to have important repercussions in shaping public perceptions of punk as a violent, uncontrolled scene.

As a result of this and other well-publicized incidents, punks became the new British "folk devils" (Cohen 1972) of the late 1970s. Like the Mods and Rockers of the late 1960s, whose highly publicized beachfront clashes engendered public panic in the United Kingdom (Cohen 1972), punks were feared as dangers to the public weal. The punk subculture, in many ways, was depicted as espousing and propagating many of the "undesirable" aspects originally associated with the term *punk*. Unlike previous subcultures, however, punks deliberately cultivated an image of violence, deviance, and repugnance at the very inception of the subculture, with McLaren encouraging the Sex Pistols' public displays of drunkenness and regurgitation. The British tabloid media quickly saturated the public with stories that featured both authorities' interpretation of punk as a subversive threat to adolescents and a titillating look at punk style.

Mud in Your Eye: Punk Style

It was the style of punk dress that was, and remains, the most recognizable aspect of punk. Punk style was characterized by its fluidity and ambiguity. Using the "bricolage" described by John Clarke (1976) and Dick Hebdige (1979), punks combined apparently discrepant styles: the "poverty look" of the U.S. punks, the "workingman's" attire of pub rock bands and the drag-inspired look of the glam rockers of the 1970s. Some bands, such as the Sex Pistols, wore Sex shop clothes; the Clash and the Stranglers adopted versions of working-class attire; the Damned and Siouxsie and the Banshees opted for a more theatrical gothic look. London punks extended the DIY aesthetic, creating their own sartorial statements by using everyday objects to adorn themselves. They played with the conventions of dress in unexpected ways: T-shirts were deliberately torn in order to be held together by safety pins; businessmen's uniform suits were transformed into sexual bondage gear; garbage bags were worn as dresses, and dog collars became necklaces. Punks also appropriated military surplus, wearing combat boots, dog tags, khakis, and camouflage wear.

Punks intended their stylistic bricolage to be subversive. In his germinal analysis of punk style, Hebdige (1979) argued that style is the primary weapon in punks' "semiotic guerilla warfare" against the dominant culture. Punks conducted such subversion by appropriating items from the mainstream and reversing their original meanings. For example, combat boots, whose original meanings encompass discipline and militarism, became part of the antiauthoritarian and anarchistic punk's uniform, to be juxtaposed with T-shirts bearing slogans such as "Disarm or Die." In adopting such symbols, punks constructed parallels between themselves and the originators of the symbols. Punk bricolage not only invested objects with new meanings, but retained the original meaning as well, even when these were contradictory. Imitation, in this case, was not flattery, but parody, as the relevant members of mainstream culture did not often view such parallels as complimentary.

As a set of subcultural symbols, punk dress served simultaneously to signify membership in the subculture, solidarity with other punks, identification with the subculture, and disaffiliation with mainstream culture. Punks carved out an image of rebellion and protest, using stylistic venues to articulate their refusal of conventional norms. Early punks used inversion to create style, glorifying anything that connoted low status (dog collars), sexual perversion (bondage clothes), banality (fake leopard fur), or degeneracy (rubber clothes). In addition, punks subverted culturally valued objects connoting tradition (the tartan kilt), conformity (the school jacket and tie), and authority (police and storm trooper uniforms), creating what Angela Carter (1992) described as "sartorial terrorism." Wearing safety pins and garbage bags and adopting such

———— *Illustration 4* ————
Health & Beauty—punk parody through juxtaposition
(Photo: D. K. Rabel)

monikers as Johnny Rotten, Rat Scabies, Richard Hell, and Poly Styrene, punks
sought to demonstrate that, as lower-class youth, they were rejected by society prior to their own rejection of society (as Johnny Rotten sang, "We're the
flowers in your dustbin").

Unlike members of "outlaw" subcultures, such as bikers, punks did not embrace this image in pure defiance of social norms. Rather, they sought to challenge the validity of such rules. Through the use of mockery, irony, and parody,
punks protested against the constraints imposed by conventional norms. They
contravened social standards in an effort to challenge the integrity of the culture that produced them.

Punks' bodily adornments did not end at their clothing styles, but extended
to nonmainstream body modifications. Punks wore dog collars, bathtub chains,

and razor blades as jewelry and pierced their ears, noses, cheeks, and eyebrows with safety pins. They also used hairstyle to confront mainstream notions of appearance, constructing hairstyles that were obvious in their artificiality in a time when those who dyed their hair took pains to hide the fact. Many used vegetable dyes to create bright, unnaturally tinged hair. Punk hair also defied gravity, being teased into rats' nests, glued into spikes, or shaved in unusual patterns. Some of these styles became standard punk fare. One popular look was to spike all of one's short hair, a style popularized by Richard Hell, Johnny Rotten, and Sid Vicious. A variant of this was "liberty spikes," featuring larger spikes reminiscent of the Statue of Liberty. Mohawk haircuts, in which the head was shaved save for a strip of hair running from brow to nape, became popular in the London punk scene of the late 1970s. Dylan Jones notes in *Haircults* that this inaccurate representation of purportedly Native American warriors' hairstyles was introduced because a "punk haircut was relatively easy to revert, but the colossal Mohawk head-dress was impossible to disguise, consequently becoming the strongest visual symbol of punk's radical posture" (1990:78).

Punks' early stylistic innovations marked their appropriation of their own bodies as sources of artistic material, a corporeal expression of punk's protest and DIY aesthetic (Wojcik 1995). Everything punks used to communicate the meanings of their subculture—their band names, nicknames, and their appropriated clothing—carried a variety of connotations. Punk dress operated at various levels of meaning, often requiring a skilled interpreter fully versed in subcultural codes. For instance, early punks often used the swastika for its shock value, rather than to indicate affinity with Nazi politics. And yet, politics and class rhetoric were as much part of the punk style as were safety pins and combat boots.

Although punk was characterized as a working-class subculture, its origins in working-class consciousness or class conflict are debatable, and its articulation of young white Britons' angst was more expressive than political. In a 1977 review of the punk scene in *New Society*, Peter Marsh offered what has become the standard reading of punk, arguing that the music of the Pistols and the Clash reflected the concerns of working-class white youth: "dole queue rock." Simon Frith (1978) responded to Marsh's characterization, arguing that punk has more to do with art than with class conflict. Punk, he argued, did not originate in the dole queue, but in art school, pointing out the art school origins of McLaren and Westwood as well as those of members of the Sex Pistols and the Clash. Frith quoted U.S. rock critic Robert Christgau: "Rather than a working class youth movement, punk is a basically working class bohemia that rejects both the haute bohemia of the rock elite and the hallowed bohe-

_____ *Illustration 5* _____
A particularly excellent example of a mohawk and punk
tattoos
(Photo: D. K. Rabel)

mian myth of classlessness. Punk doesn't want to be thought of as bohemian,
because bohemians are posers. But however vexed the question of their authenticity, bohemians do serve a historical function—they nurture aesthetic
sensibility" (Frith:536). Punk's radical politics, therefore, were more on the level
of self-expression than social revolution.

Punk's style politics were also less than straightforward. Jeff Bale and Tim
Yohannen of the U.S. punk 'zine *Maximum Rock 'n' Roll* later noted: "[P]unk
has always consisted of a complex and dynamic mixture of progressive, neu-
tral, and reactionary elements" (1986:62). The early subculture was characterized by fluidity, ambiguity, and the use of contrariness and paradox in the

construction of revolutionary aesthetics. Early punks played at politics and pro-test, portrayed themselves as political radicals by drawing on imagery and themes of anarchism, Marxism, communism, Situationism, fascism, and nihil-ism. Like punk style, punk politics were fluid and ambiguous, at once anticapi-talist and antihippie, anarchist and fascist. McLaren and Westwood produced shirts with Situationist International slogans lifted from the graffiti of the Paris student uprisings of May 1968. The Sex Pistols sang about anarchy and fas-cism in songs such as "Anarchy in the U.K." and "Belsen Was a Gas," and the Clash positioned themselves as the voice of the white proletariat with songs such as "White Riot" and "Career Opportunities." Punks wore hammer-and-sickle insignia and swastikas with equal abandon. Politically, punk failed to ap-peal to working-class labor or leftists and the Young Socialists formally condemned punk rock at its 1978 conference (Thompson 1979).

Despite the prevailing use of politics as style, not all punks' political utter-ances were done in play. Factions of the subculture, bands such as the Clash and the Buzzcocks, did take their political stances more seriously. In coalition with Rastafarian and leftist groups, some punks participated in leftist organi-zations such as the Anti-Nazi League and in egalitarian events such as the So-cialist Workers Party's Rock Against Racism concerts (Thompson 1979) and Rock Against Sexism shows, which benefited Women's Aid and rape crisis or-ganizations (O'Brien 1995).

Given the complexity and ambiguity of the stylistic minutiae of punk style and politics, its meanings varied with each reading; whereas experienced punks could decipher the message, the uninitiated may have received quite an unin-tended impression. Nowhere was this more apparent than in the style of punk female dress. While McLaren shepherded the Sex Pistols, Sex shop designer Vivienne Westwood gathered an entourage of sexually ambiguous, fun-loving transvestites, dominatrices, and other gender-bending types who contributed to the creation of punk as a style that confronted mainstream norms of gen-der and sexuality. The New York scene had produced transvestite Jayne/Wayne County and the androgyny of the New York Dolls. To this, the London punks added the glam style of Gary Glitter and David Bowie, seeking to shock by playing with conventions of gender. Punks, led by Westwood and the Bromley Contingent (which included pseudodominatrices Siouxsie Sioux and Sue Catwoman) frequented Louise's, a lesbian bar, wearing clothes that were made grotesque and absurd by their extreme sexual perversity.

This stylistic innovation was one of many ways in which women shaped the British punk subculture. Early punk was the first rock scene in which women and sex were not the main focus of song lyrics, allowing punk music to avoid gender stereotyping in large measure. Punks' rejection of virtuosity—the "cock rock" idiom that maintained that women could not play "properly"—offered unexpected benefits for female performers who often had not had the opportunities nor the support that their male peers had for developing virtuosity in rock (Home 1995). This was especially true in Britain, where women formed their own bands and participated as instrumentalists in bands with both male and female members. Chrissie Hynde, a core participant in the early London punk scene (she once tried to teach Sid Vicious to play guitar) later noted: "The best thing about [punk] for me was that I didn't have to rely on being a female guitarist as a gimmick. Punk was very liberating like that. For the first time I could do what I wanted to do, and being a girl wasn't an issue. It would've been uncool for that to be a problem. Punk allowed anyone in—you could be a dwarf, short-sighted, whatever—but that was only true for about six months, I think, when it was at its purest. A total rebellion . . . " (quoted in Hoare 1991:14).

As in the U.S. punk scene, British punk women were no longer ornaments, but served as lead singers, drummers, bassists, and guitarists in punk bands. In the British punk scene, women were integral parts of punk bands such as the Adverts, Siouxsie and the Banshees, the Au Pairs, Penetration, and the Rezillos, and female-dominated bands such as the Slits, the Raincoats, and X-Ray Spex played on the same bills as all-male bands such as the Clash and the Sex Pistols. Punk fans such as Joan Jett of the Runaways and Chrissie Hynde (briefly a clerk at Sex) later went on to make their mark in mainstream rock. Until punk, the accepted style for white female rock vocalists was "confidential and 'gentle,' . . . which all too often carried connotations of submissiveness" (Laing 1985:116). As punk music was anathema to such presentations, female punk vocalists had to create a vocal style that rejected lilting tones in favor of harsher ones. Thus, bands such as the Slits, X-Ray Spex, and the Raincoats incorporated screams, cries, and laughter into their music.

Punk Chicks Rock: Women in Early British Punk

These female punk performers made important contributions to the stylistic punk parody of female sexuality, beginning with Patti Smith and Debbie Harry in the New York scene. In London, women in bands continued this process, alternately playing with hypersexual and asexual images. The songs and stage presence of Poly Styrene, lead singer of X-Ray Spex, emphasized punk parody and ambiguity. She eschewed the hypersexual Sex shop look in favor of her own brightly colored, childlike, plastic creations. Her music exemplified many of the paradoxes and parodies constructed by female punks. In her most recognizable song, singing in a voice somewhere between that of a wailing baby and that of a banshee, she screamed "Oh Bondage! Up Yours!" and began the song with the lines "Bind me tie me chain me to the wall/ I wanna be a slave to you all!" Paradoxically, the chorus ran: "Oh bondage! Up yours!/ Oh bondage! Come on!" As Styrene continued on to the second verse, she revealed that this song is not about sex, but about consumerism: "Chain store chain smoke I consume you all/Chain gang chain mail I don't think at all!" In this one utterance, Styrene transformed a seemingly masochistic plea into an indictment of consumer culture, denouncing the blind impulses of the mainstream shopper. In depicting herself as both an agent of and resister to her submission, she created a parody of both positions, juxtaposing them powerfully against each other.

Another parodic performer, Siouxsie Sioux, began her punk career by playing a typical woman-in-rock role, dancing onstage during Sex Pistols shows decked out in provocative Sex bondage wear, peekaboo bras, and a swastika armband. Sioux routinely wore black leather and rubber bondage wear that revealed her body (corsets, fishnet stockings, and stiletto-heeled boots) but her style of presentation was stiff and angular, her posture often at odds with her attire. With her heavy black makeup, Sioux, like Jordan, strove to be more sexually repulsive than attractive. When she was dropped from the Pistols' act, she teamed up with Sid Vicious to form the Banshees, debuting at the 100 Club punk festival and fronting the only band to emerge from the original London punk scene that remains intact today.

Another performer, Arri Up of the all-female band the Slits, likewise constructed an image that played on conventions of female sexuality, pioneering the practice of wearing female undergarments over her street clothes. Viv Albertine, of the same band, noted that punk style had a liberating effect for women: "You could have your hair cut in the most hideous way, but it was an interesting thing for a woman to have done. Or Siouxsie wearing something with her tits hanging out. It was like wearing your thoughts and attitudes to life, clothes reflected it in a very obvious way" (quoted in Savage 1991:195). Early punk offered female members a wide variety of stylistic options, allowing them to create their own mode of sexualized, desexualized, or antisexual self-presentation.

However, the success of early female punk performers' attempts to desexualize the clothes they wore in such a parodic fashion is debatable. Whereas punk women intended to present these garments in such a way as to discredit their effect as fetishistic, sexually titillating items, the overriding cultural view of women as sex objects may have worked at cross-purposes with their intent. Thus, Laing argues that "an attempt to parody 'sexiness' may simply miss its mark and be read by the omnivorous male gaze as the 'real thing'" (1985:94). Their attempt at resistance, when contained within the subculture's private code, could be, and was, often read by the mainstream press and by observers more in terms of its accommodation, rather than resistance, to feminine sexual stereotypes. While striving to counter stereotypes of women in rock, punk women were repeatedly described as sluts, perverts, whores, and junkies by those outside the subculture.

However, within the punk scene, women created new roles that challenged the image of women rock fans as drug- and sex-crazed groupies. In mainstream rock youth culture, female fans had only submissive roles in the consumption of rock music: they could be teenyboppers, and when they grew older, groupies, with the groupie role providing a real-life extension of the sexualized hero worship of the teenybopper. Punk provided other roles for women, not only as musicians but as consumers of the music. This is not to say that male punk bands had no groupies, as Noel Monk and Jimmy Guterman (1990) document in their account of the Sex Pistols' U.S. tour, and McNeil and McCain (1996) document in their oral history of the New York scene. However, Monk and Guterman did document at least one girl engaging in more masculine forms of punk fan appreciation: "A teenage girl named Lamar who drove to Dallas from San Francisco just for this event, has spent much of the show trying to entice [Sid] Vicious to lean down from the stage toward her.[2] When he finally gets close enough, midway through "Problems," Lamar rears her head back and then slams it into Vicious' face, opening a gash on his nose.... A short blond punk, she wears a leather wristband ringed in barbed wire. She reels from the jolt of Sid's face, and enjoys it.... He licks his lips, tastes the fresh blood, and smiles at Lamar. She points her middle finger at him" (1990:14–15). This account contravenes standards of groupie behavior; rather than enticing Vicious for sexual purposes, "Lamar" expressed her liking in an inverted form, as violence. As punk broke down barriers between the band and the audience, and redefined abuse as adulation, some girls clearly seized the opportunity to express their appreciation in less sexualized ways.

Although punk was commonly viewed as a liberating time for women in the history of rock, its roots in the machismo and "masculinism" of '60s garage rock were bound to resurface in due time. Early punk was not entirely free of misogyny, with bands such as the Stranglers, the Dead Boys, and even Blondie occasionally putting forth unabashedly sexist lyrics and publicity. The Stranglers and Dead Boys were especially objectionable, singing gleefully about beating girlfriends, having sex with groupies, and dominating women (Dancis 1978; Laing 1985). Women and femininity were not always welcome in the punk scene: Mark P., editor of the London 'zine *Sniffin' Glue*, was quite explicit about this, writing, in October 1976, "Punks are not girls, if it comes to the crunch we'll have no option but to fight back" (quoted in Laing 1985:41). Nevertheless, historians of women in rock point to punk as a pivotal moment in women's participation in rock 'n' roll music. Punk rock's disdain for virtuosity, its lyrical focus on topics other than male teenage sexual angst, and its focus on style allowed girls more access to the subculture's core than they had ever before enjoyed in any previous U.S. and British youth subculture. Yet, many of these freedoms were lost in translation when the British returned punk to the United States.

Generation Y: Hardcore Rules

By 1979, the Sex Pistols had disbanded in a maelstrom of lawsuits. Punk rock was being co-opted by the music industry it had sought to oppose and was marketed as New Wave. Designers Vivienne Westwood, Zhandra Rhodes, and Gianni Versace and the fashion industry had defused punk's sartorial terrorism. Politically, the conservative forces of right-wing parties had triumphed in Western politics and ideology. Throughout the 1980s and early on into the 1990s, in Britain, Canada, and the United States, conservative ideologies dominated public discourse. Punk was dead.

Or was it? The co-optation of early punk bohemianism and the emergence of this rhetoric of conservatism led punks to regroup and reformulate their message of protest and its means of delivery, drawing punk deeper into antiauthoritarian politics and extremes of style. The late '70s and early '80s thus saw the rise of punk subcultures as political ideologies ranging from the far-right Nazi punks to groups that were off the political scale—anarchists and straight-edgers. After the heyday of the early punk scene, bands continued to emerge and capture the dwindling punk audience. These bands, such as the Exploited, the Anti-Nowhere League, Angelic Upstarts, Disorder, Discharge, Sham 69, UK Subs, GBH, and Chaos UK drew on working-class issues and harder-edged pub rock sounds. Only the most dedicated members of the original punk scene remained adherents to this music, and punk returned to the underground from which it had briefly emerged (Laing 1985). The subculture now began to perpetuate through the joining of post-punk kids—those who had not been around for the original formation of the subculture. This new punk subculture distinguished itself as "hardcore," a label that marked its movement away from the early punk styles, lifestyles, and beliefs.

Crass, Poisonous, and Conflicted: British Roots of Hardcore

As the punk subculture consolidated musically and stylistically, its political content grew more explicit. The strongest political voice became that of the anarchists, with bands such as Crass, Poison Girls, and Conflict spearheading the musical propagation of anarchy (Laing 1985). Crass, an anarchist vegetarian collective/band comprised nine to twelve male and female musicians and artists who lived communally in Essex, England, from 1977 to 1984 (McKay 1996). Crass did more than sing about anarchy; they attempted to combine political rhetoric with practice, creating a lifestyle based on communalism with strong doses of personal and social responsibility. Crass advocated vegetarianism and pacifism, abjured drinking and drugs, and attacked patriarchy, racism, the class system, Third World exploitation, government, the war machine, and religion, among other institutions. Crass's production, distribution, and promotion networks also extended to bands with which they allied, such as the Poison Girls, who highlighted a feminist-pacifist perspective in songs such as "Take the Toys from the Boys." Led by older (and sole) woman Vi Subversa, Poison Girls explicitly challenged the machismo and youth orientation of mainstream and punk rock (Laing 1985). Crass spawned a renaissance of punk bands with more explicitly developed political ideologies than their 1970s originators. In the 1980s, Crass's punk politics and their insistence on the enactment of punk ideology sparked the beginning of a new type of punk: hardcore. However, the egalitarian impetus of Crass's brand of punk was lost on the journey to America.

Lost in Translation: U.S. Hardcore

The story of British punk may have ended in San Francisco with the Sex Pistols' demise, but the story of the new U.S. hardcore punk subculture begins there. Reacting against the dominant hippie scene, San Francisco adolescents were seeking out a new form of subcultural rebellion in the late '70s. They found this in the New York punk music of the Dolls, the Stooges, the Ramones and Blondie. Thus, by the time the Sex Pistols reached San Francisco in 1978, the city already boasted an active punk scene, with bands such as Mary Monday and the Britches, the Avengers, the Screamers, Crime, and the Nuns, bands whose underground rock sound already approximated punk. The San Francisco scene also had its own 'zine, *Search and Destroy*, that had been covering both local and New York bands since 1977. The SF punks had created their own distinctive brand of punk, which became more like British punk when members of the scene were exposed to documentaries about the London scene and to the Sex Pistols' entourage (Stark 1992).

As in the U.K. punk scenes, young women on the West Coast played pivotal roles in early punk. In San Francisco, women such as Mary Monday, Jennifer Miro, and Penelope Houston took center stage in early punk bands, as did the later all-female bands Contractions and Noh Mercy. The Nuns, led by Miro, and the Avengers, Penelope Houston's band, were the premiere punk bands of the SF scene and contemporaries of the Sex Pistols, opening for them at their final show. Miro and Houston, like Debbie Harry and Patti Smith, exemplified two very disparate takes on punk femininity. Miro sported an art deco look composed of fur collars and cocktail dresses. Houston was more androgynous, wearing her bleached hair short and spiked, with the tattered and safety-pinned look more characteristic of the U.K. punks (Stark 1992).

In Los Angeles, punk girls likewise briefly stood at the center of the emerging punk scene. The Plungers, a group of girls and women sharing a Hollywood apartment (including Trudie, "L.A.'s most popular punk rocker" and Hellin Killer) hosted all the major, legendary punk parties in Los Angeles. Other scenesters such as Trixie ("the vampire"), Mary Rat, Lorna Doom, Gerber, Delphina, and Malissa all became prominent punk figures (Belsito and Davis 1983). Early L.A. punk bands such as the Bags, the Eyes, the Controllers, the Germs, the Go-gos, the Bangs (later the Bangles), and X (named for singer Exene Cervenka) all included women as instrumentalists and vocalists. For a time, women played a major role in the L.A. punk scene: "Female bass players were almost a requirement, and it seemed that it was often the women who dominated and controlled the punk scene. This equality of the sexes was just another breakdown of traditional rock and roll stereotypes that the early scene was perpetrating" (Belsito and Davis 1983:17).

On the East Coast of the United States, girls also enjoyed a brief moment in the limelight of punk. Even as punk flourished in London, the original punk scene underwent a renewal in New York City, with new kids coming into the CBGB scene as the older punks disappeared into the fame of mainstream rock or the oblivion of drug abuse (and, in some cases, both). It was in the time between the original underground scene and the introduction of hardcore that newer bands featuring female performers emerged. Second-wave punk bands such as Teenage Jesus and the Jerks and the Plasmatics followed the original New York bands onto the CBGB stage. Lydia Lunch, diminutive teenage vocalist of Teenage Jesus, and Wendy O Williams (an amazonian ex-porn-star presence in bondage gear whose band became renowned for blowing up cars onstage) briefly became central in the New York punk scene (Kozak 1988; O'Brien 1995).

As the West Coast scene grew, the early pop punk bands were eclipsed by newer, harder, more masculine bands whose sound and politics were influenced by the newer U.K. bands such as the Exploited and the UK Subs. All-male bands such as San Francisco's Dead Kennedys (formed in 1978), Hermosa Beach's "muscle punk" Black Flag (in 1979) and Fear (in 1980) invaded the California punk scenes. These bands had a harder-edged sound than did the previous San Francisco bands, and were less interested in (feminine) arty self-expression than they were in creating a controversial expression of (masculine) punk anger, energy, and humor.

The all-male bands of the West Coast became leaders in the new U.S. punk scene. While some of these bands rhetorically espoused egalitarianism, self-respect, and social change, in reality, they edged women out of the scene. The San Francisco punks spawned a "thrash" scene, with bands such as MDC (originally from Texas), Crucifix, and the Fuck Ups creating music with an accelerated beat and angry lyrics. This scene attracted bands from Southern California, such as Black Flag, DOA, the Circle Jerks, Suicidal Tendencies, Agent Orange, Social Distortion, and TSOL (True Sounds of Liberty), all of which produced a faster, harder-edged sound accented by angry political lyrics.

It was at these hardcore shows that the pogo dance, even in its strangling version, became too tame to keep up with the accelerated pace of the music. Enter the slam dance, which then developed into "thrashing," a seemingly more violent form of slam dance, in which, in response to the choppy rhythms of hardcore punk, fans began to thrash in the area in front of the stage, hence-forth known as "the thrash pit" or, simply, "the pit." Thrashing involved flail-ing one's arms and lifting one's knees, although surprisingly little of this apparent violence resulted in serious injury. The pushing and shoving that oc-curred in the pit, and often in male punks' roughhousing, was not interpreted as fighting; fighting in earnest was frowned upon, and dancers assisted fallen comrades back to their feet. Rather, this ritual was merely a "parody of vio-lence" (Lull 1987:242). With its symbolic violence, the thrash was a dance of male hardcore solidarity. Male thrashers, surrounded by male audience mem-bers, caught male stage divers as they leapt into the male crowd below them. Girls venturing into the thrash pit were subjected to the same elbowing and smashing as were their male peers, and to some occasional groping as well. It was not always an attractive prospect.

As hardcore and thrash pervaded California punk, women were pushed out of the center, no longer band members nor active audience members. Hardcore and thrash bands had a decidedly masculine emphasis and girls were discour-aged from entering the pit. Girl bands (or bands with female members) that had been part of the punk scene, such as the Go-gos, the Bangles, Romeo Void, and Bonnie Hayes and the Wild Combo, turned to the pop of New Wave. Jen-nifer Miro, lead singer of what had been the premiere punk band of the late seventies San Francisco punk scene, noted: "Later, it became this macho hardcore, thrasher, punk scene and that was not what it was about at first. There were a lot of women in the beginning. It was women doing things. Then it became this whole macho anti-women thing. Then women didn't go to see Punk bands anymore because they were afraid of getting killed. I didn't even go because it was so violent and so macho that it was repulsive. Women just got squeezed out" (quoted in Stark 1992:93). The two scenes diverged—with

_____ *Illustration 6* _____

Punks thrashing at UK Subs show in 1992.
(Photo: D. K. Rabel)

original punk bands now dubbed New Wave, hardcore appropriated the "punk" label.

Uni(de)formity: Eighties Punk Style

As a result of the ascendancy of hardcore, much of the variety and play apparent in the early punk style of dress was lost. The hardcore punk look became highly recognizable and much more uniform, and punks became generally intolerant of very many of the spontaneous stylistic generations that had characterized the original punk subculture. The basic hardcore punk uniform was then composed of combat boots, torn jeans, leather jackets, spiked armbands and dog collars, and mohawks. Hardcore punk still retained a limited DIY aesthetic. Using markers, paint, and metal studs, punks ornamented their clothing, handwriting slogans ("No Future," "Fight War, not Wars"), symbols (the anarchist circled A), band names (Misfits, the Exploited), and song titles ("Nazi Punks Fuck Off") on their shirts and jeans; painting band logos on their leather jackets; and affixing a variety of metal studs, chains, dog tags, and patches to all manner of apparel. Male hardcore punks often wore a "butt flap," a square piece of cloth affixed to the waistband in back of their pants and that hung down past their buttocks in a fashion much resembling a loincloth. In hardcore, punk style became decidedly harder-edged, masculine, creating a look that was basically "unisex" (male) as opposed to androgynous (a mix of male and female). The hardcore look became so emblematic of punk

——— *Illustration 7* ———————————————
Punk exhibiting self-made modifications to leather jacket
(Photo: D. K. Rabel)

that its paraphernalia was even co-opted and sold in discount stores as Halloween costumes. (I once found a rubber "Baldie" wig with a black mohawk, at the same time that I sported the genuine article. I put it on my head, ran to find my mom in the checkout line and yelled, "Look ma!" as I removed the wig, to her horror and embarrassment.) Punk style had truly become codified.

The growing masculinization of punk was especially apparent in the construction of subcultural symbols. Whereas women's stylistic manifestations in early punk centered around sexual clothing and bondage gear, hardcore's masculinity and the codification of punk style contributed to the construction of a more masculine female punk style. In her examination of commodification and the hardcore subculture, Susan Willis (1991) noted that the punk style of male dress was open to some degree of feminization, while the musical style remained extremely masculine. Nevertheless, even within the limitations of the hardcore scene, punk girls created and elaborated distinctively feminine manners of dress. The few hardcore "pit girls" wore a uniform much like that of their male peers, but instead of jeans, they wore short kilts and black tights, feminizing the hardcore punk look.

In U.S. hardcore, politics once again played a central role in the articulation of style and lifestyle. As in the United Kingdom, as punk grew more hardcore, its politics became harder-edged, demanding a total commitment. Hardcore punks became increasingly politically active, but although hardcore punks were united in their antiauthoritarianism, the exact articulation of their politics varied greatly. These political factions included Peace Punks and Positive Force punks—vegetarian, spiritual, politically committed, pacifist Washington, D.C., punks inspired by Crass (Kliman 1990)—straight-edge punks who advocated a chemical-free lifestyle, as well as skinheads and Nazi punks, who espoused white supremacist fascist ideologies.

The prevailing punk ideology remained anarchy, with anarchist hardcore punks maintaining a high profile by organizing political groups and events. Early punks' Rock Against Racism concerts evolved into Rock Against Reagan events in the United States. Like Crass, these groups organized fund-raising concerts, coordinated and attended protests and demonstrations, and released flyers and 'zines. This punk anarchism was not based primarily upon textual sources, but rather on a grassroots interpretation of antiauthoritarianism and personal responsibility. Punk anarchism stressed not revolution, but education towards liberation, primarily through personal choice and responsibility, leading to an ethic of individualism (O'Hara 1995).

Although most punks espoused leftist progressive politics, some factions of self-described "working-class" punks adopted more reactionary political ideologies. The punk and skinhead subcultures thus briefly converged in the United Kingdom and the United States in the early 1980s, with bands such as Cockney Rejects, Sham 69, and the Exploited drawing mixed audiences. This brief convergence of punk and skinhead left marks on the punk subculture. Stylistically, punks adopted the Doc Marten boots and braces (suspenders) of the skinheads, along with the "suedehead" or totally bald hairstyle. Punks and skinheads began to frequent the same bars and clubs. Ideologically, some factions of punk became indistinguishable from skins, proclaiming themselves to be Nazi punks. However, this faction was far outnumbered by more radically egalitarian punk factions and expelled from the punk scene (a movement which found its anthem in the Dead Kennedys' "Nazi Punks Fuck Off!") to be absorbed into the skinhead subculture. Nevertheless, this brief crossover created a lingering effect, with punk and skinhead often conflated in the public imagination.

The Eighties' Hardcore Devil Diaspora
From its California origins, hardcore punk quickly spread throughout urban and suburban areas in the United States and Canada. Scenes started

up from the Canadian West Coast (Baron 1989a, 1989b), to cities in the U.S. Midwest (Eicher, Baizerman, and Michelman 1991) and Southwest (Fox 1987; Kotarba and Wells 1987), and on to the East Coast. With the original punk scene, both in England and North America, waning, the East Coast punks also quickly picked up on the new California hardcore scene. CBGB responded to the new scene, hosting afternoon hardcore shows in the 1980s. In the mid-1980s, the New York scene spawned all-male bands like Agnostic Front (originally a skinhead band), Prong, Murphy's Law, Youth of Today, and Warzone (Hurley 1989). As on the West Coast, punk became more masculine: "When TSOL and the Circle Jerks came out with vinyl, slam dancing got big. Whenever people did it, they were deemed cool, so everybody did it. All the girls who went to the shows sort of dropped out of the scene because it became so male-dominated. They kind of stayed on the outskirts. Some got into it—wore kilts and combat boots. Teen Idles broke up. Then SOA and Minor Threat started. Those bands were a lot tougher and everything became more macho" (Nathan Strejcek, quoted in Connolly, Clague, and Cheslow 1992:25). Once again, girls were edged out of the burgeoning new hardcore punk scene. Never again would they occupy a central role in the punk subculture.

The ascendancy of hardcore punk created a schism in the punk scene. *Hardcore* began not only to describe a type of fast, hard-edged punk music, but to denote subcultural commitment as well. In describing the social organization of a group of punks, Kathryn Fox (1987) found distinct hierarchies within the punk scene. Hardcore punks expressed the greatest commitment to the punk subculture, embodying "punk fashion and lifestyle codes to the highest degree" (352). Mostly male, and coming from lower- or working-class backgrounds, hardcore punks viewed their participation in the subculture as permanent, exhibiting their disdain for mainstream society through their adoption of the most extreme forms of punk style and lifestyle. They adopted radical alterations of their bodies (shaved heads, piercings, tattoos), espoused extremes of the subcultural lifestyle (unemployment, poverty, drug use), and verbally expressed strong commitment to the punk ideology and the local punk scene.

Distinct from hardcore punks, softcore punks expressed less commitment to punk values and viewed their membership in the subculture as transitory. More numerous, and including a higher proportion of females, softcore punks were less likely to adopt the extremes of punk style and lifestyle. However, they did verbally endorse punk ideologies and beliefs and associated with hardcore punks, occasionally resolving to make a deeper commitment and moving from their peripheral position to the center of the hardcore scene. Stephen Baron (1989a, 1989b) found a similar hierarchy and gender breakdown in a Canadian West Coast punk scene. Again, the hardcore punks were mainly male, whereas softcore punks tended to be female, and to lack the subcultural support to integrate more deeply into the tough, street-based lifestyle increasingly demanded by hardcore.

As they had in Britain a decade before, and as skinheads would a decade later, North American hardcore punks became the "folk devils" of the 1980s. Unlike previously demonized youth subcultures however, punks had purposely assumed the positions of "society's alienated outcasts" (Lamy and Levin 1985:157). Punks fashioned this stigmatized group identity by using style to directly confront the middle-class values of mainstream culture. Harold Levine and Steven Stumpf found that the prevailing themes of the punk subculture center on "the interrelated imagery of death, violence, perversion, loathsomeness, chaos, victimization, and the like" (1983:430). They argued that punks not only were well aware of the effect created by the confrontational nature of their symbols, but that they enjoyed being cast as social misfits, arguing that "punks want to repel those in the mainstream culture and to challenge them with what the latter would regard as negative symbols" (431). They concluded that punk is a "reflexive" subculture that draws on "loathsome" images and constructs social rejection in order to construct a critique of mainstream culture.

The subtlety of this message of protest was frequently overlooked, and it was often solely the image of deviance that punks successfully projected. The achievement of this constructed image of deviance exceeded even the original expectations of its punk progenitors. Thus, in a pretest for a social psychological study on the relation of personal space to granting requests for small favors, Glick, DeMorest, and Hotze (1988) asked ten persons to compare and rate punk and nonpunk confederates (research assistants who would later ask strangers to participate in a survey) on such measures as mainstream appearance, attractiveness, and "punk traits." The punk confederate was deemed to be not only statistically deviant ("highly dissimilar in appearance to the general population" [319]), but to be pathologically deviant as well ("significantly more likely to commit violent crimes, use drugs, hold subversive political beliefs, be more threatening, and less trustworthy"[319]).[3] Not surprisingly, Glick, DeMorest, and Hotze discovered that the likelihood of the punk confederate being granted her request for a small favor (participation in a survey) increased with her physical distance from members of the general public.

As in the punk explosion in the United Kingdom in the late 1970s, during the ascendancy of hardcore and the American punk revival of the mid-1980s, parents' fears regarding their children's espousal of punk style were addressed in a number of media. Parents ostensibly dreaded the following scenario: "One

morning, let's say, your hitherto nicely dressed teenager comes down for breakfast with hair dyed green and teased into a shark-fin, a safety-pin in one nos-
tril, skull-and-crossbones earrings and enough clanking metal chains to hold
down King Kong. Confused about the meaning of this transformation? Wor-
ried that the change may be permanent?" (Mays 1991:C13). Advice articles
urged parents to examine additional aspects of the child's behavior, such as
school performance, prior to concluding that the child was not only "spiking
his hair, boasting metal studs," but "shooting drugs" as well (Kogan 1991:D5).
Instead, articles reassured parents that "[w]hether your child wants to be a
punk rocker or a preppy, there's no need to worry. Wanting to make a statement is part of normal development" (Comer 1989:132).

Despite the ultimately sympathetic message of such articles, most media
coverage served to reinforce the notion that punks are offensively, and even
dangerously, deviant. As punks were demonized, parents became concerned
with their children's involvement in the subculture. Even advisory articles that
cast punk as a "phase" did not instruct that membership in the subculture is
benign, but rather that it should not be considered the sole indicator of juvenile degeneracy. Youth authorities likewise took a dim view of punk "deviance."
Efforts at formal control of punks flourished, especially in the southern California birthplace of U.S. hardcore, where groups such as Parents of Punkers
and the Back in Control Training Center used both conferences and media
coverage to advocate various means by which parents could go about "de-
punking" (and "de-[heavy] metaling") their children, usually through empha-
sizing "family values" by using "tough love." Such measures garnered a great
amount of media coverage, with Serena Dank, founder of Parents of Punkers,
appearing nationwide on television programs such as *Donahue, Hour Magazine,* and *The Today Show* in the early 1980s, accompanied by punks currently
under her care (O'Hara 1995; Wooden 1995).

This moral panic even became encoded in judicial procedures in the mid-
1980s, as various southern California judiciaries, drawing from the Back in
Control Training Center's manual, *The Punk and Heavy Metal Handbook,* instituted programs to "de-punk" adolescents who were placed on probation
(Broeske 1985; Lewis 1986). Darlyne Pettinnicchio, former probation officer
and codirector of the center, advised, "[T]he parents have to go into the child's
bedroom and remove the posters, the albums, and the clothes. . . . Then they
have to take him to the barber to get his hair cut, or to the hairdresser to get
the color changed" (quoted in Benet 1986:1). In addition to these stylistic prohibitions, adolescents were also forbidden to associate with known punks, frequent punk shows, listen to punk music, or doodle anything punkish. Back in
Control held day-long Sound and Fury conferences, at which they sought to

sensitize parents, educators, and police officers about the dangers of punk and heavy metal (Conklin 1985a, 1985b; McLellan 1985). Although codirectors Pettinnicchio and Boedenheimer admitted that not all punk (or heavy metal) adolescents were delinquent, and that it was impossible to determine which would be, they advocated parental measures aimed at eradicating any signs of punk identity in their teenagers despite the presence or absence of other behavioral factors.

These restrictive measures were adopted and instituted in the face of a lack of research demonstrating any causal (or even casual) link between membership in the punk subculture and delinquency. Conducting research on the effects of punk and heavy metal music on adolescents in response to a call by the Back in Control Training Center, Jill Rosenbaum and Lorraine Prinsky (1987) found no link between musical preference and delinquency. Later, Christine Hansen and Ranald Hansen (1991) did determine that fans of punk rock not only were more likely to reject authority than were those of heavy metal, but that they also perceived higher rates of antisocial behaviors such as shoplifting and committing various other crimes and misdemeanors among their peers. However, this was a general perception held by these punk fans, and not a self-report of their own activity. Nevertheless, in a later study, Rosenbaum and Prinsky (1991) discovered that 83 percent of psychiatric institutions catering to adolescents in southern California recommended admitting a youth for treatment solely on the basis of his/her adoption of a punk style of dress, regardless of the presence or absence of other behavioral factors. According to a newspaper report on the psychiatric abuse of adolescents, at least one teenage punk, a fifteen-year-old California girl with no history of emotional problems, was unwillingly committed to one psychiatric institution for forty-five days and to another for nine months simply because her punk style "offended and embarrassed her father who was president of a local university" (Leaf 1984).

Such extreme reactions to subcultural membership show that American punks' construction of a deviant image became accepted at face value, with few recognizing or acknowledging the subtleties of political and social protest implied in punk style. As Stephen Beaumont, columnist for the punk magazine *Maximum Rock 'n' Roll*, wrote in the *Toronto Star*, "Punk may have become a victim of its own success. The vision of a volatile, rebellious youth attracts a number of disaffected teens, drawn to the prospect of anti-social violence and rampant drug use. Although this perception of punk bears little semblance to the core of the movement, it reinforces the public's view that punk is a negative subculture to be feared" (1989:A27). By the late 1980s, American hardcore punk had achieved a level of recognition and notoriety on a par with that of the British punks of a decade before.

Generation Z: Subcultural Schisms

In the early 1990s, punk underwent yet another "revival," largely due to the popularity of "grunge." The mainstream music media finally "discovered" the previously overlooked impact of punk on rock music, and the fashion industry once again turned to punk for inspiration. In an outstanding example of the homogeneity of media products, two U.S. television stations produced and broadcast accounts of rock and roll in 1994. Both TBS's *History of Rock 'n' Roll* and PBS's *Rock 'n' Roll,* multi-episodic documentaries, featured episodes dedicated to punk, finally recognizing the early punk musical underground as an important moment in the development of rock. While these documentaries diverged in some of their content (TBS included a vignette on Elvis Costello, in which he protested that he was never a punk; PBS delved briefly into reggae), both ended on a similar note, proclaiming grunge to be the resurrection of this long-disregarded rock form. These documentaries, while splendidly documenting New York and London punk and bemoaning its decline into New Wave, glossed over the '80s; they implied that punk had died in 1978, soon after the Sex Pistols' *Never Mind the Bullocks,* and was revived in 1991, with Nirvana's *Nevermind.* Media documenting this as a revival tied punk, erroneously, to the grunge scene. It was as though hardcore had never happened.

Rather than being the salvation of punk, grunge was more of a hybrid of punk DIY aesthetics and hippie slovenliness. Grunge was not the revival of punk, for punk was still alive and thriving, not only in Seattle, but in pockets and enclaves all over the United States. Punk had survived the conservative '80s, and in the late '80s and early '90s renewed itself in a variety of offshoots such as grunge, Riot Grrrl, and "queercore." The hardcore punk scene declined somewhat in the '90s and fractured into two factions: punk rockers and gutter punks.

Old, New, or Spirited: Punk Rockers

Most punks today are much like the original punks of the late 1970s and early 1980s. These punks tend to be localized, living at their parents' home, in apartments, or in well-organized squats. Many are employed or attend school, and are active in local bands, 'zines, political groups, or independent music production companies. These punks have strong ties to the local scene, helping to organize shows and conscientiously attending local bands' shows in order to "support their local scenes." I refer to these punks as "punk rockers," although they include very different groups such as old school, new school, or Spirit of '77 punks, as well as remaining vestiges of the original hardcore and straight-edge punks of the 1980s. These punks dress in more typically recognizable punk style, featuring neatly shaved hairstyles, brightly colored hair, and colorful plaid clothes.

Old school punks, or "original punks," are usually punks who have been into the punk scene since the late '70s or early '80s. These aging punks tend to adhere to some modified version of their punk look, but usually have made concessions to mainstream society in order to be able to hold onto jobs. These punks are recognized and respected (but not revered) as "old punks." They tend to be employed in artistic fields and retain their connections to the local punk scene, sometimes documenting the scenes in academic (O'Hara 1995), historic (McNeil and McCain 1996; Savage 1991), autobiographical (Lydon 1994; Matlock 1990), or artistic (Stark 1992) works.

New school punks are usually younger, are just finding the punk scene, and find the original punk style appealing. This group is expanding, as more punk music undergoes a revival in the popular sense. "Power-pop" or "pop-punk" bands such as Green Day, Rancid, and the Offspring, with hit songs in the so-called alternative market, provided adolescents, once again, with media access to punks, sparking the most widespread popular interest in punk since the late 1970s. Most punks tend to have a fair amount of disdain for the new school adolescents, who view punk merely as a fashion without understanding its underlying ideologies or meanings.

Some punks constructed and maintained allegiances to the original British punk scene. These became known as "Spirit of '77" punks, adolescents who argued that the new hardcore bands were no match for the intensity and passion of original punk bands. Spirit of '77 punks take their version of punk style and ideology not from the original New York scene (although they may revere the Ramones and Iggy and the Stooges), but from the London version of punk, which remains very much alive in some enclaves. They idealize not the early, ironic and playful, British bands such as the Sex Pistols and the Buzzcocks, but the more political bands of 1977 to 1979—the Clash, UK Subs, the Exploited, and so on. Spirit of '77 punks dream of traveling to London to attend shows by original punk bands that have remained together or re-formed and to meet original British punks. However, whereas U.K. punks originally wore the Union Jack as T-shirts or jackets in order to degrade the flag, Spirit of '77 punks tend to do so reverently, and often become anglophiles. Ironically, in constructing London as a punk Mecca, they contravene much of the original punks' dissatisfaction with and disdain for British society.

These many types of punk rockers adhere, with varying amounts of fervor, to the more recognizable punk styles and ideologies. When lumped together as punk rockers, they make up the majority of most punk scenes in the 1990s and are the most active in preserving the punk scenes in which unique punk culture—recordings, shows, and style—emerge. Their subcultural commitment is more one of style and political expression than it is of protest as lifestyle (*à la* Crass collective). Many punk rockers are employed, working in the service sector, construction, or retail, while a few support themselves through artistic endeavors, including music and photography. Many punk rockers attend high school, college, or graduate school. Many are supported by their parents. These punks tend to live fairly conventional daily lives, insofar as their activities, if not their physical adornment, are concerned. Their involvements in bands and organizing shows are often relegated to weekends and evenings, although some punk rockers do manage to support themselves exclusively through their musicianship.

Crusty, Street-Living, and Squatting: Gutter Punk

Throughout the 1980s, the most hardcore (both in the sense of being fans of hardcore and being committed to the punk subculture) of hardcore punks often adopted forms of street living, squatting in abandoned buildings or "couch surfing" from one acquaintance's home to another's. This type of subcultural participation evolved, in the late 1980s and early 1990s, into its own faction of the punk subculture, whose members are known as "street punks," "crusties," "travelers," or "gutter punks." Unlike the street punks and squatter punks of the 1980s, who were local adolescents remaining in their city of origin, gutter punks adopt an itinerant lifestyle, traveling throughout North America by hitching rides, jumping trains, or obtaining gas vouchers, which are provided by many municipalities for ridding themselves of undesirables (or, more charitably, for aiding stranded travelers). Like the "new age travelers" (descendants of the hippies) in the United Kingdom and the deadhead contingent that, until 1995, followed the Grateful Dead throughout the United States, gutter punks travel in order to attend events; they may attend Rainbow Gatherings (quasi-hippie annual festivals), but they are usually on their way to evens such as Punkfest, Chaos Days, or the Beer Olympics, day- or week-long festivals that feature punk bands, political protest, and booze. Most gutter punks drink alcohol excessively, and many consume illegal drugs. They travel a circuit that links Seattle to San Francisco to Austin, Texas, wintering in New Orleans (or at least arriving there for Mardi Gras), and often ending up in New York City. Gutter punks tend to travel in small groups of two to five, often splitting up and serendipitously reuniting with friends in other cities.

Gutter punks come from both middle-class and working-class families, but uniformly express low levels of social aspiration. Some are homeless because they have been pushed out of their families or have run away from abusive situations or foster homes. Others, usually older, claim to choose this lifestyle in order to opt out of a mainstream society that they view as overly concerned with status, power, and the accumulation of capital at the expense of the virtues of compassion, integrity, and freedom. Often, however, the punks who explain their lifestyle as a choice also have family backgrounds that are marked by abuse, neglect, or parental drug abuse (see Fisher 1996).

Gutter punks' daily lives center on obtaining food and shelter. Many alternate between panhandling and hanging out, once they have obtained sufficient money for food or drink. On rainy, cold, or hot days, they may remain in their squats (where they often live for weeks or months before being evicted by police) or seek out youth shelters and other indoor hangouts, such as restaurants. Gutter punks pursue all these activities in pairs or small groups, sharing the goods they obtain with their companions, hanging out, "doing nothing," and conversing.

Many gutter punks hold very antiauthoritarian views, maintaining that submission to the regime of work and family responsibilities is antithetical to punk. Gutter punks are highly individualistic, self-sufficient, and resourceful, and often consider themselves to be survivalists. In addition to squatting for shelter and panhandling for money, some engage in busking, selling handmade items, or "dumpster diving" (digging through trash) for food or sellable items. A few resort to dealing drugs, in order to support their drug use or abuse. Some own dogs, for whom they often provide food at the expense of their own meal. Some also own pet rats, which live on their bodies or in cardboard boxes at night. Many gutter punks dream not of getting off the streets per se, but rather of establishing some form of communal, often agrarian, living arrangement with other like-minded antiauthoritarian punks.

Gutter punks have a distinctive style of dress. Many still wear recognizable punk fashions, spiking their unusually colored hair, wearing torn clothes and leather jackets, and ornamenting their clothes with graffiti, patches, and studs. However, unlike the brightly colored Spirit of '77 punks, gutter punks dress in a muted, earth tone palette of gray, khaki, black, brown, and white. In addition, gutter punks decorate their clothes with folded-over caps from beer bottles or with chrome tabs pulled off disposable cigarette lighters. Due to their homelessness and itinerant lifestyle, few gutter punks have regular access to bathing facilities, and so are often grungy. One faction of gutter punks—the crusty punks—takes this uncleanness to an extreme, viewing regular bathing as a bourgeois ritual and thus cultivating grime, vermin, and body odor.

The growth of the gutter punk scene has not gone unnoticed by the media and youth authorities, with punks in the '90s sparking yet another "moral panic" in which they are cast as "folk devils" (Cohen 1972). Punks in the '90s retain their negative reputation and police are pressured to control this menace. Currently, the gutter punks of New Orleans and other cities have begun to receive the media's attention, with feature articles on these "nihilistic, angry, ironic spawn" (Booth 1996) appearing in major national newspapers (Booth 1996; Yardley 1996; Fisher 1996) and in at least one major national magazine, *Details* (Orenstein 1995). Such articles usually portray gutter punks as drugged-out losers, thieves, and menaces to public safety. Shopkeepers in New Orleans' French Quarter, the gutter punks' preferred winter destination, repeatedly pressure the police to rid the streets of homeless adolescents (all of whom are mistakenly labeled "gutter punks") in order to improve the tourist trade. Likewise, the Montreal press reported an incident in which subway police, allegedly, brutalized a punk who had bumped into an officer (Leger 1994) and in the summer of 1996 Montreal police "cracked down" on punks squatting in a downtown park, sparking riots. The press's focus on gutter punks and police crackdowns are only the most recent manifestation of the serial characterization of punk as a deviant subculture composed of dangerous undesirables.

The schism between hardcore and softcore punks in the 1980s is replicated in the split between gutter punks and localized punk rockers in the 1990s. Gutter punks argue that punk rockers who have homes and jobs are inauthentic, are "poseurs." The two groups may associate with each other, but the gutter punks refer to punk rockers as "postcard punks" (for being the picture-perfect consumers of punk paraphernalia often depicted on tourist trade postcards, especially in London), "house punks," or "safety punks." For their part, many of the punk rockers find gutter punks perplexing, and often revolting, accusing them of giving punk a bad name and labeling them "scum punks." These punk rockers, who create each local punk scene, accuse the gutter punks of freeloading off the local scene, rather than supporting it, and dislike having unwashed punks join in the pits at shows. For punk rockers, then, the emergence of squatter punks challenges the purity of their preservation of what they see as the original punk style and ethos. Gutter punks, on the other hand, view their interpretation of punk as the epitome of the embodiment and practice of punk ideals.

Girls on the Outside: Conclusion

From its origins in the underground music scene of New York City to its current incarnations as hardcore, Spirit of '77, gutter, crusty, postcard, new school, or old school, the punk subcultures retain certain core punk ideologies, remaining subversive, political, parodic, and oppositional throughout the many mutations of punk. Punks still use stylistic devices to counter mainstream political, vocational, and moral imperatives, creating a type of "sartorial terrorism" or "semiotic guerilla warfare" (Hebdige 1979) against mainstream society. The various punk subcultures remain oppositional in their norms, beliefs, rituals, and styles of dress, hair, and body adornment; as members of a "reflexive" subculture, punks seek to remain outside the dominant culture, while "illuminating central features of it" (Levine and Stumpf 1983:433). Punk continues to offer adolescents a site to construct rebellion against mainstream mores, by allowing them the freedom to express, verbally, stylistically, musically, and politically, their disaffection with the state of the world. Punks have created new forms of literary and artistic expression, a type of viscerally exciting, expressive music, and a network of underground institutions such as independent record labels, alternative radio programming, small concert venues, cheap local publications, and squatters' networks.

As it has been from the start, punk remains a predominantly white subculture. The early fusions of punk and reggae and the progressive politics and Rock Against Racism events of the 1970s and 1980s did establish a crossover between the subcultural worlds of black and white youth, a process Hebdige (1979) describes in detail. This crossover carried over into punk's relation with a contemporaneous resistant subculture, hip-hop, in the late '70s and early '80s when bands such as Blondie and the Clash drew on the talent of New York rap artists in their recordings (the crossover extended in both directions, with the former punk band Beastie Boys gaining much subcultural approval from both punk and hip-hop subcultures as a rap group in the 1980s). However, the rise of fascist and white supremacist factions of hardcore in the '80s did much to destroy the dialogue between punk and black youth subcultures. While the contemporary punk subculture is largely non- or anti-racist, the origins of punk in the concerns of white British youth, the ongoing image of punks as racist, and the presence of other forms of stylistic resistance such as hip-hop function to exclude all but white youth.

Thus, despite the continued development of punk, despite the subculture's oppositional, reflexive symbols, rituals, norms, values, beliefs, and ideologies, despite the critique of a break-away faction (Riot Grrrl), at the beginning of its third decade of resistance, revolt, and refusal, punk remains a predominantly white, masculine youth subculture. Punk is still a site where girls remain marginalized and silenced. These girls' lives, experiences, and opinions have remained unarticulated within the subculture, and invisible to the public. Even within punk, the most rhetorically egalitarian and oppositional of youth subcultures, girls are still on the outside.

Three

"I Grew Up and I Was a Punk"

Subcultural Stories

My mother once claimed that I became a punk because I wanted to be like the popular kids at school. Nothing could be further from the truth. In fact, by the time I became a punk, I had finally *stopped* wanting to be like the kids at school. Now, my aspirations were much higher: I wanted to be like Joan Jett, raven-haired guitar goddess of the '80s.

To achieve that end, I finally persuaded my mother to help me dye my hair black. Sick of being rejected by the preppies, I figured I'd try the metalheads. In that moment, I was transformed from a geek to a rocker wanna-be. That didn't quite work out—the metalheads in my high school, I suspect, could still catch the whiff of geekiness on me, and would have nothing to do with me. Besides, I was just a girl, and not a particularly cute or sexy one at that. There didn't appear to be a place in the metalhead world for girls who wanted to be rock stars.

Then I decided to be Pat Benatar, early feminist icon of the emerging rock video medium. As my adolescent sense of identity appears to have depended entirely on hairstyle, I had my hair cut by a hairdresser who made me look absolutely nothing like the picture I had brought with me. And this is basically how I became a punk: someone walked up to me at school and told me I looked like a punk. "What's that?" I thought, all the while acting like I knew what he was talking about.

Soon after, the other weird kids at my high school, the New Wavers, arty, punk, and alternative types—kids I had never before seen in my life—showed up at my locker in the science wing one day and moved all my stuff into a locker close to theirs, near the hairdressing program in the vocational wing. I had been adopted.

They exposed me to the Sex Pistols and the Exploited, to second-hand suits and torn fishnets, to slam dancing and clove cigarettes, to patchouli oil and hot Earl Grey tea. They gave me a place to go during lunch, a place to hang out after school. And, at my instigation, they helped me give myself a mohawk one afternoon, using dog-grooming clippers—the first in a long series of self-inflicted haircuts. My dad, picking me up that afternoon in his truck, quietly freaked and said nothing. My parents continued to freak, and eventually said something. And then something else, and so on.

But it's not like I woke up one morning, fired with the passion of resistance, and turned from nerd to hardcore within the space of hours. Rather, my becoming a punk was a gradual process involving equal parts rejection, rebellion, conformity, imitation, and boredom, with a large dose of botched haircuts. Jessie, one of the punk girls I later interviewed, summed it up perfectly: "You just fall into it. I never thought, 'Well, I'm going to be a punk. That's what I want to do.'"

So when the principal, while kicking me out of high school, claimed that I was a punk because I wanted to be Wendy O Williams, lead singer of the Plasmatics, I laughed, because he was dead wrong. Wrong, but not too far off. What I really wanted to be was Joan Jett. Trying to emulate my female rock heroines, I just accidentally became a punk, and serendipitously ended up becoming myself.

In the past five years, as I traveled to conferences and presented my research, I often encountered a good deal of curiosity about punk. I was often asked how punks differ from skinheads and whether punks are like gangs. When I talked about punk girls, however, I encountered much more tentative questions. *What* kind of girls? Who are punk girls? How old are they? Are they all from bad families? Aren't they exploited, like girls in motorcycle gangs? Don't they have low self-esteem? Often, the question underlying all of these queries was more simple: Why do girls become punks? This is certainly a legitimate question, and one that I wanted to answer when I started this work. In chapter 1 I offered the example of Sue, a green-haired fifteen-year-old whose experiences in the subculture were not always unabashedly positive, and asked myself why such an intelligent and articulate girl would put up with everything she described. I then asked a more general question: What attracts these girls to male-dominated youth subcultures such as punk? As I sought to answer this question, more arose: What happens to girls once they become punks? How are they treated by those they love? Why do they remain punks when, surely, they are maltreated because of their subcultural identity? And, most importantly for a scholar, where could I turn for answers to these questions?

Books were no help to me now. Research and theorizing on youth subcultures have been gendered masculine since the beginning. In the United States, subcultural studies from Frederick Thrasher's 1927 study of gangs, to William Whyte's 1943 research on the Italian slum, to Jay MacLeod's 1987 (updated in 1995) ethnography of inner-city black and white youths have focused almost exclusively on males. In the United Kingdom, such germinal research as Stan Cohen's 1972 work on Mods; Paul Willis's studies of working-class "lads" (1977) and motorcycle gangs (1978); and the foundation work of the Birmingham Centre for Contemporary Cultural Studies (Hall and Jefferson 1976) place working-class males at the center. Within the context of such male-focused and male-generated subculture theory and research, girls who participate in youth subcultures have been described as passive, ancillary, sexual, and "less resistant" than their male peers.

Both American and British feminist critics of subculture studies have posited a number of arguments accounting for this. One argument is that much of the research has been conducted by male researchers who focus on and sympathize with male members (Brake 1985). For example, American subculture theorist Albert Cohen wrote of male gang members that the "delinquent is the rogue male. His conduct may be viewed not only negatively, as a device for attacking and derogating the respectable culture; positively it may be viewed as the exploitation of modes of behavior that are traditionally symbolic of untrammeled masculinity, which are renounced by middle-class culture because incompatible with its own ends, but which are not without a certain aura of glamor and romance" (1955:140). Glamorous and romantic to whom? Feminist critics since the 1970s have argued that the male researchers attracted to the "glamor and romance" of male-dominated youth subcultures' "untrammeled masculinity" tend not only to glorify the masculine, but to disparage the feminine, uncritically reflecting the male members' evaluations of subcultural females (see Chesney-Lind 1973, 1989; McRobbie 1991; McRobbie and Garber 1976; Millman 1975; Shacklady Smith 1978; Wilson 1978). Thus, just as images of "rogue males" were lauded though celebrations of the masculine, images of "deviant girls" have always been distorted by lenses of paternalism and misogyny.

As a result, precious little is known about girls who join male-dominated youth subcultures. This is hardly surprising in the context of research on subcultures that are constructed by male members to solve status or economic problems faced by males. Clearly, young men create and join subcultures such as skinheads, gangs, graffiti crews, and other delinquent groupings to validate their masculinity (see Arnett 1996; Blazak 1991, 1995; Cohen 1955; Ferrell 1993; Gaines 1992; MacLeod 1987/1995) . In order to account for the purported absence of women from male-dominated subcultures, even feminist Angela McRobbie (1991) argues that girls are not attracted to the subcultural solutions to masculine identification, as these do not address nor interest them. And yet girls *are* present within such subcultures. A number of researchers have argued that, due to the male-domination of these subcultures and the masculinist norms, or due to the girls' adherence to norms of femininity, girls' positions within the subculture replicate their positioning in mainstream culture: their participation is ancillary and they are subordinate to the males. Girls' subcultural participation has thus been described in primarily sexualized terms, with their constructions of deviance assumed to be sexual and conducted primarily through affiliation with a male member. And yet it is hard to imagine why girls would join, and remain, if they were only accepted as toys for the boys.

Male ethnographers' reliance on male members' accounts of girls' and women's motivations result in what Leslie Shacklady Smith (1978) calls "sexist assumptions" about female participation: that girls are passive; that their roles are sexual; that they are ancillary or peripheral in the subculture; that they do not construct nor engage in forms of resistance. Yet, finding that girls are marginal is inevitable when ethnographers use research methods that give voice only to males. When researchers focus specifically on gathering first-hand accounts of girls' and women's positions in male-dominated subcultures, they find that these are much more complex and central than was previously thought.[1]

In the specific case of the punk subculture, this tendency to focus on males, to validate their constructions of the subculture, and for male ethnographers to identify only with male members has led to similar misrepresentations and misunderstandings of punk girls. In his study of West Coast Canadian punks of the late 1980s, ethnographer Stephen Baron concluded that within punk the "severity of resistance was related to gender" (1989a:289). While never specifically defining resistance, Baron described it in terms of male punks' resistance to the institutions of home, school and work. Male punks, he argued, are more likely to squat, drop out, and panhandle, and are thus more resistant than females:

> Males tend to adopt the more severe forms of resistance. They have little
> work experience and few skills, and face a labour market where there is a
> declining demand for manual labor. At the same time, they do not desire the
> employment that is available since the pay is poor, provides little status, and

is alienating. For the male, the subculture is an alternative source of status. The others share his problems and by dismissing the dominant ideology he can attain status via subcultural criteria. . . . Female participation was less severe perhaps because the service sector areas where they are most likely to be employed are still in need of cheap labour. Furthermore, they are still likely to be subject to parental supervision and view the subculture as a social vehicle. [2] (Baron 1989a:312)

This leads Baron to argue that punk is almost two gendered subcultures: For girls, punk is a type of social club, while for boys, it is an avenue of resistance. According to Baron's implied criteria, girls do not engage in the same type of resistance and hence cannot attain the same type of subcultural status.

Baron does note sexism in the punk scene, in that its members discourage girls from engaging in the more masculine forms of resistance: "The subculture does not provide support for females living on the street. The males in the subculture may discourage this option, or make it difficult" (1989a:304). But his argument is tautological: he constructs a definition of punk resistance based on his observations of males, and then states that girls exhibit less severe forms of resistance than do their male counterparts. At no point, however, does he take into account the dangers young women encounter in adopting a street-based lifestyle, their sexist exclusion from subcultural activities, nor the pressures of femininity these girls experience. He thus fails to recognize the ways punk girls encounter gender oppression, and thus how they construct forms of resistance to both cultural and subcultural gender norms.

Subcultural Stories

Are punk girls less resistant than punk boys? Do any engage in "masculine" forms of resistance, such as dropping out and squatting? Do they view the punk subculture merely as a type of social club? Or do they, like their male peers, see punk as an avenue of resistance? If so, what do they resist, and how? What are the consequences of such resistance? Finding no answers in books, I turn to girls' own subcultural stories.[3] I begin with two very different, full narratives, stories that offer the most comprehensive and detailed accounts of each type of subcultural involvement I studied—punk rocker and gutter punk. I present Sue and Candace's narratives much in their own words, as reconstructed from tape-recorded interviews.

Sue: Punk Politics and Parental Rebellion

When I met Sue in the summer of 1993, she was fifteen years old, a petite punk with a large green mohawk. I interviewed her on a park bench while skinheads played some ska music nearby. At the time, Sue was about to start her junior year at a high school that specialized in art, majoring in visual art. She hoped someday to go into the field of broadcast communications. Articulate and funny, Sue was a young punk rocker with reverence for the old school. Sue's narrative of her entry into the punk subculture, and her subsequent experiences in it, were informed equally by her adoption of punk political ideology and her rebellion against her parents.

Sue began her narrative by talking at length about her relationships with her parents: "My parents just got divorced, thank god. Well, see, I hate my dad's guts. He's a Klansman. I mean, I just can't stand him. I'm not sure if he's in the Klan, but he may as well be, he may as well tattoo a swastika on his forehead. I can't stand the man and he hates me. He owns a hair studio because he's an uneducated redneck with a football scholarship that fell through. An' he tawlks lak a redneck too. He owns a hair studio and I have a green mohawk. We don't get along." Following the divorce, Sue became closer to her mother. "I'm living with my mother. She works for the Social Security administration, she's a big corporate manager. She went to university and she's got all these wonderful degrees. She's got her master's. But my mom's a government worker. She used to run off anarchist material at work for us. She's cool. I love my mom and she just moved to the coolest part of town and everything and she's really great. I don't want to leave, I don't want to go squat or leave home or be all rebellious because I love my mom and she loves me. She doesn't mind the way I look, she's like, 'Did you get a new nose ring?' 'Yeah, Ma.' She thinks my squatter boyfriends have been cute and sweet and she's fixed them dinner, and I'm just like, 'Okay.' No kidding. I had this boyfriend who smelled like rotting cheese and she loved him. I could bring home a Polo prep and she'd be like 'Are you on drugs? Is he a dealer?' 'No, Mom.' So we get along."

Becoming a punk approximately a decade after the subculture originated, Sue was introduced to an already-existing scene. She first encountered punk through the media:

One of my first memories is [of San Francisco punk band] Fear on *Saturday Night Live* in 1984. Halloween. I didn't trick-or-treat because I wanted to watch Joan Rivers and this punk band played, and I was like "Omigod!" 1984. I was, what, six? But I do remember them. And my parents are just total right-wing suburbanites, and they were just like, I was making this joke about the band or something, and [my mom] goes, "You'd better not get into that shit!" And I was like "Why?" A few years later, I was like "Do you remember when Fear played *Saturday Night Live*?" That just came to my mind. I watched a lot of TV when I was young, so I saw it on TV, but never saw it downtown. I couldn't leave the suburb. And I guess when I started going to the shows, downtown in 1986, GBH and X were playing opposite each other the same night. Downtown looked like a fucking shark fight, there was so many mohawks. It was great, but that's not when I was really into it.

When I was about nine or ten years old, there was a punk band who lived down the street from me and thought it was really amusing to let me and the drummer's little sister baby-sit the tomato plants while they went to shows. And after a while, they started taking us to shows and we became the "punk babies." The scene kind of sucked us in.

Like many other punks, Sue was also involved in other subcultures prior to choosing punk: "We were both going to a white middle school, everybody hated our guts, we were skater kids, typical rough kids. We skated, we were such bad asses." Sue described her entry into the subculture in familial terms:

We kept going to shows and they adopted us like a family. [My friend] kind of stuck with it in a way. She kind of tends to keep to herself. We came in at the exact same time. I got in a band immediately and I met everybody, and I've been into it since. I guess I really started getting into it when I was about twelve, but [I was] in the groups when I was about nine.

Sue's account of her "adoption" into the punk scene is typical; many other punk girls used familial metaphors when describing punk as their "family" or when referring to their entry into the subculture as an "adoption."

When I asked her what had attracted her to the punk scene, Sue reported that her feelings of social distance from her adolescent peers played a role:

I never really did like Laura Ashley. I never got along with those suburban kids, because we lived in the "low-rent" district of the richest neighborhood, so that immediately separated me from everybody else. I went to a private school where everybody else was like sons of senators' sons and I was like, "Yeah, my dad cuts hair." I'm not saying we were working-class; we were loaded, but I was poor for the atmosphere I'd been surrounded in. I didn't see black people unless they picked up the trash until seventh grade.

Her rebellion against suburban adolescence was also spurred by her disagreement with her father's racist ideas:

And so once I'd started realizing that my dad was just dead fuckin' wrong, I started hanging out in all the places he had told me not to, which happened to be where all the punks hung out, and the highest crime area of town. And then again, the band brought me into it, and it just grew on me. My family was kind of, my mom's nice to me, but my dad was a dick.

The punks in that scene offered her a substitute family:

> And the kids that were covered in tattoos and piercings were like big broth-
> ers, and so I loved going down to see those guys, even if I couldn't drink,
> and just watch them all get really drunk and listen to albums. It was just,
> like, "Wow, I worship these guys." They were so cool. Anyway, I ended up
> like that, and now we're the weirdest-looking kids in the city, looking at the
> nine-year-old kids now and going, "And I have to be a role model for you!"
>
> If I needed to pick a label, while I'm in the South, I would say "punk." If I
> were in New York, where there's been punks that have been around since
> punk began, I wouldn't go "Yes, I'm fifteen years old and I'm going to claim
> your title that you started and then I mooched." I'm not going to go, "Punk
> rock." I'm going to say, "Well, I'm into the political aspects of punk, I love
> the lifestyle, I love the music." But I'm still learning. I'm not saying "I'm not
> worthy," but in D.C. they were cool as hell to me, and so I would say that.
> When I talk to other fifteen-year-olds in town there, they just strike me as
> babbling fucking idiots. But I think, I consider myself intelligent and in a way
> that's kind of why I went and went wild with my hair. It's because when I
> was a little pixie model, people didn't look at me, they were staring at my
> ass. And now when I wear giant clothes and a belt made of bullets, they're
> going to listen to me because they're scared out of their fucking skulls. And
> that's cool. And also, I'm rather small, I'm extremely defensive, and I want
> to argue politics. I will argue politics till the day I die. The left wing is right.
> I'm sorry. Fascism should have been stopped in Italy. It shouldn't have gone
> any further and I have very unkind words for fascists. I'm politically active.

Sue saw the subculture primarily as a political outlet. For a fifteen-year-old
in a generation often described as "slacker," she was surprisingly politically
involved:

> I'm political, of course putting out a bunch of 'zines, of course putting up with
> anarchist networks. I'm really not sure of what my political stance is. My fa-
> vorite form of intangible never-happen government is all the anarchists move
> out to a damn island, call themselves anarcho-communists and reap the ben-
> efits of the free world, but *Lord of the Flies* happens and they start dying off.
> But that'll never happen. And so, I think democratic socialism like they have
> in Sweden is really cool. But I haven't really been involved in that much. I've
> written my 'zines here and there, put out newspapers. I've been to [an] an-
> archist conference in Atlanta, actually. All sorts of stuff. I'm starting to re-
> ally get burned out on it, so I just argue with local fascists. Help start up an
> antifascist group this year.

Thus, for Sue, punk offered more than a style or a social outlet:

I think intelligence signifies punk. And political correctness, to a point, signifies punk. I'm not talking about these kids that go out and wear loose-fitting
garments and hang out at Rainbow Gatherings and say "We're politically correct because we don't eat meat." That's vulgar. Politically correct is how you
live your life. I don't care how many punks wear swastikas to shock people;
that's full of shit. Even though punk was started in England and it was mostly
white, I don't think it should have been a racist movement whatsoever. A lot
of racism does exist within punk, but it shouldn't.

I'm friends with most of the punks downtown, but then again, I go to an
art school chock-full o' hippies, and so, I have to hang with everybody or I
can't. And I'm not homophobic because the gays are oppressed by the
[skinhead] Nazis just as much as much as the punks are. I'm on their side
about it. And so, I'm friends with people into politics, people into punk, people
into whatever. I'm friends with punks all over the country. I love punk. It's
my family. And the old school punks will take you in as a friend and the new
school punks, a lot of them don't have a clue. And I hate being my age and
automatically being labeled "new school" when the old school punks kind of
raised me. It's like its own world within itself, but it kind of branches off into
other little things, like lots of skins hate punks and punks hate skins. It's a
big soap opera, but I try not to get involved, I just kind of hang out with anybody but a Nazi. Road trips are always great. Going out of town, you meet
these punks you've never seen before, you swap addresses, you write each
other, you keep up with what's going on in other parts of the country so if
eighty Nazis maul one kid, you can find out about it.

As Sue became more committed to what she described as the core political
ideology of the punk subculture, she also became very intolerant of the more
superficial aspects: "I don't go around the city trying to earn P[unk]-points at
all costs. I'm not like, 'Hey, there's an old lady, let's mug her.' I'll talk to people
about punk or whatever." She saw her commitment to punk extending throughout her life:

I think I may change my hair, I may change how I dress, I may moderate.
It's like half the other old school punks do when they get in their late twen-
ties when they finally just say "I'll never get a job," or, "I got razor burn for
the last time, damn it!" I think I may not always look different, but I'll always
be different. I'm not going to turn into one of those, when hippies turned
into yuppies, I don't know what the ex-punks would be. I don't think I'll go
yuppie on purpose. Well, I'll sort of be like [Dead Kennedys lead singer] Jello

Biafra and run for mayor. I'll always kind of like the music, no matter how normal I may end up looking. And even if I do look normal, I won't consider myself to be a sellout to the cause, because it's not all how you look.

Sue claimed that punk provided her with an outlet for the type of frustration and dissent that she experienced:

> If I weren't a punk, I'd just probably be a totally schizzed-out little person. Have you ever noticed, out of normal people, you've always got those few that are off? I think I'd probably be way off. I probably would have ended up, if I hadn't gotten into punk I would probably have made better grades. I'm not saying, "Oh, everybody, Tough Love. Punk rock makes bad grades." I know some punks get straight A's. I'm just really lazy. And if I weren't into the punk scene, I don't know what the hell I'd do on weekends, so I probably would make better grades. I'm not saying I'd be more intelligent, I'm just saying I'd make better grades.

Sue still struggled to reconcile some of the norms of punk with her own ambitions and dreams:

> A part of the punk thing is to print up anarchist literature, get screwed, and don't care about good grades anymore. It's just like, "High school? Fuck high school." I mean, I'll finish it and hopefully get to a college, but it's not like I care about it. I want to go into broadcast communications and if I'm good, then they're not going to care. I've talked to a lot of people that are college graduates, who say they look at the school, not the grades. As long as I'm personally getting something out of school, that's fine. I don't care about what grade I get.

Sue's ambitions for the future were divided between punk desires and mainstream expectations:

> In five years, I want to get a band up. I'm not saying I want to get big. I want to have a band the kids will like, that people will show up at shows and they'll have a good time, but I also have to think of college in five years. Broadcast communications, TV or radio. I really don't want to do the photojournalist thing, the demand's running out. Radio's dead. Television. Installation art's also really cool, but that might be a minor, a minor in theater and something like installation art, but it might help me in broadcast communication to have that. But I have no idea what the hell I'm going to be doing. I know I want to be going to college, hopefully New York, but I have a feeling New York's going to shy me off a little. I might get kind of reclusive, you know, resurface after. I want to adopt a kid. I want to adopt a teenager. Because my parents

have put me through all sorts of little institutions to "cure" me, and I met teenagers in there that were up for adoption and had no damn chance. I want to adopt a teenager and just kind of hang out with him, not even come off as an authority figure because they obviously haven't had any authority in their entire lives and I'm not going to change and be a little fascist to them. It's going to be like "You can live here as long as you don't get arrested or really cause any trouble and I'll be really nice to you. Feed you and clothe you, and maybe even send you to college for good."

Sue characterized her participation in punk as the result of many factors. Rebelling against her parents played a key part in her seeking out subcultural options, as did her feelings of isolation from the other adolescents in her high school. She reported having participated in the skater subculture prior to becoming a punk, a pattern of participation in other subcultures which I would find repeated in many girls' stories. Finally, she described her entry into the subculture as being affected by media exposure to punk music and by immediate exposure to other punks. As did many girls, Sue characterized the punk subculture in familial terms: older punks are like "big brothers" and her entry was a process of "adoption." This family, for some punk girls, was a supportive peer group; for others, it was their sole means of survival.

Candace: Thrown into the Street

When I met Candace, she was twenty-one, very much an individualist, and hanging out with gutter punks, having lived as one and now gradually getting away from the more radical aspects of the lifestyle. She was working as a stripper and living in an apartment with her ex-boyfriend, a roommate, and her precocious three-year-old daughter. Candace is a survivor; she talked to me at length about her parents' abuse and neglect. For her, punk was more than a social or political outlet; it was a supportive community and a survival network:

My mom does some sort of marketing type thing, works for some big business. I know there's a 1–800 number I can call and talk to her. My dad fixes heating and air conditioners. My parents kicked me out of the house when I was fourteen, and it wasn't the first time I'd been kicked out, but this time when I got kicked out I went and stayed with my friend and her mother as opposed to, sometimes if it was summer, I'd go off in the woods, or I'd go into the city and I'd go find an abandoned house and stay. Or I'd stay with friends. This time I moved in with my friend and her mother, and it was stable. A week after they kicked me out, my parents came by in a moving truck and they moved to another city. And I didn't know where for about a year, where they moved to.

Candace's stability was short-lived:

When I was fourteen, when my parents left and I lived with my friend and her mom, I eventually got kicked out of that house. That wasn't even my fault. That was her daughter's fault. It was more her fault, because she repressed her daughter really heavily and her daughter, her mom would go out until six in the morning, and claim she wasn't an alcoholic, but she'd be gone until six in the morning and her daughter would take upon herself to like invite all our friends over, and buy a keg of beer. And so I got kicked out of the house for it. So her daughter got the cops called on her. By her own mother. . . . So I was kind of on my own. I saw my parents again once I had her. Once I had my little girl, they started to, then my mom started to try and they started trying to keep in touch. Now I talk to her about once a month. Once every couple of weeks.

Like Sue, Candace was exposed to punk through other members of the subculture, in her case a member of her family:

I've been into punk since I was twelve. My stepbrother used to take me to Black Sabbath concerts and Deep Purple concerts. I know that's not so much punk rock back then, but it definitely started me out. From there it was like, listening to the Circle Jerks and the Meatmen and stuff like that. He just took me to a lot of shows where I would just get lost off on the side. And he'd take me places where I wasn't supposed to go, like bars and stuff like that. I'd be trying to hold him up when we were walking out the door. He influenced me and once he influenced me, all the people he hung around with [did]. I liked the fact that my parents were always down on him, and I didn't see anything wrong with what he was doing when I was younger, and I was just starting to be at that age where I was about to rebel, that natural phase that every kid goes through. That and the music, because sometimes I feel like, "Arrrgh" and the music exactly. That and I know I didn't fit in to the norm of the way my parents expected me to be. And I know that most of my friends that were punks then didn't either. I was not wanting to listen to the same kind of music, not wanting to be like everybody else. Feeling like you weren't happy all the time, even though you're supposed to act that way. It's totally unrealistic to me. Even then, I know I wasn't happy. And a lot of it was my parents not wanting to admit my father abused me when I was younger and I still to this day hate him. When my brother left town, I hung out with his friends, and they kind of took me in.

Candace's entry into punk exacerbated the tension of her family situation and her feelings of rejection: "My parents definitely didn't like me being punk. They reacted in the same way as school, thinking I was going to just be nothing, having no confidence in me because of classification. It was real generalized, like, 'Oh, you're depressed all the time. You're unhappy. You're nothing but hateful. What's your problem?' Whereas I was just expressing my feelings." The only supportive network which Candace could access was her punk friends. Not only did they offer emotional sustenance, but they provided for her physical needs as well:

> I kind of felt like I had a sense of understanding from friends, whereas I'd been going to school and none of the people in school, people used to make fun of me. "Look at her. Look at her funny hairdo." Stuff like that. I definitely had a good sense of understanding from friends. When my parents would kick me out, after my friend's mom kicked me out, I lived with these four guys that were friends of my half-brother, and they pretty much raised me until I was sixteen and I split. We all ended up leaving, the house we were staying in got sold and cops started coming in and I was underage and so I had to leave. But they totally helped me feel like I had friends whereas I didn't feel like I had anybody that understood or wanted to be friends with me or anything when I was really young.
>
> But once I got the taste of the music, I kind of followed it, and I kind of had this same style of living, living in an abandoned house, I did a lot. Just trying to find anywhere to live. For a long time I just stayed in a abandoned subway station in Boston. Even in the winter, it was the warmest place I could be. This one, the downstairs was wet and I had lots of garbage and stuff in it, and there was two metal spiral staircases that went up on either side of the subway, and it was a really old station. But upstairs, there was an area, and I could sleep in there and all the heat rose to the top, and so the steam, I guess, from the subway would come up. And it was loud. At night it wasn't so bad, but early in the evening, every fifteen minutes you'd hear the subway go by there. But it was always dry and it was always somewhat warm, so it was the best place to stay.

While trying to find the resources to survive, Candace experienced trouble from school authorities:

> I was kind of forced to resign from school when I was sixteen. I got a petition from school saying—it was actually from the school board—saying that if I did not cut, it was basically saying that my hair was a health hazard. I had dreadlocks, basically. I had shaved on the sides, all shaved underneath

and there's a big circle of dreads. I had that and it did get me kicked out of school, but that was just one of the things that I should have expected, "You have a funny hair-do, you're never going to be anything in life." It was clean, I washed my hair. I didn't live with my parents, and they knew that, and that kind of bothered them, so they thought I wasn't clean. I was forced to resign. I could either cut or comb, somehow get my hair out of dreadlocks and take all the stuff out. I had a lot of wire and just stuff that I had found wired into my hair, and they felt that to be a health hazard and that it wasn't clean, so that I had to either resign or do something about it. I pretty much was at my wits' end, as I had been on my own since I was fourteen and I had chosen just to resign and say, "Forget it." I tried going to summer school after that, but it was hard for me to go to school and try and feed myself at the same time. I plan to go back when my daughter goes to school, I plan on going to school myself and kind of going through it with her.

Candace's adherence to the punk subculture was a survival strategy. Other punks had helped her to survive both physically and emotionally at a time when everyone else had turned her away:

If I'd never become a punk, I'd be really scared, confused, and probably in a mental health sanitarium. Because I could not live like my mom. I know when I go and see her, it's like, "I want to come and, I want to see you and your baby," and then it's like nothing but, "Why do you do that to her? Why don't you feed her meat? She's going to be unhealthy." I feel I'm raising her a lot more healthy than my mom. My father sexually abused me and my mom still will not admit to it. She won't even talk to me about it. Whereas it would help me a whole hell of a lot if she would, but she won't. She won't even admit that it ever happened. She'd just as soon yell and go, "I don't want to hear about it! I don't want to hear anything about it!" I didn't talk about it at all until I was about eighteen, until after I had [my daughter] and I told my midwife and I told my husband, but I never really talked about it to anybody until a couple of years ago. I couldn't talk about it. I would just start crying immediately when I started talking about it. It's just the past couple of years I can talk about it and not think about it like for four days after that. It's somewhat out of my head, I still have a lot to get out, but I've gotten a lot of it out. I can deal with it now. I can actually, when I'm talking to people, I can actually tell them about it, whereas before, I'd keep it a secret. Knowing that I can talk about it, mention it to people, makes me feel a little bit stronger.

In her ongoing process of recovery, Candace takes a stance for individualism: "I'm just kind of myself. I don't follow any sort of norm as far as like what society says. . . . I don't take on anybody else. I'm definitely influenced by the world around me, but I try to keep myself like as sacred as possible. Because if you don't have yourself, then you don't really have anything." With a home and a job, and planning to return to school, Candace is working hard to improve life for herself and her little girl.

"Somebody Everybody Hated": Adolescent Alienation

Sue's and Candace's narratives suggest that girls become punks for very different reasons and that the subculture offers them a variety of challenges and resources. In many cases, girls' attractions to punk are the result of a number of factors: rebellion against their parents; attraction to the music, style, and lifestyle; agreement with its political ideologies; rejection of mainstream conventions; desire for a support network. For those for whom the subculture provides a way to rebel or to express a political opinion, becoming a punk involves rejecting the mainstream norms enforced by parents, peers, and school authorities. For others, especially for the girls who experienced abuse, who ran away from home, or who were pushed out of their families, the subculture serves as a survival network.

One of the commonalties among all of these girls' narratives is their general sense of alienation from the mainstream adolescent culture of their neighborhoods or schools. Many girls reported being outsiders even before becoming punks, being barred from the popular friendship groups in mainstream adolescent culture. Some girls attributed this to their economic situations:

Sheila: Most, most people, they just, their parents, even when I was younger, they just thought I was a weird kid or whatever, came from a poor family, and some mothers wouldn't let their kids hang out with me, because I was a "bad influence" or whatever.

Others discussed their relative deprivation, not having the connections, cars, and clothes that are central in most North American adolescent culture. Sue's description of herself as the daughter of a hairdresser among "sons of senators' sons" is one such account, as is that of Denise:

I grew up in this totally upper-middle-class, white neighborhood . . . and my parents sent us to public school because my parents have very different values. My dad grew up poor, so he's just like, "You need a sense of value." All this stuff, all these things that nobody around me had any sense for, and it was like all these people in my neighborhood were like, "She bought a Volvo station wagon down the street we've got to get one too" kind of thing. And my dad's like, "Well, I guess whenever you have money to buy yourself a car, I guess you'll do it." . . . [P]robably even up until eighth grade, it was like even though I didn't really feel like the people I went to school with I couldn't really relate to that well and I really didn't get along with them, but I still wanted to, I was like, I really wanted to. I was like, " I want to be popular. I want to wear Guess jeans" and all that. And then I got to ninth grade and I was just like, "I'm not going to play anymore. I don't care." . . . Over that summer I was just like, "I just don't want to, why should I pretend? This is not me, this is not what I want to do, this is not the people I like, this isn't music I like, this is nothing. I just, I go out and I'm like, 'This is boring as hell.'"

Whether upper middle class or poor, girls described themselves as nerds, loners, or social rejects, highlighting differences between themselves and their more mainstream peers that even predated their construction of punk identities: "A nerd. . . . That's what I was before I was a punk. I still am, I just do it now with green hair. . . . That's what a lot of people that I knew got into it were when they were younger" (Anna). Allie, who grew up in foster care, said: "People always kind of looked at me with disdain. I was always kind of like not given a fucking break. . . . When I was growing up I just never could fit in anywhere." Jennie echoed this: "I've always been that kid that sits alone. . . . I was just a loner. . . . I was definitely a loner at the time," as did Carina: "I would go on walks by myself, just spend a lot of time by myself and that, that really sucks because you bring yourself down when you're by yourself. I'm glad that did not happen." Hallie added: "When I was younger, I wasn't exactly a nerd, I was just kind of somebody everybody hated."

Girls sometimes based their perceived differences from their peers on their family experiences of divorce, parental conflict, abuse, or neglect, as Candace did. This sense of alienation could also be a consequence of being labeled antisocial, depressed, or learning impaired:

Andie: Since sixth grade, see, everybody started beating me up for no reason, because I was a little bit different, because I was so-called crazy . . . and the thing was is that, see, I would get all pissed off at them, so I said, "Well, fuck it. I'm just going to look what I am." And I started wearing all black all the time, and never wore earrings in my right ear, always wore them in my left, shaved my head and just wore all black all the time, and was really quiet, and everybody just said, "Oh, let's leave her alone."

Basilisk: My father just died and I was sad, so I had to go to the doctor and he said I was depressed, so they sent me to a hospital, and then I was in a hospital ever since, for five years. Thirteen to eighteen. And I think part of the reason was because I wasn't what [my mother] wanted me to be, the cheerleading type and that.

Clara: When I was ten, people were already telling me that I was rebellious and that I would always be anti-social. Because I had been in a session with a psychologist, and she told me that I was hyper rebellious because of my parents' divorce and all that and that I was anti-social, all that. The whole story. But in my ten-year-old brain, I didn't understand that. But now today I know . . . they're qualities.

In seeking out the subculture, these girls sought out others with the same "defects," and redefined these, as Clara stated explicitly, as being (good) qualities. When turning to punk, these girls sought a reference group of outsiders, an alternative source of status and support. Their description of seeking out such a reference group is quite in keeping with Albert Cohen's (1955) findings on delinquent boys, even to the redefinition of perceived faults as virtues within the subculture.

"Just Slowly Drawing Me into It": Exposure to Punk

Many of these girls had formed other subcultural affiliations prior to becoming punks, trying out different forms of youth rebellion before finding one that fit:

Wanda: I sort of went from sort of the New Wave type music, I was into that sort of music and, it, you kind of ease into, because it's—branches out. A lot of these people that started out listening to a lot of New Wave they, they either went towards heavy metal and metal or the other way. That's what I noticed, even when I was in high school. And because I, these other girls, we used to hang out and we all wrote short stories and stuff together and, and then we sort of, they branched into the, to the heavy metal thing and I sort of branched the other way.

Alexea: Probably when I was thirteen or something. I got in really, really into the skinhead scene. And then into Gothic. I don't understand how those two relate to anything, but you just hang out with a lot of skinheads and shit.

Jennie: I was probably twelve or thirteen. Right when you get into junior high. You start to break away, you're like, "Wait, I'm my own person." It's like, "I don't have to have Mom take me to the mall and buy me the Gap. Wait. I like this instead." I did that. I got in, it was more New Wave than, there was a little punkish crowd in there and then I got into the skinheads and played with them for a little while and then I moved out of that about two, two and a half years ago, I got back into punk. Started getting into other things, stuff like the Sex Pistols, getting into the harder bands.

In many cases, these girls joined subcultures that had close ties to punk: skinhead, which was frequently associated with punk in the 1980s; Goth, which is an offshoot of punk; skater, which is a blend of punk and surfer subcultures; and New Wave, which is a more mainstream, palatable interpretation of the punk style of the late 1970s. Many girls claimed, as did Camille, "I went through a bunch of styles, just to find out that what I was thinking, it was the punk mentality."

Most girls also encountered "the punk mentality" through exposure to peers with whom they were emotionally close. Punk girls discovered punk and learned about the minutiae of punk style, lifestyle, and behavior through close associates who encouraged and influenced their choices. One source of such influence was (full, half, step and foster) siblings, especially older brothers and sisters who actively encouraged girls to dress like punks. Candace's stepbrother had been an important source, as were siblings in other punk girls' accounts:

LL: How long have you been a punk?

Chloe: When I really started to empathize was when my sister . . . She ran away to live in London, squat scene down in London, and she used to come home, my mother would say she looked like death itself. . . . She was what made me a punk. Because she was my surrogate mother. Because my mother was always away at work, and she was the major black sheep of the family, I admit it. And everybody in my family hated her. And when I was a little kid, my mother would always say, "You're just like your sister. You know that? You're just like your sister." And I'd be like, "Cool. My sister must be pretty cool." And then I started. She turned me on to the Sex Pistols and shit. Because she used to drive my mother crazy, I admit it. Because she hated my sister, my sister left the house and I was her legacy unto my mother or something. I was her little punk baby.

Lisa: Actually, my older brother, who actually was probably my primary caregiver when I was from maybe two years old to five years old, he then split out west and he got into the scene there. . . . [My parents] did send me out there and we, and he dolled me up in his photo studio and took all these wild pictures of me. I was eight years old or something.

Carnie: When I first started, I liked getting into the whole thing with the music and friends. I was around twelve, but it was because my older brother, because he's, that's the way he is. And I kind of grew up with him my role model and so I started listening to his type of music, getting my hair shaved in different haircuts, wearing different clothes. . . . Well, he's not my real brother. He's my foster brother. But mostly that and his friends and stuff and his girlfriends. I really thought they were really neat. I liked them. . . . He used to take me with him to shows and stuff. And then take me out to the city, and hang out with people, just hang out and do stupid stuff.

Clara: It started little by little. I was twelve, thirteen years old. I was in a fos-ter family and there was this girl, she had a super big mohawk, she was shaved with all the big things. All wow. And she started getting me into lis-tening to the music. And I went on from there. . . . When I met that girl, I lived with her every day, and I progressed from there on my own. . . . I didn't necessarily hang out with punks. But I started having the mentality and all that, to understand things and all.

Cousins were also a source of influence:

Cora: With me, it's my cousin Sully. I hung out with him, I saw him, but he, he made me listen to the music and I liked it. His hair was colored and I thought it was nice.

Ava: I was a little New Wave skater girl and then when I was around thir-teen, my cousin shaved my head and got me really drunk and put Docs on me in Rhode Island. And he was a total punk and I was like, "Oh, I worship you." I started going to shows when I got back [home] and *Rocky Horror Picture Show*, nothing really very punk, but they were pretty rad. Just started getting into the scene from there.

Elle: At first I'd see it on TV. Then my cousin would come around with his hair all sorts of colors and spiked up in the air. And I said to myself, "I'll do that too." So I shaved all my head, I left a little line here [in the middle], then I was seven. . . . I'd hang out with my cousin, a bunch of sixteen, seven-teen year olds. I always hung out with people that were older than me. It was really fun. That was real life to me.

Finally, as in Sue's case, friends were also a source of exposure and influence:

Emily: My first introduction to punk was, I was in seventh grade and I was good friends with this girl named Kristen and her brother was a skinhead. And I was hooked. I guess he was pretty much my introduction, him and her. I remember when I was in camp, there was, the end of sixth grade I was in camp, this guy had a [pop-country-punk group] Violent Femmes tape and they were, that was the first band I ever listened to.

Sheila: I hooked up with some friends, I met people in the States and they were punk rockers and I guess I thought they were really cool and stuff, and decided to hang out with them and listen to their views on everything, and I just dropped out of school and from then on moved down to the States and just started hanging out. . . . I wasn't influenced [to drop out]. I'd started to not go to school . . . and then I met people and they had a big influence on me. Now they're my family.

Jessie: I was fourteen and living in New York and I had an apartment with, I lived with my sister. She lived there and I used to go up there and stay with her for long, long periods of time. And then I was in the park one day, I was hanging out with this bum—he was only sixteen and he was a crackhead— and for some reason I was attracted to all those fucked up kids that I never, are just so screwed up. Anyway, I was hanging out with him and he knew a bunch of punks and the next thing I knew I was hanging out with them and they took me in. They were like, "Hey, let's cut your hair." And they just, I just, I liked it. I liked the way they looked, I liked the way they talked and stuff. . . . So basically, I was influenced.

Family members and friends were therefore important sources of information and influence in these girls' adoptions of the punk style. Girls spoke repeatedly of being "influenced" and "taught," of having others cut their hair into punk styles and of looking up to older siblings, cousins, and friends who were punks as role models. These peers encouraged the girls' first steps into the punk look and lifestyle, modeling appropriate dress and behavior, and then teaching them punk lifestyle and ideology.

The media also played an important role in these girls' decisions to become punks. Girls who became punks in the 1980s had encountered the subculture primarily through media sources:

Anna: I had the short-wave radio, I could pick up the BBC, so I got a lot of music that I didn't hear in the very small town I was living in, and that's how I kind of got introduced to some of the music and stuff. . . . It was a lot of things. Really, when I, growing up, I read a lot of comic books, fantasy, things like that. I was into science-fiction, and I just always thought it was interesting, different hair colors and stuff like that, without really associating it with that movement and the music. And then I started hearing some of the music, and I liked it, and I saw what came with it. But I was, I guess, avant-garde, or dressing weird, or interested in more theatrical appearances before I knew what punk was, so I just happened to see the marriage in it. It was like, "Cool. Here's something, other people do this too." So that was, I was like, like I said, comic book characters or book characters, and things like that inspired me, until I knew there was something else beyond that. . . . It was neat, I must say.

Many who became punks more recently, such as Sue, reported having seen and been impressed by punks on film and television long before they actually became punks themselves:

> Jennie: I grew up in a little small hick town and I remember watching TV and seeing punks. I'd be like, "Oh, they're so rad. I want to be one of those." And then when we moved to [the city], I remember seeing my first punk rock girl and I was eight, and I was like, "I want to be that." So that would be probably the first time. I was eight but I just met someone into it and it was just slowly drawing me into it and I went from there.

> Courtney: I knew what New Wave was when I was a little kid, because you heard about Sex Pistols and you heard about different things on TV and stuff, but you didn't really know, Sex Pistols, that's punk or it, or this is New Wave and this is whatever, so I would see New Wave people around and it was like, "Oooh, weird." And I was with my mom when I was six or five or something, and I saw this really cool sandal-type of shoes and they were all different rainbow colors and I was like, "Mom, when I grow up I want to be a New Waver."

> Tori: I got in when I was eight, I think I was eight years old when I first heard Fear. And I was just like, "Yeah, that sounds really good." The Germs, I've always been a big fan, ever since I was just a little kid. I remember, my babysitter, my parents' friends having their records or LPs around. And a lot of movies back then too, like *Repo Man* and shit like that. The kids were just glued to the TV and that's what we were brought up on. And I loved, I always loved that.

What is especially interesting about these girls' accounts is that they tended to recollect not instances where punks are depicted negatively (such as the "*Quincy* punks" of police dramas, the maniacal punk killers of *Class of 1984*, or the obnoxious punk of *Star Trek IV*), but rather depictions that are laudatory. They had detailed recollections of radio and television appearances by bands such as Fear, the Sex Pistols and the Germs, and films such as *Repo Man*, which depict punks in a positive light. This may be an example of selective recollection—many may have seen negative depictions of punk, or positive depictions of other subcultures, on television as well, but they did not assign the same weight to those events. Although their relationships with siblings, cousins, and friends who were punks may have had stronger influences on their decisions to be punks and on their learning the styles, norms, and rituals of the subculture, the media played an important role in introducing them to punk, in making them, in Jennie's words, "want to be one of those."

However, wanting and becoming are different things, and becoming punks required an education in subcultural style and substance.

"Any Idiot Can Shave Their Head": Commitment Processes

Learning both the minutiae and ideology of punk is an important process in joining and committing to the subculture, in creating an authentic punk identity. In an interview study of adolescents, social psychologists Sue Widdicombe and Rob Wooffitt found that, according to punks, genuine membership in the subculture "requires a moral, personal commitment from the individual" (1990:262). The punks they interviewed stated that the length of one's involvement had a positive effect on others' recognition of one's authenticity, with old school punks being accorded more respect than new school punks. To this, Kathryn Fox (1987) adds that a punk's willingness to radically alter his or her appearance in conformity with the extremities of punk style counted toward authenticity; punks with mohawks and tattoos were deemed to be more committed to the scene than those who had "convertible" haircuts (punk when worn one way, preppie when worn another). Commitment to punk beliefs, along with the willingness to eschew employment, abandon schooling, and forsake conventional housing are often strong indicators of subcultural authenticity (and resistance, according to Baron 1989a, 1989b). Thus, as adolescents affiliate themselves with the subculture, they learn that style is insufficient grounds for claiming a subcultural identity. In order to gain acceptance in the group, they must learn, espouse, and exhibit punk beliefs, attitudes, and "mentality."

Becoming a punk was the result of such a process of commitment for the girls I spoke with as well as for their male peers. Although style, behavior, and attitude are the most tangible and recognizable components of subcultural affiliation, these punk girls soon found that commitment to the subculture includes more than displaying the just the right look, attitude, or lifestyle. Whatever attracted girls to punk, they soon learned that the espousal of punk beliefs is a core component of the creation of punk commitment. The girls repeatedly cited the importance of behavior and beliefs superseding punk appearance:

> Amalia: Punk is not dead. Punk is much more about the way you look, because [some people] with all the shiny studs all over them, and they've got their hair all charged up or spiked or whatever. That's not punk at all. Punk rock, just punk actually, is the way you are, the way you act.

> Rosie: And that's [what] my whole expression is, it's more inside of me, it's not so much outside of me. I know I look this way and I have bright pink

hair and all this stuff and tons of metal on me, but it's not, it's more in my head. I can dress up super nicely and still think the way I think. It doesn't change anything for me.

Sue cited lyrics by the punk band Subhumans in order to explain this:

It's not just "dye your hair," like the Subhumans say, it's "Die for your beliefs, not just dye your hair." I think punk was a political movement, and any of these little Sex Pistols fucks that want to argue with me can bring it on, because punk is based on politics. It's like, punks and hippies are brothers. Hippies are trying to see the light side of revolution, saying how great the revolution can be, and the punks are saying "Fuck this, we're pissed off." It's just the dark side of revolution, in people's faces, and that's how I see punk. I don't label someone a punk just because they have a mohawk. Any idiot can shave their head. It's not a technically hard thing to do. Just get a razor and shave your head. But it does in a way take balls to do that when you're really young, living with your parents in their all-white rich suburb to shave your head and dye [the remainder of your hair] green. Then it's saying, "Well, fuck society, fuck the corporate world, I'm going to be against all this shit."

As they delved deeper into the subculture and learned that the "punk mentality" includes rebelling against authority and questioning conventionality, these punk girls saw punk as being particularly congruent with their own opinions:

Courtney: There happened to be some people at school that opened my eyes to things. I always felt very uncomfortable with the way I was because my mother always bought my clothes, my mother always decided what to do. I didn't know what I liked because my mother decided everything for me. And then I didn't know anything about, really, punk. I mean, all I knew was Nina Hagen because she was German, and so . . . In high school, somebody made me listen to something and I said, "This is cool!" I don't remember what it was, but it was like, "Whoa, I like this." And then I just started finding out and trying to see what music there was out there.

Sophie: The way I thought when I was young, I'll explain it to you. . . . I thought like [the punks], I found them to be super cool. They thought with the same mentality as me, "Eat my shit." I was always thinking like that and I always found their mentality to be cool. So I joined up. That's it.

Hallie: I think punk is different for each person, because everybody has a different perspective on life, everybody has a different reality. Punk is a perspective on life and it is a reality for me. I believe that you don't have to look punk to be punk. I believe it's a mentality and an attitude, and basically it's something you're born with, because you're born with your mentality. I believe that when I was younger, that I was a punk, even though I didn't look punk or stuff like that. I just basically had anarchist views, and I don't think you have to be anarchy to be punk, but I just had the whole mentality of it

As they integrated into the subculture, these girls learned that, although the style and lifestyle are the most recognizable aspects of punk, their espousal of the punk subculture also required commitments to more ideological, political, and attitudinal aspects. Thus, as they became socialized into the punk subculture, girls learned its norms, its attitude, and its "mentality," even bringing their own values and beliefs in line with those of punk. Punk identifications required both an attenuation of their commitment to mainstream institutions (e.g., work, school) and their belief in mainstream values and norms (e.g., "the American dream," the value of work and education, the validity of the democratic process), and a subsequent commitment to subcultural style (i.e., music, dress, hairstyle, etc.) and ideology (e.g., anarchism, survivalism, do-it-yourself). Although not all punk girls reject mainstream institutions outright, nor adopt all facets of punk, they characterize these aspects of punk as being what they sought out, as being basically congruent with their prior beliefs, or as serving to resolve problems they experienced.

The construction of subcultural authenticity continues throughout punks' tenure in the subculture. Although all the girls I interviewed identified as punks, they represent different stages of subcultural development. Craig O'Hara describes the process for the subculture as a whole as an attenuation of the focus on style in favor of a focus on substance: "Punk has evolved past the 'shock tactics' of colored hair and dog collars to have a fairly cohesive philosophy with little or nothing to do with one particular style of dress. While useful at the time, and still fun today, shocking people with appearances has taken back seat to shocking people with ideas" (1995:17–18). As punks move through the subculture, they either adopt the ideologies and politics of punk, becoming the hardcore punks Fox (1987) described, or they move away from the style, never "graduating" from softcore to hardcore. While older hardcore punks are fairly uncommon, I did meet punks in their thirties during the course of my field research, who had remained part of the subculture, even retaining the sartorial style, since its inception. More commonly, however, in my graduate school career, I met fellow students who confessed to me that their flirtation with punk had long since passed and not left any permanent scars of either a physical or an ideological nature.

"It's Just a Part of Me": Why Punk?

Girls turn to the punk subculture for a variety of reasons. Although ethnographers and others have documented and described a wide variety of youth subcultures, the factors precipitating adolescents' choice of one particular subculture over another have not been addressed. What role did the subculture play in these forty girls' lives? Why did they choose to become punks rather than remain members of other subcultures, such as skaters, skinheads, or Goths, or become members of other contemporary youth subcultures, such as deadheads, preppies, hippies, and ravers? Many, like Sue, argued that they found the "punk mentality"—its progressive politics, its attitude of aggression and refusal—to be congruent with their own already-articulated attitudes about the world. Rhetorically, the punk subculture presents itself as a site for rebellion. For some, this rebellion occurred on a personal level:

> Arizona: The rebelliousness of it. I've always been rebellious . . . just rebellious against certain types of people and society itself. And I was, I've always been rebellious, . . . I've never been a follower. . . . I'm more of an independent punk.

> Alexea: Just probably being rebellious and doing what the fuck you want, and not giving a shit about what everybody else thinks.

> Sheila: It was the rebellion part, and I was, you can be your own person. And I, I would sit and look and watch people and how just blind they were to everything. I didn't want to be like that because I never was like that as a kid. I always wanted to know, and I wanted to find out and that's why, I just wanted to learn.

For other girls, such as Sue, this rebellion was more ideological; they saw punk as being a way in which they can change the world. The reflexivity of the punk subculture, its aim to illuminate and critique the central concerns of mainstream culture (Levine and Stumpf 1983), was particularly attractive to these girls. It was this rhetoric of rebellion that attracted many girls to punk, just as it did their male peers.

> Denise: I would see things that I just didn't agree with, things that really bothered me. And so I just, I had all this energy, I had all this frustration, but I didn't know where to channel it. So [my punk boyfriend] more like gave me a direction to channel it in and that's the direction it took.

> Rosie: I heard about anarchy and I, and I understood it and I read, I know a lot, a lot of stuff about it. . . . I started being like this when I was fourteen. In

a way it's important to me, because I want to work through society. I want to work through the system. I want to change it, to make it better. I want to make it so the people who need help get it. . . . First, I believed in communism and stuff, but then I figured it out and I said, if I was in a communist society, in Russia or something, I'd have to work, because in Russia you either work or you go to jail. So, you have to work and all this stuff. So then I reconsidered that and I said, well, Jesus Christ, people should be allowed to do what they want and stuff.

Within punk, these girls found avenues of personal expression and political protest, seeing punk as a means for both personal growth and political rebellion. These girls saw their lifestyle as part of the punk rebellion. Those who lived on the streets and had no conventional goals—gutter punks—saw their form of retreat from mainstream society as an embodiment of this rebellion. Many who were pursuing conventional goals—such as being photographers, artists, sociologists, and stockbrokers—through conventional means (schooling and job training) also couched their aspirations as being rebellious: working within the system to change it. Likewise, the innovators, who were seeking to be professional musicians not through going to school, but through being in bands or performing as street musicians, saw their lifestyle choices as expressing aspects of punk rebellion. To many of these punk girls, almost anything could be, and was, described as rebellious.

Other punk girls, such as Candace, turned to punk not solely for reasons of rebellion, but also as a form of survival network. Girls who had run away from home or group homes found that the punk subculture gave them a supportive group, assisting them with both physical and emotional needs:

Basilisk: I lived on the street, mainly, in a bonding-type thing. We all took care of each other. A lot of times. If it really comes down to it, like if someone makes trouble, we'll all back each other up.

Hallie: I was on my own, I lived on my own for a long time. There was this one period where I was hanging out with this guy Izzy, who was punk as fuck, right, and we were the team for six months. And he got busted. And I was still on my own and then I had this other running-away partner or whatever, she was female and she got busted. I was like, "Damn, I'm going to be busted." Right? And I was just hanging out with some friends of mine and this thirty-year-old punk named Dan—at the time he was twenty-six or something, but now he's thirty-two—and we were hanging out around his house and we were talking about things I could do to not get busted, because it just happened, and my adrenaline was going and everything, and Dan said some smart-ass remark like, "Get a mohawk, turn punk, they'll never recognize you." And so I did. I was like, "Oh, yeah, that sounds like a good idea." And I was just like, I got a mohawk, just totally overnight deal. And then I still liked hanging out on State street and a lot of other real punks were like, "Oh, there's a new punk in town." And they started hanging out with me and they were like, I could relate to them like I could relate to no other people ever before. . . . It was just really cool. I just totally related to them and then I started going to shows and stuff, and I just totally loved the music, I totally loved shows, I love the music. Just basically it became part of me after a year or so. That was when I was twelve, just growing. I just started to like it more and more, it became part of me and now it's not even so much anything. It's just a part of me. It's something I couldn't even . . . It's just a lifestyle for me, it's just the way I am.

Lola: We're all sort of, whether we like it or not, we take care of each other. We take care of each other a lot. We have our bouts but it's nothing that we can't get over. Some people beat the shit out of each other and then an hour later, they're drinking a beer and hanging out and it's cool.

Because punk remains the primary subculture among squatter and runaway adolescents, its community is most attractive to newcomers on the streets. Today, punk survivalism flourishes, with small groups of gutter punks traveling together, while larger groups share squats, food, and the proceeds of their dumpster diving, panhandling, and busking. When members of their group are threatened, other punks can be counted on to help them by physically defending them. Punks help hide runaways from the police, and assist their peers in leaving town if they get into trouble with the police. For runaway or "throwaway" punk girls, joining the gutter punk subculture is a more appealing prospect than squatting alone or engaging in prostitution. Aspects of the punk subculture, in some cases, serve as survival networks.

Both gutter punks and punk rockers I spoke with characterized members of the subculture as being like-minded and supportive. They described punks as a family, one in which bonds of support were often stronger than those in their own families:

Carina: A bunch of happy people. Everybody, yeah, they fight a lot but it's more like we're family. It's more of a family fight. And then we're, we're best friends the next day. It's just how it was with my brothers and sisters.

Amalia: I like the unity that all of us have. We're all really, really close. Well, at least most everybody is. There's some people I don't get along with. Most of us are all really, really close and all take care of each other and we're all like brothers and sisters. We're like a big family. And we all stick up for each other, we've always got each other's backs. And that's what I like about it.

Tori: When I got into, down to New Orleans, this dominatrix lady took me in and kind of like sheltered me for a long time. And she introduced me to all, all the punks, all the heavy twenty-year-old punks, twenty-four-year-old punks, and I'm just this twelve-year-old little girl, starting out, and they took care of me like I was their daughter, so it was kind of cool. . . . I felt like I had a family. I mean, these were freaks that, that felt, because when you're that young, eleven, twelve, thirteen, you go through the thing of suicide, you go through the thing that nobody loves you, everybody is out to get you or whatever. And there were other people that were saying, "Hey, that's not how it is. We're here, we want to be your friend. We want to be your family." And that's how it's been ever since is the street people, gutter punks have been my family.

Wanda: As far as the squats and stuff go . . . it's kind of a family type thing. Because there's a million people in this, this building right now. Well, not a million, but there's a lot of people here, and yet everybody is getting along. And I, and I like that, the whole . . . and it's nice there's a lot of people that— I'm off and on the streets all the time because of my situation—and it's nice to know there's, where you go and, and have the family-type bond with people, where you know that if there's something, and you need somebody, they're with you. There are people there.

Punk girls repeatedly characterized their entry into punk as being an "adoption," creating within the punk subculture a chosen family. Punk girls describe this family relationship as a sibling bond, referring to each other as "brothers and sisters." Some of these girls had experienced incest, abuse, and neglect at the hands of their biological families, incidents that had precipitated them into the streets. Once there, however, they found that other punks offered them constructed kinship bonds that were more nurturing than those they had left.

In some measure, this chosen familial relationship was based on the reciprocal sharing of goods and services:

Tori: I've gotten jobs and I've gotten an apartment and it's been trashed within a couple of weeks, and I think a lot of it is because I've got too good of a heart. Because any of my friends come into the town and I'm in and they've got a place, they're there. They don't, they're not squatting. I make sure they've got food and I always make, I always look out for people, my friends, my family or whatever, and that's what brings me down. It doesn't matter, because then I still have somebody else to lean on and they help me out.

Rudie: I had an apartment, I paid $950, a two-bedroom apartment on the Lower East Side. I worked eighty hours a week and got fifteen people at a time to be in my apartment—before I got kicked, got kicked out—keeping warm all winter. I had, you've got to see what it's like to have a rented yuppie apartment, have dogs, junkies, crusties, punks, oh, just drunk fucking cold people. . . . They would bring food. They'd stand in Diane's line, there's this food line, and there's this annoying lady and she would scream for hours about religion and if you stood there and took [it], she'd give you a bag of food. And it was great. It had a big carton of juice. It would have Devil Dogs, it had all kinds of candy and pasta and some tomato sauce, so we, people always brought food to my house. . . . And when people got checks or money from different places, they would kick me down [give me some]. . . . It was good. People would always say, "If you need someone to walk your dog . . ."

This communal sharing often prevented these punks with income from breaking out of the poverty they experienced.[4] In sharing their goods with other punks, they augmented the well-being of the entire group, rather than simply accumulating wealth. This sharing served the purpose of strengthening the communal bond through reciprocity ("what comes around goes around") while simultaneously preventing some members from capitalizing on their own hard work or good fortune.

For these girls, the punk subculture served a variety of needs. Some, especially punk rockers, were attracted to the subculture for its rhetoric of rebellion. They found that the progressive politics of the subculture resonated with their own beliefs. Their decision to become punks was affected as well by their exposure to punk through friends and family, who facilitated their entry into the local scene. Many who had tried other subcultures found that punk was simply the best fit. For gutter punk girls, punk as a survival network allowed them to escape intolerable family situations and maintain a style of street living in the safety of the company of others. Girls in both groups talked about punk as a form of family, which satisfied the needs that their own families could not address. Thus, the selection of one subculture over another included such factors as opportunity, exposure, and need.

"They Drew Away": Consequences

In addition to the family difficulties they experienced prior to becoming punks, many girls found that becoming punks—although it satisfied their needs for rebellion, survival, or self-expression—created or exacerbated existing family problems. Some did find that their parents were open-minded and accepted their daughter's unconventional appearance or lifestyle, as did Lisa:

[My parents] are really open-minded, so they were just like "Well, if that's what you like . . . you pay for it. Pay for your hair dye." That's it.

Jessie's parents were also supportive:

I'm not into that whole rebellion against my parents thing. It was never like that. They thought it was a phase, when I grew up . . . And so they were always real cool about it. They were like, "Well, you gotta do what you gotta do. We're not going to tell you how to be." And, and since then I've just had a lot of respect for them.

Ava received not only support, but encouragement from her mother:

Well, my mom gave me my first Sex Pistols tape, my Clash tape, and my first Stray Cats tape. My first tapes I ever had and they're from my mom. . . . It was awesome."

Sadly, these girls' experiences were very much the minority of cases.

Most girls related experiencing not support, acceptance, or even tolerance from their families. Instead they told heartbreaking narratives of being rejected by their parents and their extended families. For some, this rejection involved their parents pressuring them to change their unconventional mode of self-presentation or lifestyle:

Sophie: My mother totally freaked out. She went into a depression, the first time she saw me. "You're too young. . . . You won't start this." She was freaking out. It's not like I was doing prostitution. I was wearing fishnets, she was really scared. Every time I'd go to my mother's . . . I'd show up in lace and makeup that I'd do. For a while, she freaked, but then she got used to it. So now she's used to it. It's been long enough. . . . I called her yesterday, but she won't change that way. As long as I haven't changed my looks, she'll be: "It's not nice looking. When are you going to let your hair grow? How are you going to work?" It's annoying. She wants me to do that. She wants, she wants me to do what she says. Me, I'm like this for a reason. I can't do it.

Carina: [My mom] hates my style and it's like she's embarrassed of me, to be with me in public places and stuff, and it kind of makes me mad, because I'm who I am. Why be, why hate me for who I am? Because I, I don't tell her how dress. I don't, I don't tell anybody how to dress. So that kind of upsets me, because that hurts. Why should she be embarrassed of her own daughter? I can see her point, that she doesn't like it, and she thinks it's a bad image and stuff, but I have my life too. And I get so mad at her for that, because my dad wanted me to be this little prep girl and he took my life away for thirteen years. I just did it to make him happy. And now she's wanting to do the same thing to me. So that's another reason why I left [home], because it was just too much on me. She put her problems on me and I have to worry about my own. It was a big commotion. I couldn't handle it. It was making me depressed. There were so many times I sat in my house and just was, felt like I was going crazy. I just wanted to scream and just tear the house apart and kill myself. I just couldn't handle everything that she was putting on me. Because I couldn't explain to her you can't, you can't judge my friends by the way they look. You can't judge me either. It's not right to judge. I, I hate people that do judge people.

Some family members employed forms of ostracism, refusing to be seen with these girls, meet them, or even acknowledge them in public:

Rudie: My mom, she used to walk three feet behind me all the time. And one day I said, "Would you come on?" And she was like, "No, I don't want anyone to know I'm with you." I was like, "Damn."

Connie: My mom won't hang out with me. I haven't seen my mom in two years. She won't hang out with me at all. I called her the other day, probably three days ago, and she asked me, I told her, I said, "Yeah, I'm going to be coming through Texas, can I stop and see you?" I asked if I could stop and see her. And she said, "Do you still have those scars on your face?" And I said, "Yeah." And she said, "No." She doesn't want to hang out with me. . . . I have one family member that will talk to me and that was my uncle and he totally accepts for who I am and he wouldn't, he walks in public places with me and he'll go anywhere with me. How I look . . . I haven't talked to my grandparents or my mom or my mom's parents in a really long time. Or my dad's parents. Because the last time I went and saw my grandparents, I was sitting there on a chair and my grandpa took a really big comb to the back of my head right there, with a comb in my dreadlocks and all this stuff and he tried to comb out my hair and he didn't want to take me anywhere. I was hungry, me and my cousin were sitting in there and we were hungry and they wouldn't take us to eat with them or anything. Went out to eat, be seen in public. They'll say hello to you if there's no one around them. . . . If there's no one around, they'll say hello to you.

Other girls found that their families viewed them with suspicion and contempt:

Justine: Want it or not, when you dress like a punk, you have a big, big label. For me, it doesn't bother me more than that, but it changed, without my wanting it, some people distanced themselves from me. Some friends . . . My family, they drew away. . . . On my father's side, I go to Christmas and they're always watching to see if I steal anything. My family, the other family, I only talk to my grandmother, and to my mother, my aunt Esther, my aunt Clorisse and my aunt Martha. The others—there are twelve children in all—my grandfather is dead. Of those twelve children, there are just four aunts and my mother who'll talk to me, the three aunts and my mother. And my grandmother . . . And the other aunts are trying to give my grandmother a heart attack. They call her to tell her that I'm doing heroin and all that, and it's not true. They don't even want to hear from me and it seems that I'm doing heroin and that I'm close to dying. My grandmother was very upset and she was happy I called.

Finally, one reported that she had been abused by her father because of her style of dress:

Rosie: My dad, he punched me and stuff. My dad says, he tells me that I'm a prostitute, and he says that I'm a junkie. And then I ask him, well, "Where do I do drugs?" And he's like, to me, "Show me your arms." And I show them to him and I don't have any marks at all, I don't do needles. I'm terrified of them. Because I'm scared of them. And he's like, to me, "Well, I think you shoot in your toes or something." And that's exactly the thing. . . . And that's the thing, that's why I left home. My parents, they cause so much shit for me in my life. It's too much, you know? I finally said, "I can't take this anymore." I go home and I get all this stuff, I get degraded. I get put down. I get so much stuff there. And at least in my apartment, people, my friends they don't degrade me. They treat me like a human being. They're not like, "That's disgusting, the way you look," or, "How you dress is really slutty." They don't hit me and stuff. They're not like that. They're not like my father.

Some girls' parents tried to employ restrictive measures, like those advocated by Back in Control Training Center and Parents of Punkers in order to regain control of their punk daughters:

Basilisk: My mom always hated, she, she always tried to give me, she's real, tried to be real upper class and stuff. She always tried to have nice things. A nice house . . . she never wanted me to be like that. . . . Well, she would burn my tapes and posters, and thought I was doing drugs and I wasn't.

Courtney: I couldn't put my mohawk up in front of them. It was too painful for them. They always, they'd take away my clothes when I was living there. They'd take away my clothes, read my diary, check my bag, follow me everywhere.

Girls who had been in foster care and group homes reported similar efforts on the part of the state:

> Clara: In a group home, it's unbelievable! It's insane! Shit! They do every-thing to get you to change. They do everything, everything, everything. The first time I went into the group home where I was, I had a mohawk on my head and I was really seriously fucked up. I was really in the streets, I was nuts. And then I got there, and it was crazy. They took everything, they took all my stuff that was the least little bit marginal seeming, they took it all and they put it in a locker. I didn't get it back until I got out for Christmas. Even this [small spiked bracelet]. Even this they confiscated. I wasn't even allowed to wear it. . . . They call me a slut when I wear [my tank top]. . . . They make you put on a sweater. An ugly fucking white sweater with green squares on it. And jogging pants! . . . I entered the group home in August, April '93. It's been nearly a year and a half and there's not one week that they didn't bother me. Because before, when my hair was shorter, I would spike it up a little sometimes when I would go out on weekends. I was happy, I was going out to see my friends. But no, fuck. Every time, I'd get caught—"Go wash your hair, you!" Oh, yeah. Every week. They'd leave me be, and then they'd make me go wash it. It's nuts.

Other parents, as Sue related, turned to psychologists in an attempt to per-suade their daughters to conform:

> Wanda: I had a really hard time even when I was younger. They had sent me to a psychologist, and my mom would be, they wouldn't even go shop-ping with me. . . . And my dad had the nerve to sit there in—at one time, we had family counseling—he had the nerve to sit there and say, "Oh, I can un-derstand"—I didn't even do drugs when I was younger and I was probably a lot weirder than I am now. I didn't even do drugs then—but he had the, he sat there and told the little people, he was like, "I can understand my son being all strung out and having all these problems with drugs and alcohol, but I don't understand *that*." Meaning me. He didn't understand me.

Girls repeatedly told me that their parents' and families' reactions to their adop-tion of the punk look contributed to their adoption of more extreme versions of punk lifestyle. Girls argued that by ostracizing their children, abusing them, or pressuring them to change, these parents precipitated their running away. Such measures were ultimately unsuccessful in persuading these girls to aban-don their punk identities, and, in some cases, even drove them to the extrem-ity of street living. On the other hand, parents who openly accepted their daughters' choices, as did Jessie's, prompted further closeness: "since then I've just had a lot of respect for them."

A number of girls also reported experiencing problems at school once they had become punks. Some found that their more mainstream peers were less than accepting:

Joanie: Once I got into high school—I went to a rural high school, complete switch, and I was probably one of the weirdest people there. . . . When I transferred to that school, it was really awful, because they assumed that I was a rich kid, which I wasn't, and they used to kick me in the back of the legs, push me down the hall and stuff like that. . . . They used to call me every name in the book and it was really funny, because they would call me everything that I wasn't. Like a lesbian or a druggie and just every . . . I didn't have sex. I didn't do drugs. But because I was so strange anyway, they didn't know what to put on me, so they kept on. It was, it was a very strange thing. But they were [eventually] somewhat friendly. They voted me "Best Hair" of my class.

Chloe: When I was in high school, I used to be a weirdo and stuff and wear really crappy clothes and raggedy clothes and stuff all the time. And all these people that I used to go to school with used to say, "Why do you do that? Why can't you just be normal? Why do you always have to get attention? And now I see them a couple of years later, and they are doing monkey tranquilizers, shaving their heads, piercing their nipples, this and that, doing everything in their power to be "different" and these are the same people that a couple of years ago were saying to me, "Why are you so messed up?"

Others, like Candace, reported having problems with teachers and school administrators, due simply to their adherence to punk style:

Carina: The principal hated me, the vice principal hated me, just because I wasn't a prep. They'd love to pick on us. It made me sick. They just don't like you. At all. Because they don't think we're dressing proper in their terms of proper. There really shouldn't be any terms of properness. Who can label what? Who can label what color eyes you have, what color hair you should have, what's the right color? It doesn't matter. . . . It gave me a hassle at school because I couldn't get away with what the preps could get away with.

Basilisk: A lot of the teachers—some teachers didn't mind, the teachers were real nice to me. They like that, the colors I wore and they wanted to see what I was wearing the next day. A lot of teachers just hated it. I mean, a lot of teachers were just awful, pick on me.

Rosie: In school, they used to say that I was dealing drugs to all these people. And I wasn't even. I didn't do that. I wouldn't do that in my school, Christ, I was too scared of my dad. Or do anything. I'm terrified of my father. . . . And then I had principals phoning, and the kids' parents would say, "Keep them away from this girl. She's bad. Find her a hole. Just get her away. Don't let our kids within a fifty-mile radius of her if you can," and stuff.

Girls reported that their adherence to punk style even resulted in their expulsion from school. This type of episode still occurred over a decade after my own experience of being expelled, and for many of the same reasons:

Cora: When I dyed my hair, at school, I was the only one at school . . . All the teachers, okay, I was "distracting the people in my classes." So then that started kicking me out of classes. After that, I wouldn't do anything. After that, I got kicked out of school.

Clara: I think I was in seventh grade. . . . The principal really did not like me, he did not like me. And one day, I don't know why, I had dressed a little more strangely than usual, I was dressed really provocatively, and he said I was a slut and he told me to go home, "I never want to see you in my school again!" And he closed my file and sent it to another school. That was it. He didn't like me, he didn't like me. He didn't like my red hair and the way I dressed.

Carnie: I got suspended from school. I had a mohawk. They would suspend me from school if I put it up, but it was only that big (about one inch). . . . That's because I was "disturbing other students' class work." I don't see why, if a kid, a straight-A kid can do work while there's construction going—because at the time there was construction going down on the other side of the school and it was really loud—I don't see how if a kid can go through school, concentrate during that hell, a little piece of hair is going to disrupt the whole classroom. I think, I know that's so stupid. And also it's a shirt I wore once—it didn't say anything offensive or anything . . . it had holes in it. I was like, holes all in it, but I had a T-shirt on under it, and it's because I was "exposing" myself to the school and blah, blah, blah. I got suspended because I showed off my tattoo. I was "disrupting classmates' work," but the second bell hadn't rung yet, so class hadn't technically even started yet, but I got suspended for that. If anything ever, if people were smoking in the bathroom—I thought that was so stupid, I wouldn't even bring cigarettes to school, that was just dumb—so if someone's smoking in the bathroom during lunch or whatnot, if I just even happened to be in there, I'd automatically get blamed for it. But there were no cigarettes on me or a lighter or anything. I didn't even smell like the smoke. But I'd always get blamed for it.

Older punks who were working or looking for jobs felt pressured to change their looks in order to be hired, and those who already had jobs found that they were not immune to discrimination on the basis of style. Rudie, who worked as a stagehand at a major network soap opera, told the following story:

I was told one day when I went to work, and I went to work with my first face piercings—a lip piercing—and my boss had come back from vacation, and I was in a group of people and we were talking. . . . And he looks at me and he says . . . he looked, turns around and gets up and he went, "Omigod!" And I was like, "Ha!" Everyone starts laughing. . . . And my boss turns around, he goes, "That ain't staying." I was like, and everyone starts laughing. I was like, "Yeah right. . . You're my grandfather, right?" And he was like, he was like, "No really . . . that's not staying. . . . I don't like it. . . . I don't care what you do in your off time, but I don't have to look at it." I was like, "What do you mean, you don't like it? That doesn't matter. . . . I like it." And he got really standoffish, he said, "Well, I don't like it and you have to take it out." And I said—for once in my life, my brain worked right away—and I was like, "That's discrimination. . . . You can't tell me that." He goes, "Okay, fine. It's a safety hazard. Take it out." And I said, "What do you mean? . . . You just said in front of ten people you don't like it. I was like, "I'm not taking it out." And he says, "Well, we'll talk about this later." And I, and only recently have I become really strong and started to stand up for myself and felt secure enough that I didn't have to cower down to people. And my next five minute break, I went to the phone and I called the union and I said, "Is there a dress code set by our union?" And they said, "No, what are you talking about?" And I said straight off the bat, I said, "Look, you know I'm a freak. I'm into the crazy punk thing. I know you don't like the way I look, but I'm a good worker. . . . I work all the time. . . . No one has a problem with me. . . . I got my lip pierced. . . . I know a lot of guys that have, who have their nipples pierced . . . and I know a lot of pierced ears and people wear rings and necklaces around here. . . . I was just told by my boss that I cannot come to work with my lip piercing and I want to know if there's a code set by the union for safety or dress." And they were like, "No, the only ones that would have a code would be the company employing you. If at all." So I went right down to the fourth floor . . . and I went to the top money guy and I sat down. I knocked on his door, and I said, "Hello, Ed." And he said, "Hi, Rudie." And I said, "May I talk to you?" And I was shaking, I was like, "I have a little problem." And I told him, and I said I wanted to find out if the company set a standard, because if they did, I'd abide by it. "If not," I said, "I'd like to keep my look. This is what I choose to wear." And he was like, "You know, Rudie, I think [your boss] is an asshole . . . and he made a big mistake. . . . You can keep your lip ring . . . I don't care if it's a wedding ring, a ring in your nose, a ring in one of your private parts, I don't care. . . . Of course, if it gets torn out, it's your fault, but . . . wear what you want. And I was like, "Yeah!" By the time I got upstairs, the union had already called my boss and he was fuming for twenty minutes, yelling, "She went over my head! She went over my head! . . . You went over my head!" . . . I was like, "You told me you didn't like it . . . and you had no right." "You went over my head!" But I didn't get fired.

These punk girls repeatedly experienced intolerance, ostracism, harassment, abuse, threats or expulsion from sources of conventional socialization—families, peers, school authorities, and employers. They argued that these pressures did little to bring them into conformity with mainstream standards. This is not to say that such pressures are always ineffective; those who succumbed were, by definition, outside the purview of this research. However, these girls' narratives do show us that such pressures can not only be ineffective, but may cause further alienation from the support of friends and family.

Boy Toys? Conclusion

So, are girls in male-dominated youth subcultures only boy toys? Or do they become punks for the same reasons as males? In many ways, punk girls' narratives of entry into the punk subculture conform to the process of subcultural formation and identification detailed by numerous theorists of subcultural deviance: like the subcultural males whose experiences are well documented, punk girls turn to the subculture in order to resolve status and other frustrations.[5] They learn deviant lifestyles and ideologies from role models and from the media (Akers 1985; Sutherland and Cressey 1974). They embark on deviant careers characterized by their conformity to and involvement with groups of similar individuals. Their subcultural participation is furthered by their lack of commitment to and belief in traditional values, as well as their lack of attachment to mainstream others and involvement in conventional activities (Hirschi 1969). These girls revealed through their narratives that their reasons for joining a youth subculture involve many of the same motivations and processes as characterize the subcultural participation of their male peers.

However, for a male to join such a subculture is for him to reassert his masculinity, as the norms and codes of such subcultures are often constructed to buttress masculinity.[6] Unlike their male peers, girls who enter the punk subculture must engage with the discrepancies between subcultural masculinity and mainstream adolescent femininity. The timing of girls' entry into punk is a clear indication that subcultural participation is an aspect of resistance to female gender roles. Girls who become punks do so at the onset of puberty, a pivotal age in female development. Of the forty girls I interviewed, thirty-seven recalled an age at which they had become punks: four to eighteen, with the median, thirteen. This is the age which researchers of adolescent development describe as critical in girls' development, the stage at which femininity becomes entrenched in girls' identities. (See Hancock 1989; Orenstein 1994; Pipher 1994; Brown and Gilligan 1992; Gilligan, Lyons, and Hanmer 1989; Gilligan, Rogers, and Tolman 1991.) It is at this stage that girls are expected to forgo the freedoms of childhood in favor of the restraints of adolescent femininity.

For this reason, any account of girls' decision making at this stage in their development must examine the role of the norms of femininity. For punk girls, entry into the punk subculture is a way to circumvent the process of internalizing and enacting femininity. As Ava put it, her subcultural affiliation allowed her to experience her adolescence differently than would a mainstream adolescent:

> When I was growing up, I didn't grow up and be a teenager. I grew up and I was a punk and then I was a teenager. It was like, no one really knew me for being anything else but a little kid. I don't know how people would treat me if I was sixteen and I turned into a punk, but I was twelve when I turned into a punk. . . . See, I grew up being a punk. Well, punks, New Wave, whatever. Being weird and fucking . . . I just really never knew what it was like to be a normal kid. I like it.

For some girls, their dissatisfaction with norms of conventional femininity in large part precipitated their entry into punk. Not only do these girls resist the same strictures as their male peers, but they fight femininity on the most hostile of battlegrounds: the boys' turf.

Four

"The Punk Guys Will Really Overpower What the Punk Girls Have to Say"

The Boys' Turf

"We beat the shit out of Rattler last night." Wattie leaned on the counter of the drop-in center.

"Which one's Rattler?" I asked.

"You know, the tall skinny guy with the black curly hair and the crooked teeth that's always over here talking to Tommy."

"That guy, yeah. Who beat him up?"

"Me and Tad and Saber and Andrew and Indigo and Cooper."

"What for?"

"He was, like, molesting all the girls that were passed out on the riverfront, so me and the guys beat the shit out of him." Wattie smiled, "I heard that he jumped a train this morning."

"I heard that he was in the hospital and that he got arrested," Cooper chimed in.

I confess, I wasn't particularly heartbroken at this news. Loud, obnoxious, and opinionated, Rattler hadn't been a particularly pleasant person to have around the drop-in. If he had sexually assaulted punk girls, he had certainly encountered swift justice. Besides, from what I had observed of the police, they were likely to arrest everyone for public drunkenness if the punks had turned to them for help in this matter.

Still, I began to see this event in a different light two days later when I had to intervene to prevent the same punk guys from beating up another boy, a street hustler who had insulted me. Chris had approached me that morning, asking me to do him a favor: could I please shave my armpits? Surprised and indignant—the last thing I ever expected was that one of the street kids would object to *my* grooming habits—I told him he was being an asshole and to fuck off. We had a bit of a discussion and then he left me alone. Later that day, as I sat by the riverfront with the other punks, I told Wattie about the incident. Honestly, I was just making conversation. I had dealt with the situation, and I had no residual animosity toward Chris. We were just talking.

Wattie's reaction surprised me. "Hey, Tad, Cooper, we gotta beat the fuck out of Chris," Wattie yelled. The guys were getting visibly agitated, fired up. Just then, Chris showed up.

"Did you say that stupid shit to Lauraine? 'Cause she's our friend, you know." Wattie yelled out. Chris did not reply.

I jumped in, "No, really guys, it's okay. It's cool. It's no big deal. He was being an asshole at me, and I dealt with it. End of story." They backed down, but it was a week before Chris showed up at the drop-in again, and then only after I had told his friend to convey the message that no one was going to hurt him.

Having been inducted into the local punks' "tribe," it seemed that I was theirs—the guys'—to "protect," regardless of whether or not I wanted or needed such protection. My emotions about this incident remain deeply conflicted. On the one hand, I was pleased that the guys considered me a part of their group, for I had worked hard to earn their friendship and respect, mostly by putting up with insults, doing them small favors, and showing no fear when Indigo jokingly (I think) threatened to cut off my finger to get my engagement ring. Despite the fact that I had always done so without a thought when I was a teenager, hanging out with the punks in squats and in the streets at night now seemed to me to be a fairly dangerous activity, and so I was glad to be in the company of friends who could be relied upon to help me out if I got into a jam. Yet at the same time, I was angry that these *boys*, most of whom were a decade younger than I, assumed I was in need of their protection, especially for such a trivial incident. Punk lives, and I guess chivalry's not dead either.

I have always found that punk girls have a very pithy way of summing things up, and when Sue stated (with no prompting on my part) that "punk is a male-dominated scene," I could not help but agree. "Male-dominated" is somewhat of a slippery term, though. What did she mean? That there were more guys than girls in the scene? That the guys dictate what punk is, and is about? Sue's next sentence, "It's kind of 'survival of the fittest' among the girls" seemed to indicate that "male-dominated" also means that the girls have to conform to some male-determined standard, and that not all girls achieve this "fitness." In this chapter, I examine the ways in which punk is constructed and enacted as a discourse of masculinity: a scene that is male-dominated by numerical preponderance; a subculture whose norms are constructed to be "masculinist"; and a group in which punk girls are constrained within male-defined gender expectations.

My primary aim in this research was not to discover male punks' constructions of masculinity, but rather punk girls' definitions of femininity. These constructions of gender are neither complementary nor inversions of one another, for male-dominated subcultures support masculine identification in boys, while challenging feminine identification in girls. Thus, the process by which gender is constructed within such subcultures differs dramatically for males and females. Clearly, the social construction of masculinities within subcultures such as punk is a topic worthy of investigation, and an interview study of male members of such subcultures would do well to discover such accounts. However, this was out of the purview of my research. Rather, I draw on my interview and observational research not to discover how males construct *their* masculinity, but rather how their relations with punk girls construct the masculinity of the punk subculture. I then explore how, in turn, this masculinity affects punk girls' constructions of both feminine and punk identities (which I explore further in the next chapter).

Ultimately, the masculinity of the subculture imposes contradictory standards for female punks' behavior and effectively isolates girls from each other. Furthermore, I was dismayed to find, this internal form of oppression is one which punk girls accommodate, rather than resist. Although I had originally committed to representing punk girls' realities as they constructed and presented them, I found myself seeing aspects of male punk culture which oppressed punk girls. Yet only some punk girls acknowledged that this oppression existed, and even these did not resist this oppression, but accommodated male punks' limitations on them. In the end of my analysis, I will conclude by examining their motivations for such accommodation.

Male Domination as Numerical

Since its inception, punk has been a numerically male-dominated subculture. Historical accounts of the subculture, such as McNeil and McCain's (1996) *Please Kill Me* and Savage's (1991) *England's Dreaming* detail the preponderance of males in both the U.S. and British punk scenes of the seventies. The masculinization of hardcore in the 1980s further heightened male participation and decreased punk's attractiveness to girls. Sociologists' accounts of punk highlight the male domination of the scene as well. Researchers who study punks (except for Leslie Roman, whose sample was predominantly female) tend to have more male than female participants. Thus, in an epidemiological study, Burr (1984) drew on a sample of nineteen punks—eleven males and eight females. Of Levine and Stumpf's (1983) punk "informants," three were female and four male. Likewise, ethnographer James Lull (1987), while offering no numerical account, writes at length about the male domination of punk.

Field researchers also note the numerical dominance of male punks. Although Kathryn Fox claims that the number of men and women within the punk scene she studied in the 1980s was "fairly equal" (1987:348), Stephen Baron (1989a, 1989b, Kennedy and Baron 1993) reports, in his contemporaneous ethnography of the Victoria, British Columbia, punk subculture, that males outnumbered female participants in a ratio of three to two. As well, Wayne Wooden (1995) found that males constitute roughly two-thirds of the California punk population he surveyed and four-fifths of the punks in New Zealand. In my own field research, I observed that the males made up two-thirds to three-quarters of the populations of the various punk scenes I encountered. Thus, at its most basic level, punk is a male-dominated youth subculture in the sense that males constitute the majority of the punk population. However, this male domination is much deeper and more complex than mere numerical dominance.

"That Total 'Punk Rock Attitude'": Male Domination as Masculinist

The numerical preponderance of males in the punk scene is not the only way that punk is male dominated. As they are in other numerically male-dominated youth subcultures, punk's codes and norms are heavily masculine. A number of subculture theorists have argued that males create youth subcultures in order to satisfy their need to express, affirm, and celebrate masculinity. As early as 1955, Albert Cohen argued that delinquent boys specifically constructed their "subcultural solution" to draw on and express masculinity: "The reader will sense, although he [sic] may find it hard to articulate, that in some way both the middle-class pattern and the delinquent response are characteristically *masculine*. Although they differ dramatically, to be sure, they have something in common. This common element is suggested by the words 'achievement,' 'exploit,' 'aggressiveness,' 'daring,' 'active mastery,' 'pursuit.' ... The delinquent response, however it may be condemned by others on moral grounds, has at least one virtue: it incontestably confirms, in the eyes of all concerned, his essential masculinity" (139–140; emphasis in original). British sociologist Michael Brake later noted that as a result of such domination of male concerns, subcultures develop male normative standards: "subcultures are male-dominated, masculinist in the sense that they emphasise maleness

_____ *Illustration 8* _____

Males outnumber females in a ratio of three to two.
(Photo: D. K. Rabel)

as a solution to an identity otherwise undermined by structural features"
(1985:163). Thus, the numerical dominance of males in these subcultures is
only the tip of the iceberg—these subcultures are indeed specifically constructed to be hypermasculine in order to compensate for perceived challenges
to working-class boys' masculinity in mainstream culture.

Thus, theorists have argued that when adolescent males encounter constraints of class they turn to a celebration of masculinity in their creation of an
acceptable "subcultural solution." Ethnographers have documented the ways
in which postwar subcultures of the past four decades were masculinist, from
Teddy boys (Jefferson 1976) and Mods (Hebdige 1976) to working-class youths
in the United Kingdom (Willis 1977) and the United States (MacLeod 1987/
1995). The numerical preponderance of males creates subcultures that are
masculinist in their norms and practices. What often remains unexplored in
these writings are the operative definitions of *masculinity* and *masculinism.*
What do these theorists mean when they celebrate the masculinity of youth
subcultures? What is the content of these "masculinist" norms? What is the
source of such definitions?

In his groundbreaking examination of the link between gender and crime,
James Messerschmidt (1993) draws on feminist and social-constructionist accounts of gender to examine the various sources and enactments of what he
describes as "multiple masculinities." Beginning with a critique of criminological

theory's gender blindness, Messerschmidt argues for an examination of crime (and deviance) which is attentive to various feminist theories of gender. He then describes the complexities of race- and class-specific masculinities: white middle-class masculinity reinforces achievement in sports and academics, while working-class masculinity often emphasizes quite the opposite. For both white and minority working- and lower-class youths, attributes of toughness, coolness, and aggressiveness connote manhood.[1] Despite the multiple iterations of male gender norms, Messerschmidt does argue that there is a dominant ideal of masculinity in the United States. This model transcends boundaries of class and race and involves characteristics of dominance, control, and independence (93). The norms of working-class male subcultures merely reflect the valorization of working-class masculinity: the cool pose, the sexual objectification of women, the disdain for the feminine world of learning, and the valorization of violence. Masculinity becomes codified in these subcultures, rendering them "masculinist" in their value orientations and norm construction.

The masculinity of punk is especially apparent in the construction of subcultural symbols and rituals. The history of punk shows that punk was not originally constructed as a site for female participation, with the earliest of punk 'zines proclaiming that "punks are not girls" (Laing 1985). Lydia, who has been a member of the North American punk subculture since its inception, noted:

> [The guys] had all the power too, we have to admit. They did. They had all the power in that movement in the beginning. Women were seen as an accessory like in every fucking thing almost. I think it changed though. I don't think that's totally true. I'm sorry, I shouldn't be saying this, but a lot of women were there . . . they were there as groupies. There were a lot of groupies, right, but this was one of the first scenes where women did start to play in the bands. But it took a while, because in the beginning it was still all guys and if you look at any chronology of bands, it's still mostly guys from that period.

As Lydia remarked, throughout the history of the subculture the majority of punk bands have been all male and, as did other rock bands, they wrote and performed songs with misogynist lyrics. As the subculture grew, punk may have offered girls in a variety of scenes in both the United States and the United Kingdom the means and opportunity to develop forms of rebellion and self-expression, but by the 1980s, punk had become resolutely masculine. Even today, the thrash pit remains male punks' territory. As participation in the pit is a marker of subcultural authenticity, the male domination of the pit had repercussions in punks' assessments of who is a "true" punk.

In addition to their construction of punk rituals as masculine, male punks are instrumental in establishing the "rules of engagement" of the subculture. They often discuss authenticity (who is a real punk and who is a poseur) specifically with reference to who most closely approximates the masculinity of the ideal punk. This involves aspects of ideology, behavior, and dress. The uniform punk style of dress, with its shaved head, combat boots, tattoos, and leather jacket, was constructed along male lines. Aspects of punk behaviors, such as tough posturing, rebelliousness, confrontation, roughhousing, snarling, spitting, and displaying a "cool pose," are traditionally constructed to be masculine. The ideal punk, deemed hardcore for adherence to the extremes of punk style, lifestyle, and ideology, is most often male, as it is males who are most likely to adopt modes of street living, to have multiple tattoos and shaved heads, to engage in the ritualized violence of thrashing, and to exhibit attributes of "cool" (Fox 1987). It is these very attributes of masculinity which so define punk that ethnographer Stephen Baron (1989a, 1989b) described them as hegemonically defining "punk resistance," which, to no one's surprise, he then characterized as a property of male punks.

While male punks and their ethnographers may fail to note the masculinity of these norms, punk girls are not blind to it. For some punk girls, their encounters with male punks' definitions of punk norms were the least attractive aspect of participation in the subculture:

> Lola: I don't like the so-called, if you're not dirty [then you're not punk], that kind of thing, or that you have to hate other people, like hippie bashing. Because I don't think, I don't like that part, I don't. I think that's pretty, that's pretty crass. And the whole so-called macho—these men, the guys will get the big, when they get drunk and they try to beat the crap out of each other and they're the big, they're so "punk." They get that total "punk rock attitude" kind of thing. I don't like that association to it.

In describing the "punk rock attitude" as being crusty, hating others, bashing hippies, and roughhousing, Lola pointed out the stereotypically masculine behavior of punks. These behaviors, along with fighting, vandalism, and tough posturing when drunk, are aspects what male hardcore punks consider to denote authenticity. Other punk girls also found these behaviors and expectations to be particularly distressing:

> Nikita: A lot of people that consider themselves punk, or label themselves "punk," if you don't have an eighteen-inch mohawk, you're not cool, or if you don't have something on your body pierced or blah blah blah, have this many tattoos, or . . . It's the whole "punker than thou" bullshit.

Alexea: I hate it when people do stupid shit, fucking stupid shit, like throwing a bottle through the front windshield of a cop. Oh yeah, that's "punk rock." That's stupid as fuck. Don't blame it on punk rock. It didn't make you do it. . . . I hate it. Or when people do really dumb things. Like, blatantly stupid, childish things and blame it on being punk rock. "That's hardcore!" Hardcore, my ass. . . . I don't really fall into that shit either, whether or not people think I'm hardcore. I could fucking care less. If they don't think my look's hard enough, then they can eat my shit.

The behaviors that Nikita and Alexea described as normatively punk, Lola further labeled "that macho kind of thing." These behaviors, in turn, are inherent to the subculture's definition. Punk girls recognized that participation in the subculture necessarily meant an association with those norms associated with punk masculinity:

Lisa: My experience has been—because there's also—a lot of people associate with a certain aggressiveness with the music and with the scene so . . . and always that's been something that's been associated with male behavior and maleness.

However, this does not mean that punk girls agree with this masculine definition of punk. In Lola's view, such behaviors may be historically correct for punks, but do not reflect the reality of what she and her friends, self-identified punks, define as punk: "We're pretty laid-back." Counterdefinitions, such as Alexea's rejection of others' determinations of her as more or less hardcore are derided as not being "punk enough." These girls may have quite different definitions of what is punk, but because the male punks outnumber the females, it is usually their definition of the subculture that prevails. Failure to conform to the hardcore standard created and enforced by male punks, can, as we shall see, be grounds for expulsion from the scene.

In theory, punks oppose the norms and values of mainstream culture. In practice, punks adopt many of the gender codes and conventions of mainstream adolescent culture. In the many mixed-gender groups I observed, it was the male punks who most closely approximated and typified what is commonly regarded as punk behavior. More so than the girls, they tended to be abrasive, loud, and obnoxious. They adopted very combative stances toward each other, often jokingly insulting and threatening each other. At some points, this verbal combat escalated into physical fighting which, more often than not, was play fighting, or roughhousing. None of the punk girls I observed ever engaged in such rough behavior. They often bantered with the male punks and sometimes engaged in the more mild physical altercations: "They treat us as equals.

I'm treated, they, they spit on me. If I spit on them, they'll spit on me back. It's just a total equal thing. They don't see gender, actually" (Lola). In verbal exchanges, the girls often could not give as good as they got. Given the plethora of degrading terms for women in the English (and French) language, and the comparative lack of comparable profanities referring to males, girls found it difficult to escalate any badinage. Even when angry at being insulted or when engaged in such banter with each other (which was extremely uncommon), the punk girls' exchanges with both male and female punks never attained the point of physical combat or roughhousing. Thus, when punk is described as a "subculture of violence" (Kennedy and Baron 1993), it is usually the male punks' behaviors that, as Lola put it, give punks a bad name.

Punk girls' accounts of others' perceptions of them also reflect the ways in which punk is constructed as masculine. Some punk males exercise their power in labeling behaviors as acceptable for punk males, but not for punk females:

> Carnie: When punks like Cooper look at you, they're like, "It's cool for a guy to be dirty, but for a girl it's not. Girls should be clean and girls should shave and should wear makeup and . . . " Safety punks, they're the ones that look at girls different than they look at guys. Because they're, they're little house punks: "I can be punk on the weekends, but from nine to five Monday through Friday, I'm going to be a little conservative McDonald's-working employee."

Carnie argued that "house punks," especially, retained a more conservative, traditional outlook on appropriate gender attributes. However, Carnie, as did other girls, found that punks were much more of a mixed group when it came to defining norms and treating punk girls with respect or abuse:

> Some of them are really cool, they respect you just as they respect another guy, and some of them are just like, they call you a prostitute and call you . . . it's a normal thing. They make fun of you and pick on you, but it's kind of, just a friend thing. Just kidding around. Like a big, they normally treat you like a big brother. . . . They're big assholes to us but they know, you know they love you because if something bad were to happen, they'd be there for you.

> Candace: The lifestyle, getting drunk and passing out somewhere . . . getting drunk or being in a pit, a lot of, you have a tendency to get a lot more violence put on you, I feel. I know I've been raped in squats by other punks and by crack fiends wandering in. I know I've been put down because I was a female. A lot of them are chauvinistic. But I also run across a lot of really cool male punks, also. So it's just, it's the same everywhere. . . . Even in the

punk rock culture there's people of all sorts, that are real assholes and that are really cool and that just kind of sit off to the side and watch everything. It's the same.

Amalia: We all treat each other as equals. Some, I'm sure, I know actually there are some guys who [are] like, "I'm a man," got the testosterone going on, but usually, to me, all my boyfriends have been really, really cool. They treated me as one of the guys or something.

Although not all punks are as blatant as Cooper in expressing what is appropriate for punk girls, most of the girls I spoke with did report that some punk guys were openly opposed to the presence of girls in the scene. As a consequence of their actions in maintaining gender boundaries and delimiting the range of acceptable gendered behavior, the role that these male punks play in defining entry into the subculture is quite important in defining punk as masculine. Baron (1989a) notes that male punks discourage girls' adoption of a street-based lifestyle; while I found that many male punks were supportive and protective (see below), some did indeed openly discourage girls' presence, while others merely circumscribed appropriate female behavior in the scene.

In addition to the pressures exerted by male punks, members of the mainstream public play a role in reinforcing the masculinity of punk, by holding what punk girls perceive as a double standard. Carnie, who identifies as a crusty street punk, attributed variations in mainstream people's reactions to their attribution of gender ideologies:

When people, other people look at you, they think it's okay if a guy is digging in a trash can, just a guy, people won't look at him the same way as a girl digging in a trash can. They're like, "Girls shouldn't do that." But then there can be a guy a few blocks down the street, eating trash out of the trash can or whatnot, "That's okay, it's a guy. Guys can do that because they're [guys]." So it's kind of different.

While it is debatable whether most members of the general populace view digging in trash as acceptable for anyone, Carnie's point that it is more disturbing to see a crusty girl draws on notions of chivalry, a paternalistic standard:

People look at you differently. Well, it's okay for a guy to do it because they're male—they're masculine. But you, you're a girl, you're a symbol of purity and this and that and you should be clean. You're the bearer of children and this and that. And it's just like, yeah, so? I can have children dirty as well as I can clean, and I think it's kind of dumb.

Carnie perceived the link between ideals of cleanliness and maternity (femi-

_____ *Illustration 9* _____
Male punk "cool pose"—snarling and grinning
(Photo: D. K. Rabel)

nine attributes of domesticity) as informing public gender bias in their perception of punks' behaviors. Justine echoed Carnie's assessment of the paternalistic standard with respect to the punk norm of street living:

> A girl in the streets is more pitiful than a guy. Guys can defend themselves better. Not necessarily, but according to them . . . That's what they think, but I know very well that if someone got in my face and wanted to hit me, I'd be

very capable of hitting him. Except that I'll admit that you put my boyfriend in the street and me in the street and I'm pathetic. He's stronger than I am.

Besides the gender bias in the judgment of punk girls' behavior, Carnie also perceives gender bias in public perceptions of punks' appearance:

> It is different because people look at you different. Guys can have a bald head, but girls can't. Guys can wear boots, but girls can't. Girls should wear pantyhose and dresses. But not ripped ones.

The effect of this, argued another girl, is that punk girls are taken much less seriously than are punk guys:

> Sheila: People won't, will listen to a man more than they would to you. Because some, some people are just like, "Oh, you're a girl. You don't know what you're talking about." I get that in a big way.

As a result of this perception, being a punk girl can lead to more unwanted attention than that to which the males are subjected:

> Rosie: I think seriously, I think that guys, at least the guys definitely get away with it a lot more than the girls do. They still get the same shit and everything, but it's not as bad for a guy as it is for a girl. Like the comments, and the shit. I mean, girls get beaten up by skinhead guys too and stuff. Things like that happen. It occurs. I think in a way it's really bad.

Punk girls are, indeed, subjected to forms of public sexual harassment as well as harassment for being punks, which I explore in later chapters. On other occasions, however, with a different audience, being a girl can also result in a lessening of public censure or of police attention:

> Allie: I think that girls and guys are totally treated different. I know I get away with murder. I've done a lot of things. Cops always look at me and they say, always like . . . I've been caught drinking with friends in public and stuff like that and they'll pull my friends aside, they'll give them tickets, and then they'll pull me aside, tell my friends to leave, and they'll, they'll say, "Oh, you shouldn't be with these people. They're just bad influences on you." They always assume that I'm a runaway, that I'm some little girl and these boys are taking advantage of me or trying to get me drunk or whatever. . . . People always just assume that I'm some little helpless child.

Thus, gender is always salient in the eyes not only of male punks, but of the larger society in which the subculture is encapsulated. More often than not, the mainstream public reinforces the male definition, and hence male domination, of punk.

Ironically, given that some male punks so blatantly uphold gender divisions and different, gendered, standards of punk, the punk subculture often portrays itself as being egalitarian with respect to gender arrangements. In a survey of both California and New Zealand punks, Wooden (1995) found that 71 percent of both groups affirmed that "females are equal to males." In the California group, this far exceeded the 55 percent affirmative response of metalheads and the 57 percent affirmative response of the comparison group; in New Zealand, 80 percent of metalheads responded affirmatively and 70 percent of the comparison group did. Based on this finding, Wooden concluded that "a more egalitarian view with respect to females being treated equal to males was shared by the punk rockers in both countries" (106). Indeed, although punk is a male-dominated and predominantly white subculture, the subculture does present itself with a veneer of egalitarianism with respect to race and gender, as Sloopy put it:

> That's one of the things it's about, equality and nonracism and stuff. . . . But generally it doesn't matter if you're a boy or a girl in this scene. That's one of the cool things. That's why it's not sexist and stuff, because there's equality and it really doesn't matter.

Another girl was even more explicit regarding the egalitarian expectations and rhetoric of punk:

> Andie: The guys, some of the punks want you to be a feminist. The thing is that they're not, they don't have total control of you. They want you to tell them what to do. That's what's great about them: they want you to tell them what to do.

However, not all punk girls were satisfied with these expectations. Andie continued:

> But I like, I like it better when I can look what I look like and have a guy tell me what to do. That's why I hang around with Jed, because he's always like, "Bitch, get over here. Play me a song. Entertain me. Now!" I like that. It's cool. I'd like to just have a collar and a leash so he could just walk me around. It would be fun.

What is striking about Andie's account (besides the play at sadomasochism she described), is that the male punks' desire for her to be a feminist runs counter to her own wishes, contradicting the self-determination that is one of feminism's tenets. Furthermore, the male punks Andie described who wanted punk girls to be feminist were very much in the minority. Overall, punk's reflexive reversal of the structural features of the mainstream culture does not extend to the reversal of gender norms. In both my observations and interviews with punk girls, I found, instead, that male punks are very active in creating and maintaining the masculinity of the punk subculture throughout their interactions with punk girls.

"Just One of the Guys"?: Male Domination as Expectation and in Interactions

These ideologies of masculinity profoundly affect the position of girls within the punk subculture. It is not only that the values, norms, behaviors, symbols, and rituals of the punk subculture are masculine, but the male punks construct and reinforce the masculinism of the subculture though their everyday interactions with each other and with punk girls. Through these interactions, they set up contradictory expectations of how punk girls are supposed to behave. Girls most often encounter the norms of punk masculinity in their daily contacts with punk guys. It is in these interchanges with punk girls that the males reinforce the masculinity of the norms and controlled gender relations within the subculture.

In my months of fieldwork, I had numerous opportunities to observe interactions between male and female punks, many of which conformed to the same pattern as the incidents described below. Often, I would get to know punks as a group before interviewing the punk girls. I discovered predictable patterns in male punks' perceptions of me and of my research. They accused me of reverse sexism for focusing only on punk girls. They asked to be interviewed, asserting that they would pretend to be girls. They would check me out before "allowing" me to interview girls. They would encourage reluctant girls to be interviewed, and, in one case, attempted to discourage a girl, Jessie, from coming to our scheduled interview. The punk guys would occasionally interrupt interviews, asking for money, volunteering information, and asking once again to be interviewed. In one case, when I allowed a male punk to sit in on an interview (this was early on in my research) he became extremely disruptive:

LL: Are you . . . involved with someone?

Jessie: Uh, no. Just broke up. [Marcus is] just my friend.

Marcus: She's lying, we've been married for some time now.

Jessie: I met him, like, four days ago.

Marcus: We have a nonsexual relationship. It's one of the best-type things we ever had.

LL: Good.

Marcus: She's got two husbands.

LL: That's good. I wouldn't let that get about too much.

Marcus: Well, that's what I call rolling in the hay. Hey hey hey.

LL: Where do you live?

Jessie: I live in Midtown.

LL: With roommates and stuff?

Jessie: A roommate, yeah . . . I rent a room from this guy.

Marcus: Quit that lying. She lives in a cardboard box . . .

Jessie: Yeah, I live in a pipe, I live in a pipe under a bridge. That's it.

Marcus didn't stop interrupting us until I finally gave him money to go away and play video games while Jessie and I talked.

All of these interruptions, requests, and comments were made in a jocular manner, which made it especially difficult to respond in such a way as to end the interaction without seeming uncool or uptight. Over the course of my field research, I tried out a number of tactics to deflect this attention. I began by telling the guys that other researchers were doing research only on male punks. I would explain that I was constrained by university regulations, setting up the Women's Studies program as a meddlesome arbiter of my research. I told them that if I was going to cheat by letting them impersonate girls, I might as well just stay home, make up my interviews, and save myself a lot of time and money (I swear, I didn't). Eventually, I started allowing the punk girls to deal with interruptions, a strategy that emerged as one girl responded to a male punk's request to be interviewed:

Guy: Give me five bucks. Two questions.

Clara: You're such aunties. You want to talk all the time.

LL: I can't. Because I'm only collecting information on girls. It would be useless to me.

Guy: Two questions, five bucks.

LL: I don't need you.

Clara: Can't you see that girls are more interesting than boys?

The punk males' intrusions into interviews and on the research process underscored, for me, not only the omnipresence of males' encroachment, but also the ways in which they shaped punk girls' experiences. Even in this project to uncover girls' voices, we operated under the "benevolent auspices" of male punks.

Punk girls' own accounts of they ways they were treated or perceived by the males fell into four categories: males as standoffish, sexist, or abusive; males as "respectful" or egalitarian; males as protective, chivalrous, or gentlemanly; and males as flirtatious or sexual. Often, a punk girl's account would reflect aspects of more than one of these stances. For instance, when I asked Alexea, a very tough, hardcore gutter punk, "How do male punks treat you?" she replied, "They treat me fine. If they talk shit, we can brawl." Like the male punks, she reported that she is willing to engage in roughhousing or fighting when the males "talk shit" to her (if you knew Alexea, you'd believe her too). I then asked her if she considered this as being treated like one of the guys, to which she replied, "Well, yeah, but they always want to schmooze on you. Especially when you're drunk and shit. Get down your pants, but that's a guy thing and . . . it just ain't happening." Despite her ability to "talk shit" and "brawl" with the best of them, Alexea still found that she was often treated as a sex object. Such incidents show how males maintain the masculinity of the punk subculture by shaping and enforcing its gender norms, and by presenting girls with contradictory sets of expectations.

"The Sneered Look": Condescension and Abuse

In some instances, female punks reported that male punks behaved in a manner that was standoffish, sexist, condescending, or even physically and sexually abusive. Although some girls attributed this behavior only to the worst individuals in the subculture, "real hardcore assholes," as Lola put it, encounters with male punks who were condescending to female punks, or even downright verbally or physically abusive, were fairly common.

> Cathy: Usually first, and I find this in almost all things, [guys] usually, just like with any stereotype that boys are mostly in, they usually at first won't talk to you, they just look at you, kind of like the sneered look and then even after they get to know, after they've talked to you a couple of times and realize—I don't know about all girls, well at least with me, that I'm like, that I goof around and I'm silly—then they usually just, then after that they usually just kid around me and goof around.

Cathy's attribution of this behavior to the majority of male punks stands in contrast to Lisa's description of the offending behavior as being perpetrated only by some male punks:

It really depends. Some of them are very definitely, yeah, all range of experiences. Some of them are really condescending, some of them—of course you'll find out this from other people—some of them are nice to their friends, but obviously not very respectful of their partner or whatever. And some of them are very, very gentlemanly and nice.

LL: What do you mean by "condescending"?

Lisa: Just sort of disrespect sort of tinged with a "Well, who really cares what you think?" . . . I think it's more sexist. Just [a] basic gender thing.

In addition to being standoffish or condescending, in the protection of male punk turf, such as the thrash pit, punk guys can become downright physically abusive:

Lola: We get our ass kicked. We have to fight ten times harder in a pit, just because you're a female. I went to—you've seen L7 [an all-female punk band]—I seen L7 at the Pantheon a year ago, and they had to, [the lead singer] had to stop the show and she started cussing out the guys at the Pantheon and was picking up the mike stand and started kicking them in the head with it and tell[ing] them—because there was a couple of girls there, and they were there, and the guys were literally forefront and beating the shit out of them, and just going way more than the other guys.

As well as being battered in the pit—more so than are male punks—girls reported other examples of male punks being physically abusive, and two girls reported having been raped by male punks.[2] Connie reported a milder, yet still abusive, incident stemming from punk drunkenness and banter:

I had a fight with Indigo last time I saw him too. . . . Fuck him, dude. He walked up to me and said, "I wouldn't hit a woman, but I'll slap a bitch." And he slapped me. Fucking, he's totally . . . He's totally cool when he's sober. . . . He's totally cool whenever . . . he's sober around me, but when he's drunk around me, he's just fucking, such a fucking prick, man.

It is noteworthy that Indigo was one of the guys who had beaten up Rattler, chivalrously protecting the punk girls whom he later abuses himself. He was also the one who threatened to mutilate me, but who later became a good connection in the field.

In being condescending or abusive, the males who participated in the scene directly reinforce the masculinity of the punk scene by subjecting female punks to punitive attention if they dared to enter the males' territory. In this way, they directly reinforced and perpetuated the masculinity of the punk subculture, keeping the streets, the pit, and the squats as boys' turf. However, other aspects of gender interactions within the punk subculture also reinforce these norms, often in a more subtle manner.

"Always Just the Pal": Becoming a Virtual Boy

While some male punks try to maintain the masculinity of punk through the exclusion of girls from punk turf, others recognize the inevitability of girls' encroachments. How do male punks deal with a female presence? One solution is to masculinize girls, to encourage them to become virtual boys. Lola, much battered about in the thrash pit, described the typical scenario of male acceptance:

> If you're a chick and you choose to get in that pit, they're going to go at you with full force, so you have to fight a lot harder. But when you do, when you come out in the end, you get respect, but you have to earn [it]. Yeah, you have to earn it. Because they all, they'll knock the hell out of you. And a lot of them won't, a lot of them will take care of you, but most of the real hardcore assholes, they'll just knock the shit out of you. And so you have to—when I go in the pit, definitely go with my steel-toed boots on and something in my fist, because if I have to go . . . I'm ready for assault in my battle gear.

Lola's strategy included both behavioral and sartorial adaptations: she entered the pit ready to fight, dressed in the steel-toed boots of punk masculinity, ready for the inevitable assault. Lola reported that male punks, upon perceiving a girl's toughness—that is, her successful adoption of traditionally male characteristics—would grant her the "respect" that she had "earned." In other words, it is only in proving herself to be as masculine as they that a girl can gain the type of camaraderie that male punks accord each other.

For punk girls, integration into the punk scene through friendships with males is contingent upon their attainment of the males' "respect." That "respect," however, can be gained only through the adoption of masculine characteristics, such as aspects of male punk dress (e.g., a mohawk or boots) or aspects of male punk behavior (e.g., toughness or coolness). For Anna, it was adopting the male style of dress that led to this form of "respect":

> Usually I was always just the pal, I was always treated like another guy, because I dressed a lot more androgynous.

Others found that toughness gained them "respect":

Ava: Male punks? Well, the majority of them are really cool to me, I think because I don't consider . . . I don't think I'm like a lot of girls, and they're just . . . I think the majority of them treat me with a lot of respect. Because I won't take their shit. . . . [I'm] mostly just one of the guys.

Arizona: More like a pal. I'm one of the guys, going strong at the end of the day. They don't, I'll get some shit from them sometimes, but I stand my ground. . . . Just, they'll get drunk and obnoxious and I'll get in their face and they'll get in my face and then we're done. So just get obnoxious, drunk. . . . But I get treated pretty equal. I would say. If I don't, I don't realize it.

Jennie: I'm treated like one of the guys. And they go around, I've been called "little brawler" because I do everything that they can do and that's the feminist in me coming out, but whatever a guy can do, I can do it too. . . . That's what it all comes out to is I want to play with them. But just one of the guys.

Dressing in a more masculine fashion, and especially being tough or cool (not "taking their shit") was a recurrent theme when girls spoke of attaining punk males' "respect." Joanie noted that once this respect is earned, it remains constant:

A boy. They treat me like I'm a boy. . . . It's fine with me. I forget what I am a lot. And then every thirty days I go, "Whoa! Shit! I am a girl!"

Girls who fail to attain that "respect" because they become punks for a traditionally feminine reason (meeting guys) are treated in derogatory ways and are not accepted by most punks in the scene:

Jennie: Girls just, they can't get into it. Or if they do, they did it because of a guy. Because I've seen that happen too, where they start seeing a punk rock guy: "Oooh, we'll shave our head and give ourselves a mohawk." And then they get kicked out [of the scene] because it's just like, "No. That's not what it's all about."

Thus, while some perspectives on deviance argue that girls become deviant for the sake of boys ("she did it all for love"—Millman 1975), this motivation is the kiss of death for girls wanting to be punks. This form of exclusion also highlights the gendered power dynamics of the subculture.

Girls are disadvantaged not only by their gender, but by their youth as well:

Emily: The little girl punks that come out here, they're younger and stupid and just into it because they think that punk rock boys are cute, and [the guys] treat them like stupid little girls. Most of the guy friends that I have, they all know me and they all respect me.

Thus, while young punk males are taken into the subculture by older males, the youth and naiveté of younger girls prevents their integration, further limiting the number of girls accepted into the scene. Moreover, the aloofness demanded by cool, the aggressiveness demanded by toughness run counter to female gender role socialization. Girls who want to be punk have to break through a subcultural glass ceiling imposed by the males.

In addition to this, as Emily's description shows, even other girls adopt these criteria, working against newer girls entering the boys' turf. Those who had earned "respect" then colluded with the males in making sure that all subsequent girls would be subjected to the same tests. These normative standards, therefore, become subcultural, adding once again to the hypermasculinity of punk. And yet, although the males rewarded girls' adoption of masculine norms, and encouraged other girls to maintain that standard, they also retained gender boundaries in the construction of their own behavior toward women.

"They're Not Really Mean": Chivalry and Protection

Punk girls reported that male punks accord a sort of protective chivalry to the girls in the subculture. In contrast to the behavior of the "real hardcore assholes" girls encountered, some male punks act toward females with a sort of gentlemanly demeanor. For example, contrast this account of Wanda's experience in the thrash pit to Lola's above:

> Wanda: Generally, they treat me fine. They're nice and they're not really mean. Especially moshing. If you're a girl and you're moshing and you fall, like during Lollapalooza, you fall and there are ten guys standing around you with their hands out. They're real gentlemen about it, sort of. And I thought that was real funny.

Jessie, who described herself as "ladylike" despite her shaved head, combat boots, and painted leather jacket, appreciated not being subjected to male punk rudeness:

> They treat me like one of the guys, I mean, they don't treat me anything, they don't like . . . They're real cool. They treat me like a lady. They don't like give me a hard time or anything. They're real nice to me. I don't have any problems with the guys.

Jessie's assumptions here are particularly interesting: she supports her definition of male punks' gentlemanly behavior by stating that they don't give her a hard time and that she doesn't have any problems with them. While this is exceptional, given the condescension and abuse other girls experience, it is noteworthy that it is merely the absence of such put-downs that defines punk chivalry. In fact, her request for more proactive gentlemanly acts met with resistance:

> Well, I always think, like when a guy doesn't open a door for me, I always say, "Is chivalry dead?" Not open the door for me, but just anything, I'll give them a hard time about it, "Is chivalry dead?" And they're like, "Well, you fought for fucking equal rights, now you gotta deal with it."

Not only did these male punks refuse an act of chivalry, as Jessie defined it, they turned to the rhetoric of feminism to excuse their actions—not at all a very "gentlemanly" thing to do!

In addition to this type of "chivalry" (read: absence of abuse), some male punks display a type of paternal protectiveness toward the girls. For some girls, this type of protective behavior is welcome. Cathy, who noted that male punks eventually warm up to her for her jocularity, also added:

> They're usually pretty protective too. They don't let people mess around with you too much. I like that.

Lola, who had characterized male punks as abusive in the thrash pit, also remarks otherwise:

> They're like big brothers to me, Saber and all of them, they just beat the shit out of Rattler, because Rattler was feeling us all up and stuff. They're real protective and cool. They treat you as equals, really. They really do. . . . They're real protective. Yet they know that I can take care of myself. They see me, they're like. "Sic Lola on them. She can beat some ass," and all this . . . They're real cool, they're really protective.

Thus, although the male punks do accord Lola "respect" for her toughness, they undermine her sense of being able to take care of herself by being protective in some circumstances. Male punk protectiveness is thus a tool used simultaneously to care for and disempower punk girls.

This type of protectiveness creates a dependence among the punk girls, as they come to expect such protection:

> Tori: A female punk, when you're in the pit, [the guys] do look out for you. You get this little tiny girl in there, she's on the ground, I make sure *I* pick her up and make sure she's on the outside of the circle or something like that. Just, if a girl punk starts something with a male or whatever, I expect my male punk friends to have my back. I guess just maybe about the strength factor. In which, I can kick some ass, but I can't kick everybody's ass. There's always someone better.

In many cases, however, this protectiveness combines with a form of possessiveness, leading to verbal abuse:

> Andie: The other punks see me as a little baby and they're like my bodyguards, every single one of them. There's like twenty out there, they're all my bodyguards. Because I'm usually the only girl, so a whole bunch of guys, and they all like me, it's so funny. They're like "Oh what a sweetie. Come here baby. Come here. Come here, bitch."

Andie did not recognize it but this male protectiveness was actually a means of controlling her:

> And it's not like, they don't harass me or anything, it's like, if somebody harasses me, *if somebody else besides out of the group harasses me*, then everybody jumps their shit. Everybody gets up and says "Hey, this is my baby, go away." Something like that. "Hey, this is Andie, this is my girl" [emphasis added].

Andie's account shows that, although the male punks may seek to protect punk girls from verbal harassment or abuse from outsiders, they retain that prerogative for themselves. This dynamic was made especially apparent in a horrifying account related by Carnie. She recounted an incident where she and a friend had been sexually assaulted by a stranger, which resulted in a change of attitudes among the male punks:

> Earlier that day, [the guys] were like, "Fuck you, you're a bitch. You're a cunt and a whore. You're an alcowhore, ya da da da da, but then when they found out about [the rape], they all freaked out and they were like, "Fuck that." And they were looking for the guy all night. And they found us a good place to stay and got us blankets and stuff. They were real cool about it.

Thus, although the males may try to protect punk girls from outside harassment or assault (admittedly, a valuable function, given the dangers of street living), they do little to police this type of behavior among themselves. Thus, male punks' chivalry does not, essentially, contradict their maltreatment of punk girls. The males protect the girls from outside abuses, but retain forms of behavior among themselves that they would not countenance from an out-group member. In this way, although they may push punk girls into adopting masculine characteristics by rewarding them with "respect," they still maintain gender boundaries in their protective treatment of them. They also achieve this by constructing sexual scripts for punk girls and by exerting contradictory sexual pressures.

"So They Want Something": Sexual Pressure

Punk is a predominantly heterosexual subculture. Although there is sometimes room within punk for gay and lesbian self-expression, much of this has gradually been relegated to the spin-off queercore scene. Thus, the pressures of heterosexuality still dominate punk, as evinced by the seven bisexual girls I interviewed, all of whom were dating male punks. The numerical predominance of punk guys over punk girls may predispose bisexual punk girls toward selecting male lovers rather than seeking out female lovers among the few punk girls in the scene. However, given the amount of heterosexual pressure and banter within the subculture, as well as some punks' homophobic attitudes, many girls may have felt constrained into such choices. Thus, within the subculture, "compulsory heterosexuality" (Rich 1980) is as normative as in mainstream adolescent culture and romantic relationships develop among many of the same rituals of teenage courtship.

Thus, although punks may appear to be sexually deviant, their sexual relationships conform to many of the mainstream cultural standards governing adolescent relationships: male and female punks pair up, break up, and make up just like their nonpunk peers. Unlike the hippie subculture, which challenged monogamy with a "free love" ideology, punks rarely challenge the mainstream norms governing sex and romance. Beyond Johnny Rotten's purported characterization of sexual intercourse as "two minutes of squelching noises" and early punks' flirtation with homosexual and sadomasochistic self-expression, the punk subculture remains resolutely heterosexualist. The tragically dysfunctional relationship of Sid Vicious and Nancy Spungen often serves as somewhat of a model for punk relationships:

> Joanie: [Feminine punk girls are] going to end up with an asshole punk rock boyfriend that's like, "Fucking girl, blah, blah, blah." A beer-drinking punk rocker that likes his little teenage girls and kind of roughs them around and has petty arguments with them all the time . . . That's like trendy punk rock relationships. "Like Sid and Nancy!"

Filmmaker Alex Cox (Cox and Wool 1986) immortalized this relationship in an eponymous film, summarizing its lesson as "love kills." As abusive as the Sid and Nancy relationship was, and as frightening as its example is as a model relationship, its role as a punk image underscores the heterosexuality of punk.

Fortunately, contrary to popular, subcultural, and parental expectations, within relationships male punks are usually no more rude nor violent than are nonpunk boyfriends (which is damning by faint praise):

> Andie: Actually, they are really good toward women . . . other punks, punks

_____ *Illustration 10* _____
Punk couple
(*Photo: D. K. Rabel*)

are really, really sweet toward women. They have the most . . . I think that they're even better than some of the men that they bring you flowers and stuff. They got, the punks are like, "This is my little baby." They take care of you better than they take care of themselves. It's like they put you first all the time.

Sue: I've noticed that punk rock guys are the nicest boyfriends I've ever had in my life. They're not obligated to do anything. It's a pleasure-based society. . . . For the most part, they're going to actually be caring people. People have this misconception of punk guys just being ogres, but I've gone out with some really nice punk guys that were actually better than the other little boyfriends I've gone out with.

Sexual relationships between men and women within the subculture tend to conform to the monogamous style of mainstream heterosexual relations. Although punks may appear to be decadent and do have a propensity to wear bondage gear, many relationships replicate the standards of mainstream culture, with sadomasochistic practices being fairly uncommon. Heterosexual pairings among the punks, as among nonpunks, may lead to permanent commitments of cohabitation and marriage; a number of the girls I interviewed were engaged, married, or living with their boyfriends.

With this normative expectation of heterosexuality, retaining some traditional gender roles such as femininity and masculinity remains functional. This heterosexuality is further reinforced through interactions between male and female punks. Punk girls, as potential partners for the males, are expected to conform to mainstream standards of female heterosexuality, to present themselves as attractive and sexually available. These, in turn, are some of the central constitutive norms of femininity. Punk males, as are males in other youth subcultures, are instrumental in delineating the ways in which sexual expression occurs within the subculture.

Deirdre Wilson (1978) found that males in male-dominated delinquent subcultures played an important part in controlling girls' sexuality by setting up paradoxical sets of expectations. They both attempted to engage girls in sexual activity and sanctioned girls who adopted a more liberal, instrumental, "masculine" view of sexual activity. Likewise, Mindy Stombler (1994) found that fraternity brothers both treated girls in their "little sister" organizations as sexual commodities, and yet also proffered negative sanctions to those girls deemed too promiscuous or "easy." As did males in these subcultures, punk guys also set up contradictory standards for the sexual behavior of punk girls.

Flirting or other sexual banter is a primary way in which punk males reinforce gender boundaries. Many punk girls reported that the males view them (or other girls) in a primarily sexual way:

LL: How do male punks treat you?

Denise: It's very much the same as always—it's like, depending on, usually the first, guys come up to me it's cause they're hitting on me, so they want something. Almost immediately, it's always the first thing out of my mouth, all the time, and it's "No, I'm engaged," and then after that we can kind of take it on to a different level. But it always starts out as, "I don't want to talk to you about what you believe I just want to get you in bed."

This banter could even extend to overt pressures for sex, culminating in attempted rape:

Justine: There's this one guy [at "punk park"] who could only speak English, and the only thing he could say [in French] is, *"Veux-tu faire l'amour avec moi?"* [Do you want to make love to me?] And he was harassing all the girls there. He was an asshole. . . . The guys that I thought were my friends, not even a year ago, nearly the last time I ran away, I thought he was my friend. I slept at his place and he wanted me to sleep with him. He said, "Hey, you have my hospitality. What are you going to give me for it?" He was getting violent. He wanted to make me, but I grabbed my shit and left.

Even when these interactions did not escalate to attempted rape, girls resented the ongoing sexual pressures which male punks applied:

LL: How do male punks treat you?

Basilisk: Either they all, they want to sleep with me, that's basically what it boils down to. And a lot of them want to sleep with me. It gets, it kind of gets annoying, because I don't want to sleep with a lot of them. . . . That's what it goes like. You have, a majority of them, either they're nice to me, some of them are nice to me, they don't really bother me. And with some of them, they totally are like, they're all touchy-feely and oh, and if I don't sleep [with them], then they get pissed off at me if I don't sleep with them.

Although, as in Justine's and Basilisk's accounts, such sexual attention can become very annoying or threatening, some girls viewed this as harmless:

Lola: We always mess, they always tease you around sexually, of course, but nothing bad. And they're all, they never make, really, advances and stuff, and they treat me like big brothers, really.

Candace: I haven't had any problems with [punk guys]. But generally, they're hitting on you and it just depends who it is.

Cora: It depends on the guy. . . . There are guys here that will jump on any girl. . . . When I got here, not long ago, all the guys were all over me. . . . They grab our boobs and we're always hugging, but it's just among friends.

For some punk girls, this sexual attention is what they first encounter with other punks:

Clara: Here, as soon as they see a new girl, they spot her right away. . . . Well, I started coming to the park last summer. At the start I was a little shy. . . . Then, in the fall, there was a big rush, everyone wanted to go out with me one day. I was the new blood on the block.

Girls soon learned that sexual banter was an acceptable way for punk guys and girls to communicate, so the banter was not always one-sided:

Clara: It seems to me that all the guys at the park are my friends. Shit. Like Ricky. Ricky, you talk to him, you kiss him, you grab his butt. He's a friend. They're almost all like that. Ricky, he's an exception . . . sex machine . . .

Most girls, although finding this somewhat bothersome, did not perceive such sexualized attention as threatening, merely annoying:

Elle: Well, punk guys [here] really trip out on sex. I think that's really stupid. But besides that, it's okay. It doesn't bother me at all. It's fun.

The male punks who behaved flirtatiously or who engaged in sexual activity with punk girls played upon the sexual permissiveness of adolescent culture. However, male punks also set up contradictory expectations, proffering negative sanctions to girls who engaged in what they deemed to be promiscuity. As one girl reported, engaging in such sexual activity may then lead to a lessening of the type of "respect" that punk girls gain by behaving in male ways. Tori noted that this makes a difference in the ways the males treat girls:

I think they treat me just a little bit different than they treat the other girls. Because, because I have been with that one person for so long. . . . And I get, I get a lot of respect from the guys. I know I do. From, rather than when I was just . . . because there was . . . a point when I was younger that I did sell my ass when I was younger, like twelve or thirteen, down in New Orleans . . . Back then, I think maybe everybody thought I was a floozy or a hooker or whatever, which I was. I was, but I wasn't. I didn't sleep with everybody. And now I just, nobody ever hears of me sleeping with anybody anymore and I get a lot of respect for that, I think.

Thus, sexual chastity, or at least monogamy, led to girls earning "respect" as well. However, as in other parts of teen culture, males were not held to so stringent a standard. Tori went on to discuss the ways in which more sexually active or promiscuous girls were treated:

LL: You said that the guys treat you differently than they treat other girls. Is that the difference?

Tori: I think so, yeah.

LL: They treat other girls like they're . . .

Tori: There's these three girls that are my best friends—I love them to death—they've been around with a couple of guys and so the guys kind of like—maybe not intentionally in a bad way, but it does come out in a bad way—talk about how that girl was or how that girl can be to you or something like that. And so that kind of sucks. And with me, they can't do that, because nobody out here has been with me. So, but I still love those girls to death and I still love the boys to death. I get along better with the boys than the girls, most of the time.

Whereas males who engage in sexual activity do not lose status (being "studs" or "players"), females who do, even within the punk subculture, become negatively labeled as "whores" or "sluts." Thus, although the males will initiate sexual activity, it is not the case that in engaging in sex girls can gain the male prerogative of promiscuity. Celia Cowie and Sue Lees (1981) argue that this maintains a gendered double standard with respect to sexual activity: girls who "do" are "slags," and girls' who "don't" are "drags." In creating this distinction between the acceptability of sexual activity for males and for females, the males perpetuate a standard of behavior that reinforces gender distinctions within the punk subculture and highlights the relative inferiority of punk girls.

Conclusion

In all, punk males present and reward contradictory expectations of punk girls: they should be tough, like the guys, but they should also be pretty and sexually available. And yet, although they are expected to be sexual, they should not be overly promiscuous, for then they incur negative sanctions of being "sluts." Punk males also used these paradoxical expectations in order to create schisms between "types" of punk girls. Anna, who got "respect" from the males for her construction of an androgynous mode of self-presentation, reported that the punk males did distinguish between her "type" of punkness and that of other girls:

> Most of the time I was just treated like a pal or "tough girl" or, "She's cool, she's tough." That's usually how I got treated. There was always one or two of—they were more gothic, I guess, they were a little more feminine, they always wore the long black skirts and they'd have a little mohawk or the Robert Smith 'do—that they were always the heartthrobs that [the guys] liked. Because they were very, they'd never get into the pit, they'd stand on the side and stuff. And I just—I don't condemn anyone, if that's what they want to do—it's just always I get in and have fun, so I guess I got labeled more of a macho chick or whatever.

The male punks are certainly instrumental in establishing and maintaining boundaries between "tough girls" who are "respected" and other girls. As a result, the adoption of masculine characteristics becomes necessary for girls' creations of "respected" punk identities; paradoxically, however, the punk males expect and reinforce, to some extent, the girls' adoption of traditionally feminine characteristics. By expecting girls to be more masculine (rewarding this with "respect") and yet expecting them to be sexual partners who behave in traditionally feminine (read: chaste) ways, male punks set up conflicting expectations:

> Jennie: They treat me like one of the guys. That sucks in a way, but I am. . . . Sometimes you want a little bit more, but that's not how they see me. That's what sucks. . . . I wouldn't mind not being one of the guys. Because they expect you of all, they don't understand that, well, even though I wouldn't do this with you, I still have feelings and there's just sometimes you just need to talk to someone and they just don't understand it. "Well, what do you mean? You're one of the guys." You're just like, "No, you just don't understand."

Punk girls' constructions of forms of resistance often do not extend to their intimate contact with punk males. A measure of resistance, I have argued, requires three instances: a subjective account of oppression, an express desire to counter that oppression, and an action (broadly defined as word, thought, or deed) intended specifically to counter that oppression. The first category is satisfied: Girls are not blind to the oppressiveness of punk's masculinity, and even equate it with that they encounter elsewhere: "I see sexism in day-to-day life all the fucking time, so it doesn't surprise me that it comes from punk males" (Hallie). Punk girls recognize and object to the complex role that the males in the subculture play in determining membership and status:

> Sue: A lot of the punk guys think, just like a lot of the skinhead guys think skinhead girls are just "Oi toys," because skinhead girls didn't have a big role in the skin scene. Whereas punk girls and guys—have you ever seen in *The Decline of Western Civilization*, or like U.K. . . . what was it? *Social Distortion on Tour*—all the punk guys are going, "Girls are icky," and the girls were wild. They eventually intertwined. They had to at some point. But, punk is a male-dominated scene. It's kind of "survival of the fittest" among the girls.

However, punk girls are divided in characterizing male punk "chivalry," abusiveness, or control as problematic. Some, like Lola, reported pleasure in the banter in which they engage with the males. Others, like Anna and Candace, were proud of their position as tough girls or objects of "respect." Even those girls who objected to the males' treatment did not report undertaking courses of action to resist that treatment, save ignoring it or avoiding the offensive male.

Given the characterization of punk as a subculture of resistance, and girls' constructions of punk identities as a core aspect of their own personal resistance, why do these girls continue to accept this type of treatment? The answer may lie in the constraints of the subcultural role that faces these girls.

Punk girls recognize the male domination of the subculture, both numerically and normatively. Those girls who fail to recognize or reject the masculinity of punk, those whom Emily described as "the little girl punks that come out here, they're younger and stupid," who join for traditionally feminine reasons, such as wanting to meet men, do not participate long in the subculture; as Jennie stated: "[They] get kicked out [of the scene] because it's just like, 'No. That's not what it's all about.'" The girls who do achieve acceptance as punks are those who have achieved the acceptance of punk males by measuring up to the masculinist standards of the subculture. They are the "tough girls," the "macho chicks" who have commanded "respect." The girls who do "make it" in punk, in light of these masculinist norms, either self-select from a certain type or work to achieve it: "very assertive and aggressive girls" (Sue).

Punk girls thus accept, internalize, and project these norms, adopting many of these norms in their own assessments and expectations of other punk girls:

> Tori: It's harder to find a girl that can be as tough as a guy. Seriously—none, none of the male chauvinist crazy shit like that—a girl should be able to drink as much as a guy and—[for] their body weight—be able to climb rocks and go hiking with them and camping with them and be able to sleep outside in the cold and not complain twenty-four hours a day. It's hard to find girls like that, but they are out there. We are out there.

Becoming or being a punk girl therefore requires not only that one reject mainstream notions of femininity, but that one encounter and prevail over the male domination of the punk scene itself:

> Sue: The punk guys will really overpower what the punk girls have to say. I think the punk girl thing is a very aggressive scene, and very assertive and aggressive girls tend to get into it. I don't know many really passive, timid little girls who are going to shave their heads and look like a freak, take harassment from everybody all the time, and then fight off the guys in the scene.

Punk girls, therefore, are likely to collude with, rather than resist the masculinism of punk. Only a few punk girls, like the Riot Grrrls, raise their voices in protest, stating, "We are tired of boy band after boy band, boy 'zine after boy 'zine, boy punk after boy punk after boy." Riot Grrrls, realizing that they will "never meet the hierarchical BOY standards of talented, or cool, or smart" argue that if they do meet them, "we will become tokens" (Riot Grrrl 1992). In challenging the masculinist standards of punk, Riot Grrrls have been marginalized, indeed, have formed their own subculture now quite distinct from punk. Punk girls who want to remain within the subculture restrict their resistance to the masculinism of punk to rhetorical, general comments rather than to confrontation of male punks:

> Sue: I think more girls should get into punk and tell these guys that are trying to shy them off just so it can be an elite punk men's thing to fuck off. And get involved, who cares. . . . It doesn't matter how attractive you are to the boy next door.

Sue thus placed the onus on changing the subculture on girls, rather than on the males' treatment of girls or in their definition and support of masculinist punk norms. In accommodating to the masculinist punk norms, the punk girls I interviewed did indeed become tokens, often isolated from other girls, both punk and mainstream. Few reported having girl friends, and thus their forms of resistance to the masculinity of punk would enjoy little support, and little chance of success.

In some ways, this has been the most difficult part of my analysis to present, because, unlike other chapters that celebrate punk girls' resistance, this one points out and condemns both male punks' behaviors in shaping punk norms and punk girls' collusion with these constraints. Many of the girls I interviewed, I suspect, would (and will) challenge this aspect of my analysis as misrepresenting the actualities of the punk subculture or as casting punk into a bad light. Throughout this project, I have sought to present, explore, and honor punk girls' accounts of their realities. In this one chapter, I challenge the validity of their subjectivities, of their accounts stating that they feel unfettered and unoppressed by their male peers. Punk girls do report experiences of oppression at the hands of males, but then fail to counter that oppression. Others, experiencing the same types of behaviors, merely ignore them or discount their effects. No form of resistance can be pure, untainted by stains of accommodation. It is in their dealings with male punks and with the masculinity of the subculture that punk girls' forms of resistance fail them, for the cost of resistance—expulsion from the subculture—may be too high. Those who do remain within the punk subculture instead use its resources to turn their forms of resistance outward to challenge both mainstream gender norms and their harassment by strangers.

Five

"I'll Slap on My Lipstick and Then Kick Their Ass"

Constructing Femininity

When I was in the tenth grade, my little group of punk friends, at the instigation of our Canadian history teacher, published a one-off 'zine: *Vomit: A Journal of Dissent and Poor Taste*. Because our high school was providing photocopying (or was it mimeographing?) services, we had to submit our materials for approval to the principal, Mr. Rogers. My friend Holt had written an earnest article contrasting the lyrical content of the Clash's "Guns of Brixton" and Van Halen's top-ten hit, "Jump," arguing that songs about police repression were much more socially worthy and important than those about jumping. My acquaintance Rosemary submitted a heartfelt piece castigating our mostly upper-middle-class peers' obsession with the upcoming prom (what to wear? which car to drive?) and their total oblivion to the inability of some of their peers to afford the trappings surrounding the event.

Not one for such direct protest, I contributed a page-long parody of women's magazines, featuring an article on the care and maintenance of a mohawk haircut (don't shave your own head; don't use a straight razor; do use shaving cream, gel, and hairspray to keep it up) and recipes for punk party food: green French toast and Baby-in-a-Bowl, which is, basically, red Jell-O in a bedpan with a baby doll floating in it. Of all the articles proposed for *Vomit*, mine was the only one censored, returned to me with Mr. Rogers's admonition that the latter recipe was "disturbing." I revised Baby-in-a-Bowl to Rogers-in-a-Bowl, substituting a Mr. Rogers doll (the TV personality) for the baby doll. The school authorities consented to print the revision, but I suspect my revised recipe, with its not-so-subtle jab at the principal, contributed to my expulsion from high school later that month.

My parody of women's magazines pretty much summed up how I felt about mainstream women's media, the *Family Circle* and *Woman's Day* magazines my mother bought and I occasionally read. What with being so busy being a punk—writing parodies and getting expelled from high school—I never did get around to learning the finer points of femininity they detailed. Nor do I recall ever reading teen magazines, trying out makeup ideas, or lusting after the latest fashion for teenage girls. I could make my face into a perfect geisha mask at the age of fifteen, but the subtleties of eye shadow and blush still escape me to this day. When I got tattooed on my shoulder and wrist, and Holt asked me, admonishingly, what I would do if I ever had to wear a strapless dress or a slinky bracelet, I could not envision ever encountering such a circumstance. Even today, when I get together with girl friends, we reminisce about our leather jackets and Doc Martens and swap notes on the most effective methods we knew to make our mohawks stand upright, and do not discuss relationships or makeup tips. It's almost as though being punks kept us from being girls, or at least typical girls. Instead, we were punk girls.

"It's hard to be a punk and be a girl." Lavender-haired Rosie said this explicitly, and other girls I interviewed made this point over and over in their accounts of reconciling the norms of punk with those of femininity. What struck me about Rosie's statement was the way she phrased it: she didn't say "it's hard to be a punk girl" or "it's hard to be a girl punk," but that it's hard to do one, and hard to do the other, and supremely difficult to do both at once. To do both at once, girls have to reconcile the ways in which these terms contradict each other, and they have to negotiate between the expectations of both. In previous chapters, I examined what makes it hard for girls to be punks—the rejection of parents, peers, and school authorities; the gender expectations of male punks—and how punk girls accommodate or resist these difficulties. In this chapter, I turn to punks girls' inventive resolutions of the paradox of femininity and punk masculinity by examining how they behaviorally, stylistically, and discursively reject, accept, and reconceptualize the norms of punk and those of femininity—how "punks" and "girls" become punk girls.

"It's Somewhat of a Front": The Femininity Game

Punk girls are subjected to the same kinds of pressures that most Western women encounter, forced to play a no-win game of femininity. We are taught the rules in girlhood, and very few are excused from the game. In order to win, women have to strive to reach an impossible ideal: the wide-ranging attributes and expectations of femininity, which include behavioral and physical attributes of gentility, passivity, beauty, domesticity, et cetera. Playing the game involves achieving the goals of femininity through actions (behavior), costuming (dress), scripts (romance), and other communicative acts.[1] As Western norms and symbols of femininity are defined by idealized attributes of heterosexual, middle-class, white women, the most likely winner of the game has the right combination of genetic and socially constructed attributes of gender, race, class, and sexuality. Because femininity is determined by what is pleasing or useful to men, it also demands heterosexuality. Indeed, the image of a strong, aggressive, direct (hence, masculine) woman is often associated with lesbianism. As a result, the ability to sexually attract one or more men is a pretty clear indication that one is well ahead of the game.[2]

Although the rules of the femininity game are weighted in favor of some, entry into the game is democratic. Every Western female, save for the very young (and, with the emergence of child beauty pageants, this age is declining) and the very old (increasing, due to cosmetic surgery) has to play. Although the goals of femininity derive from white, middle-class notions of propriety and beauty, these norms inform the gender assessments applied to all Western women, regardless of race, sexuality, or class. This one set of standards applies to lesbians and Latinas, working-class and wealthy women, African-American and white women alike. These expectations may have changed over time, but many of their core aspects remain consistent. For example, the Victorian ideology of "the angel of the house" (Woolf 1929) became, for many European and North American women, the domestic ideologies of "housewife" and "mother." Regardless of our position in the labor market, most women are still expected to provide primary child care and general nurturing, even taking on these responsibilities as a "second shift" (Hochschild 1989) in addition to paid employment. With the increasing number of women entering the work force, new norms of femininity, centered about standards of female beauty and feminine behavior, prevail; Naomi Wolf (1990) refers to the work that women perform in order to satisfy these expectations of feminine beauty as a "third shift." Girls and women are expected to play by these rules irrespective of our economic opportunities, sexuality, race, or age, and are judged according to our degree of success. Although it is becoming increasingly expensive, hazardous, and time-consuming to play the femininity game, it is still incumbent upon girls and women, regardless of our individual particularities, to do so.

The goals of the game, the attributes of femininity, are specifically constructed to contrast with those of masculinity. Whereas men ought to be aggressive, women ought to be passive; whereas men ought to be strong and direct, women ought to be subtle, coy, weak, timid, and so on. This part of the game, otherwise called the social construction of gender, not only considers femininity and masculinity as opposites, but as hierarchically related. Not only are masculinity and femininity diametrically opposed, but masculinity is set above femininity. The relative value of these norms of femininity is especially evident in the research by Inge Broverman and her colleagues (1970), who surveyed a number of mental health professionals on the topic of sex-role stereotypes. They found that these clinicians were likely to label typically male characteristics (such as "very logical," "very aggressive," "very independent") as healthy for males as well as for adults in general. In contrast to this, typically feminine characteristics ("very emotional," "very submissive," "very passive") were deemed healthy for an adult female, yet unhealthy for adults in general. By this definition, then, a mentally healthy female is also a mentally unhealthy adult. This is not to say that traditionally feminine characteristics such as caring and nurturing are in fact inferior to traditionally masculine characteristics. However, because traditionally masculine characteristics are valued highly, and because femininity is constructed as masculinity's opposite (ostensibly, one cannot be both rational and emotional), femininity is deemed inferior. Thus, she who ultimately triumphs in the femininity game has succeeded in stripping herself of many human qualities; she has made herself less than she could have been.

This arrangement becomes especially problematic in adolescence, when gender games become especially important to young people. Sociologist Barbara Hudson (1984) argues that girls in particular are subjected to role conflict as they enter their teenage years. The construction of adolescence contains interrelated themes and roles that are traditionally masculine: independence, thrill seeking, troublemaking, coolness, rebelliousness. These are quite opposed to the discourse of femininity, which connotes the very opposite. The discourse of adolescence Hudson describes is constructed in contrast to Western ideals of feminine behavior. Such norms are codified in the music and iconography of adolescent culture; in their writings on gender and rock 'n' roll, Simon Reynolds and Joy Press argue that in "the rebel imagination, women figure as both victims and agents of castrating conformity. Women represent everything the rebel is not (passivity, inhibition) and everything that threatens to shackle him (domesticity, social norms). This ambivalence toward the feminine domain is the defining mark of all instances of rock rebellion" (1995:3). This can easily be extended to instances of adolescent rebellion and subcultural rebellion. Youth culture presents masculine norms that are incompatible with, indeed, contradictory to those of femininity. Adolescent girls, not surprisingly, are especially susceptible to the negative effects of the femininity game.

The rules of the game are fairly straightforward. Psychologists Claudia Bepko and Jo-Ann Krestan provide a handy summary of these rules, which they call the "Code of Goodness":

BE ATTRACTIVE: A woman is as good as she looks.
BE A LADY: A good woman stays in control.
BE UNSELFISH AND OF SERVICE: A good woman lives to give.
MAKE RELATIONSHIPS WORK: A good woman loves first.
BE COMPETENT WITHOUT COMPLAINT: A good woman does it all and
never looks overwhelmed. (1990:9)

This "Code of Goodness" not only presents the rules which women must follow, but (not coincidentally) also describes many of the aspects of female socialization which researchers consider to be responsible for the lowering of girls' self-esteem in early adolescence. These rules teach girls to be concerned primarily with beauty and relationships, to set aside ambition, intelligence, self-efficacy, and independence.

Who are the judges of this game? The normative ideology of femininity exerts both external pressures and a form of internalized social control on women's lives (England and Browne 1992). Girls and women are judged on a daily basis according to these standards. Those who cannot, or will not, conform to these standards are punished—denied opportunities, subjected to both overt mockery and subtle discrimination (Chapkis 1986). Furthermore, it is not merely the case that others judge us, but because women internalize these standards, we become our own harshest critics. The failure to live up to these standards can create an inner dialogue of self-recrimination and self-doubt, in which even women who achieve success in other areas of life can still castigate themselves for their failures to be pretty or loved.

The social costs of the game are high. Because games are competitive, they ensure that not all players can win; women are therefore pitted against each other in seeking to achieve feminine supremacy. Girls and women are taught that it is not enough to be pretty; we must be prettier than someone else. This fostered competition divides women from each other. The costs of the game can also be fatal, as girls starve or binge and purge in vain efforts to approximate the dimensions of airbrushed supermodels, as women contract illnesses from silicone breast implants while others suffer from complications linked to surgeries of liposuction and lifts. In trying to achieve the perfection of womanly caring and nurturing, women and girls remain in abusive relationships, viewing violence as the cost of their failure to please the man, or the price of their inability to transform him. The more subtle costs of the game are even more widespread, so ubiquitous that they remain invisible. Thus, the game gives us girls with low self-esteem, girls whose sense of self is precarious and predicated entirely on their body image, their popularity, and their boyfriends.

In order to win the femininity game, women and girls must abandon the valued "masculine" characteristics of self-efficacy and self-determination. However, this is the catch: the femininity game ultimately presents girls and women with a "no-win" situation. Although failure to live up to the expectations of femininity can have devastating effects on girls' and women's self-esteem, so can success in attaining them. A "winner" of the femininity game has effectively stripped herself of valued human characteristics in adopting an undervalued identity. It should come as no surprise, then, that many women and girls who strive to win the game at all costs suffer from higher rates of depression and eating disorders and lower self-esteem than do boys and men.

As we are born and acculturated into a system that sets up these contradictory expectations and demands that we play into them, how can women and girls win the femininity game? It's deceptively simple. We just need to change the rules. The femininity game described above conceptualizes gender as a set of norms and practices, the rules for the game and the actions which girls and women perform to conform to them. Changing the rules of the game calls for a radical change in how we view gender and do gender.

"Doing gender" is an ethnomethodological concept originated by Don West and Candace Zimmerman (1987) to redefine the ways in which gender operates. As sociologists, West and Zimmerman argue against the notion that gender is innate, that is, biologically determined. Furthermore, they dispute the use of terminology such as *gender role* or *gender display,* arguing that gender is omnipresent in assessments of us as people, and also in our identities. West and Zimmerman maintain that gender is not only normative, but constructed through everyday actions and interactions

Canadian sociologist Dorothy Smith (1988) proposes a further paradigm shift in reconceptualizing gender not as a set of rules and enactments, but as a discourse. Previous social-constructionist theorists had described the norms of femininity as affecting the enactment of these norms, a one-way relation between the rules of the game and the actions of the players. Smith argues that the norms of femininity are not static, but are themselves constructed as they are enacted; the rules change as we play the game. Smith argues that the discourse of femininity, which comprises both norms and their enactment, is constructed through practice: "[T]he notion of femininity does not define a determinate and unitary phenomenon. Its deployment as a descriptive category does not locate a bounded class of events or state of affairs. The most it can produce is an extended collection of instances. The more they are accumulated, the more various and wide-ranging they appear to be"(1988:37). She argues that it is the practice of femininity that shapes the normative conceptualization of femininity. Thus, the norms of femininity can be changed through practice, and the rules change as we play them out differently.

Because femininity can be conceptualized as an activity, as a set of norms in process, as a discourse, it is open to interpretation and reconstruction. However, to paraphrase Karl Marx, women may choose our definitions of femininity, but not just as we please, because we do so under circumstances inherited from the past. Nevertheless, through the redefinition of its norms and a subsequent practical adherence to such redefinitions, women and girls can create important changes within the discourse. On this discursive model, resistance to the norms of femininity does not occur in a vacuum. Subcultural resistance, in its purely stylistic form, has been described as "magical" (Cohen 1980): it is symbolic and therefore ineffective in creating social change. However, symbolic resistance to a semiotic system, which is itself constituted of symbols, *can* change that system. In challenging the system, changing the rules through play, women and girls can win the femininity game. My interviews with punk girls reveal that, in challenging the ideologies of punk and femininity, and in reconstructing the norms, values, and styles of both, punk girls create such changes.

Punk, Girl Style

In the male-dominated world of punk, masculinity defines the subculture's norms, values, and styles. These norms, in many cases, directly contradict those of femininity, thereby requiring that punk girls reconcile these disparate discourses in constructing feminine punk identities. Because the norms of the punk subculture are created along the precepts of masculinity, gender becomes problematic for punk girls in ways that it is not for their male peers. For punk girls, "doing gender" in punk means negotiating a complex set of norms, reconciling the competing discourses of punk and femininity. For them, either the acceptance of femininity or its rejection can incur social sanction—the former seems antithetical to punk, and the latter to mainstream culture. Thus, girls within the punk subculture, whether they accept the feminine norms or reject them outright, must nonetheless contend with the construction of femininity.

Previous research on punk girls has tended to focus on punk dress, which is said to reflect class differences among punk girls. In her ethnography of punks in the mid-1980s, Kathryn Fox uncovered distinct differences in the dress of middle-class and working-class punk girls: "The middle-class punk women, who tended to be students, dressed in a more traditionally feminine manner, glorifying and exaggerating the 'glamor girl' image reminiscent of the sixties. This included tight skirts, teased hair, and dark, heavy makeup. The other punk women identified with a more masculine, working-class image, de-emphasizing their feminine attributes" (1987:349). The working-class punk girls

Fox observed appear to express commitment to the subculture by affiliating with the male working-class norms that define punk style. In contrast, the middle-class girls adopted a more traditional stance toward their femininity. In her contemporaneous study, which focuses more closely on the topic of punk femininity, Leslie Roman (1988) found, as Fox, that class differences determined the divergences among punk girls' styles of dress and behavior. But Roman's findings contradict Fox's in that the middle-class girls in her study eschewed traditional feminine garb, while the working-class girls retained more feminine styles of dress. Thus, the working-class punk girls Roman observed "refuse to sport mohawks, new spangled, spiked jewelry, and purportedly ambisexual or unisex clothing. Instead, they actively defy what they call the 'combat boot image' and retain connections to their working class backgrounds by making particular zones of their bodies spectacles for male pleasure" (176). Fox's and Roman's contradictory accounts point to the incompatibilities in the construction of girls' punk style that arise between girls' identification with female gender norms and their affiliation with the masculine norms of punk.

In my own research, I have found no stylistic differences among punk girls that could be attributed to class differences. Although the group of girls I interviewed emerged from a variety of class backgrounds, this did not affect their style of dress. Their adoption of various punk styles seemed more tied with their affiliation with one punk group than another. Thus, gutter punk girls, who were mostly lower or working class, were more likely to appear to be androgynous, while punk rocker girls were more likely to emphasize femininity in dress. This may be due to class as mediated by subcultural type. Or, it may be due to the dangers of street life; dressing in a less recognizably feminine manner may attenuate some of the sexual harassment experienced by gutter punk girls.

Instead of stylistic differences, I found that punk girls' constructions of femininity exhibited more commonalities than differences, and that ascribing differences in their approaches to femininity required more complex factors than binary class demarcations or explorations of sartorial style. Regardless of their class background and their type of subcultural affiliation, in entering what they recognized to be a masculinist youth subculture, punk girls constructed explicit challenges to female gender norms. That process begins with punk girls' explicit challenge to femininity, which they construct in joining the male-dominated punk subculture.

"I Don't Like Chicks": Rejecting Femininity

In this reflexive subculture, the possibility of rejecting or subverting her own femininity plays a large part in a girl's attraction to punk. Other researchers, such as Deirdre Wilson (1978) and Meda Chesney-Lind (1989), have argued that girls' attractions to forms of subcultural deviance or juvenile delinquency may be an aspect of their resistance to traditional gender norms. There is no clear consensus on this issue, however, with British sociologist Angela McRobbie (1991) arguing that the stylistic minutiae of subcultures hold little attraction for girls. Consistent with the work of Wilson and Chesney-Lind, I found that the prospect of constructing stylistic, behavioral, and discursive challenges to femininity is indeed one of the factors that attracts young women to male-dominated youth subcultures such as punk. Girls who seek to create such challenges turn to male-dominated subcultures in the absence of female-generated and female-dominated subcultural alternatives.

For a girl to become a punk, she must reject the mainstream culture's femininity games and embrace the masculinist ideologies of punk, as adopting punk style is anathema to conventional femininity. In his ethnography of the San Francisco punk scene, James Lull speculated that the masculinity of the subculture is indeed a component that attracts some young women: "The tough look of many punks and the strenuous dancefloor activity lacks a traditional female character. For that very reason, of course, some girls and young women are attracted to punk as an alternative to the sex-role behaviors they are expected to perform in American society" (1987:233). Full participation in punk not only indicates some resistance to the conventional model of adolescent femininity, but requires it.

Entry into punk is the result of such a process for many of the girls I interviewed, who sought out the subculture specifically for its rejection of mainstream femininity. Sue, for example, explicitly rejected the flowered and frilly consumerist ideal of conventional femininity: "I never really did like Laura Ashley." Another girl, Sloopy, when asked what she likes about the punk scene, replied:

> Because they're real people. They don't try to be fake—"Oh, I gotta look just right"—like a Barbie doll.

The masculine stylistic and behavioral norms of the punk subculture are the very factors that attracted these young women to the punk scene:

> Carnie: First, it was kind of like the way it looked on a girl—to see a girl look like a guy. I was like, "Wow! That's kind of neat!" They don't have dresses on and makeup and pretty nails and pretty hair. I like the way their attitude about a lot of stuff. Kind of just like, "Fuck you!"

The opportunity to construct a form of self-presentation that is not dependent upon traditional femininity is a large part of the subculture's attractiveness to young women. Some of the girls I spoke with became punks precisely because punk offers girls alternatives to the gendered roles which contemporary adolescence demands. These girls used the masculinity and reflexivity (or social critique) of the subculture as resources in order to construct their critiques of mainstream femininity.

The way in which they constructed their rejection of conventional femininity was ingenious, emerging not always in their descriptions of their own femininity, but in their discussions about friendships with male and female peers. Nearly all the girls I interviewed discursively constructed stereotyped images of femininity, deemed them to be negative, and then denied their participation in them. They did this by constructing "straw women," friends, family members, or generic images, whom they described as the epitome or embodiment of femininity. They then went on to express rejection of these people, thereby asserting disdain for conventional norms of femininity without, at the same time, having to reject the role femininity plays in their own self-image.

For Candace, this image of stereotypical femininity was embodied by her mother:

> I could not live like my mom. I know my mom puts on a mask every day. She wears makeup—and I don't think that's necessarily a mask—but she definitely acts happy when she isn't.

Candace's rejection of putting on the mask of makeup was also reflected in her self-presentation: although she worked as a stripper, I never saw her wear makeup. Candace's rejected ideal of femininity also included less tangible aspects, such as acting pleasant even though she didn't feel that way. Thus, Candace's description of her mother set up an image of femininity which Candace sought to deny in punk.

In most cases, girls constructed their rejection of femininity not around real images, but around generic female peers, whom they called "girly-girls":

> Hallie: I have problems relating to other females for one thing, so . . . they're all "girly-girly," that's what I call them.

> Andie: At school . . . I couldn't hang out with any of the girls because the girls were all, "Omigod! I broke a nail! Omigod!"

Like Hallie and Andie, many punk girls discussed their disdain for these conventional norms of femininity through expressing negative assessments of other girls' concern with feminine appearances, values, or behaviors, and with the constraints that these entail:

> Ava: I hang out with more guys than girls, just because really, girls bother me really bad. There's nothing that despises me more than a girl that just

sits around and puts makeup on all the time. Who'll sit there with a mirror and be all, "hmm, hmm, hmm" all the time. And girly-girls, they won't ever do anything fun. They won't go get drunk and fuck shit up, usually.

Ava went on to contrast this with the behavior of other punk girls: "Except for punk girls that usually don't get along with girls. Then they go out . . . " These punk girls did not see their rejections of girly-girls as necessarily meaning that they could not have girl friends, but rather as a form of selectiveness:

> Amalia: I love all my sisters—I hang out with them and all that shit—but girls are really stupid, I think. . . . Just, they're just stupid. . . . I'm speaking of girls in general. Like, most of the girls . . . They're just stupid. They're just stupid. They think, "Oh, everything is all right, blah, blah, blah." They're just, they're just stupid. Like, makeup and hair and blah, blah, blah. To be more like the latest new fashion or whatever for the season or whatever. I think girls are stupid because most girls are like that.

Beyond the aspects of appearance and behavior, these punk girls objected to what they described as girly communication, which they found in their relationships with both punk and nonpunk girls. Joanie described this as gossip:

> Communication with women has like this strange pattern, and they talk about certain things a whole bunch. . . . People. They talk about people a whole bunch and stuff like that. And it's really annoying. . . .
>
> *LL: Do you think that to be in the punk scene, girls have to let go of that stuff?*
>
> Joanie: Eventually.

Others characterized this as whining:

> Alexea: I don't get along with chicks at all. They really fucking . . . I don't like chicks. I don't like women. They bug me. . . . Because they whine a lot. And I can whine, because I can beat their asses.

Or as a type of underhandedness:

> Nikita: Girls are pretty catty. Guys are at least openly assholes and I can deal with it, but girls are deviously bitchy. And I just can't deal with . . . if somebody's going to be rude or whatever, I'd rather them just do it out in the open. And dudes have a better way of doing that than girls. For the most part . . .

Girls thus described cattiness, whining, and gossip as typically feminine forms of communication, and chose not to play that game.

Punk girls described the focus on relationships with males as especially prevalent in girly-girls' communication. Like Alexea, they saw female relationships primarily as competitive:

> Clara: That's what bugs me about girls . . . they want to be like you too much. There's always something that they want over you, and that gets me. I'm happy like I am. It's for sure, like [my friend Cora], I'm sure there's something . . . like, she has bigger tits than me, something, you know? I won't start putting her down for that. But girls are like that.

Thus, their rejection of femininity also entailed their rejection of what feminine norms dictate should be the focal concerns of girls' lives—boys and relationships:

> Justine: I think that girls are also too, "So, I'm checking out this new guy . . ." While the guys, when I'm hanging out with them, we don't talk about that kind of stuff. Well, sometimes we do. I think it's funny. . . . But I think that girls always talk about that.

Punk girls especially focused on the related issue of female competitiveness for male attention as a central reason for their rejection of femininity and of female relationships:

> Alexea: Women are really fucking competitive. . . . Over guys. Yeah, they compete for dominance. I mean, I don't like competition, dude. I'll stop it before it starts. That's it. I'm not going to compete.

Thus, in addition to rejecting girly-girls' purported concerns with achieving feminine appearances and behaviors, these punk girls objected to female competitiveness over boys.

Although many of the punk girls I interviewed decried such stereotypical femininity as the generic girly-girl stereotype, others found more specific examples of femininity within the punk subculture itself. Some did deny that the feminine competitiveness or cattiness they observed in nonpunk girls occurs within the punk subculture, as a rule:

> Nikita: Punk girls aren't the ones that I usually don't like. It's usually just girls in general. It's not like, I don't know, most punk girls seem to have a really much more of an individual attitude than a lot of girls I meet. So, as a whole, I could say maybe that I would like more punk girls that I've met than girls in general. . . . They're just not into bullshit. . . . Or maybe it's just in a more tolerable way to me personally.

Although a few girls denied that punk girls were competitive about males or concerned with femininity to the extent that nonpunk girls are, this did not hold across all cases. Instead, they offered accounts where female competitiveness involving punk girls soured friendships and created obstacles to their integration into the punk scene:

Carina: It's too hard for me to be friends with a girl because they'll get mad at you if you like the same guy. And you're just afraid to make them mad. I used to have this best friend, and she was such a bitch to me, man. And she'd always bitch, "He likes you more than he does me." And I don't want the hassle. That's why I'd rather be friends with guys than girls, because it's too much of a hassle. You don't want to hurt anybody's feelings.

Tori: Sometimes the girls get hostile and they're like, "Oh shit, here comes Tori. She's going to take my man." But that's not at all what I'm thinking. That's not at all my intention.

Justine: I find that among girls there's too much competition. Me, I'm not the competitive type. But I was in a bar with a girl once, I was in a bar with Marcia. It's hell. It's like, we were sitting and this guy was looking at me, and she got pissed. I said, "Whoa, now." Also, it's because it took two years before the girls in the park would talk to me. . . . Because of the competition. They saw that the guys were talking to me and thought I was cool. They were really jealous. I've had them say to me a lot "I'm going to mess you up." And on my side, "Why do you want to mess me up? We're just talking. I'm giving him my opinion." There's too much competition with the girls.

The presence of female competitiveness among punk girls, and male punks' role in promoting it, was further supported by the following incident:

Clara: Well, with girls I don't get along because most of the time my boyfriend will always take off with one. The last one, the last real close girlfriend I had, if she didn't go for all the guys I went out with, she didn't go for one. It was really, she had to get them all, she had to jump them one after the other. It was like it was stronger than her, that she had to do everything I did.

Besides finding that some punk girls, as well as girly-girls, expressed some stereotypically feminine concerns, they also saw a preoccupation with fashion and beauty among other punk girls:

Clara: With girls, there's too many that are like, "Oh! I'm afraid I'll break a nail!" Fuck, what is that? But there are punk girls who are like that. One of my girl friends, she has maybe eighty pairs of Doc Martens in her closet. She has all the fucking most bizarre dresses in town. She bugs me, she's always like, "Is my dye job all right?" She bugs me, man. She's got cash, her parents have money, so she takes advantage of it big time.

Some girls pointed out specific instances in which they contrasted their own behavior with the overtly feminine behavior of other girls affiliated with the punk scene:

Carnie: One thing that pisses me off are people like Rona. . . . She pisses me off. She's the type of women that don't need to be around. . . . People like her piss me off so bad. . . . People like her really piss me off. That are helpless without a guy. I don't need men to keep me together. I need my sisters. . . . I've had a problem with Rona since I met her. She's just a total female.

Thus, punk girls not only reject mainstream girly-girls' formations of femininity, but also detect and reject them in their peers as well.

Punk girls set up stereotypes of mainstream femininity as centering on appearance (fashion and beauty) and behavior (competitiveness and cattiness); their adherence to punk style allows them to vociferously deny their connection with such concerns. By constructing negative images of femininity in the forms of other girls and women, punk girls can refuse the dominant cultural scripts of femininity without having to challenge their own gender identities. They refer either to faceless, nameless girly-girls or other punk girls, or point out specific individuals from whom they differentiate themselves.

As a result of their rejection of conventional feminine concerns such as appearance, gentility, and the quest for male attention, punk girls effectively isolate themselves from nonpunk girly-girls. Their rejection of these conventions alienates them not only from mainstream girls, but from each other as well, for within the punk subculture they likewise dislike punk girls who espouse femininity. Some punk girls' rejection of mainstream norms of femininity leads to other girls' rejection of them:

Carnie: A lot of girls are like, "Eww, look, her arms are black from dirt. Eww, look, she's got armpit hair. Eww, look, she doesn't shave. . . . Eww, she's got a bald head." But it's stupid. Besides, a lot of girls just make me annoyed, because they're all like [that].

Although their disdain for both mainstream and punk girls who do conform to femininity gives them a tool to reject its constraining norms, it also creates impediments to friendship between punk girls, resulting in a form of social isolation. As we saw in the previous chapter, there are few, token, "macho chicks" or "tough girls" within the subculture, leading girls to associate almost exclusively with male punks:

Wanda: Most of my friends are guys. . . . I get along better with guys. I don't, I haven't been able to figure that out. I have a couple of friends that are girls at home, in just, just a few. It's something I've never been able to figure out. Most of the friends of mine that are, are girls, that I'm really good friends with, are the same way. They have mostly guy friends.

The kind of confrontational style these girls adopt is unappealing to most girls, so many girls then turn to males for approval:

Cathy: I guess girls are more scared to go out on a limb. I don't know why. I guess that's kind of why I hang out with more guys, because I'm always like, I always thought, most girls think, "I can't cut my hair because it's not girly," or something, and I'm just like, I want to cut my hair. Boys'll do it and they don't care, so why can't I?

Thus, although they reject the competitiveness that pits girls and women against each other in the femininity game, punk girls are still effectively isolated from other girls and women, precisely because their decision not to participate in that aspect of femininity differentiates them from those who do. As a result, punk girls are usually left to their own devices in constructing individual, rather than collective, challenges to both mainstream and punk norms of femininity. Often, their sole source of support in establishing and maintaining strong self-concepts are males, who reward them for adopting a masculinist form of subcultural identification. However, as we saw, punk males often present girls with contradictory expectations of their gendered behavior (wanting them to be both macho chicks and sex partners) and can even become abusive. Thus, in challenging femininity, these girls pay the price of isolation and confinement. Rather than reject femininity outright, they negotiate between the expectations of culture and subculture.

"Not Too Feminine, Though": Constructing Femininity through Punk

For these young women, rejecting the constraints of femininity through their rejection of girly-girl stereotypes or other feminine girls does not necessarily entail a rejection of their own feminine identities. When discussing their own constructions of femininity, few punk girls explicitly rejected the notion that they were themselves feminine. In fact, only two girls denied their own femininity outright: "I'm not really feminine at all. I really don't like femininity. It's kind of disgusting" (Alexea); "I guess I'm not really feminine. I'm not, I don't wear makeup and I don't cross my legs when I sit down. I guess I'm not very polite" (Sheila). These girls were the minority, as most girls did not explicitly reject femininity in such a forthright manner. Rather, in joining

Illustration 11

Punk girls as friends—sadly, a rare sight
(Photo: D. K. Rabel)

the subculture, they rejected some forms of femininity in very subtle ways. Instead of renouncing all feminine trappings, punk girls would respond affirmatively to the question "Do you consider yourself to be feminine?" and discuss the various types of feminine identities they constructed as alternatives to the feminine stereotypes they abjured. They used a variety of means to construct their alternative femininities: style, behavior, language. Punk girls also constructed such alternatives in a variety of ways: some wholeheartedly adopt the masculinity of the subculture, others negotiate between conventional femininity and punk masculinity, while still others seek to reinscribe the meanings of conventional femininity.

Although punk girls rejected conventional norms of femininity through the act of externalizing those norms and then denying any identification with those projections, in many cases, these girls still acknowledged some aspects of femininity as their own. As Justine put it: "I don't like feminine girls, even though I'm feminine myself. Not too feminine, though." Punk girls' explicit assessments and descriptions of their own femininity ranged from complete acceptance of the conventional norms of femininity to their total rejection. Most girls, however, negotiated between femininity and punk, creating alternatives by combining aspects of both in creating specifically "punk girl" identities. I now turn to punk girls' explicit stylistic, behavioral, and discursive constructions of their own femininity. I examine how punk girls recognized and contended with the normative structures of femininity, and how their constructions of femininity as a discourse serve to reconstruct both the norms of femininity and those of punk.

"Just a Little Boyish": Adopting Male Style

Having rejected the femininity game, a number of punk girls turned to male models of punk style as alternatives. Carnie, who said that one of the main factors that attracted her to punk was the pleasure of seeing "a girl look like a guy" is one such girl. Another is Lydia:

> My idea of punk, I never patterned myself after the women. I always patterned myself after the guys. And I've done that a lot in my dress always I think. . . . Even when I was into, even in the seventies before I even heard about punk, I patterned myself after David Bowie, so . . . I've always been into androgyny, and I've always tried to make myself look as androgynous as possible.

These girls rejected conventions of feminine appearance in favor of male apparel:

> Arizona: I dress in boys' clothes most of the time. Sometimes I don't wear makeup, so I just feel kind of, not gritty, but just a little boyish, tomboyish.

—————— *Illustration 12* ——————
Punk girls adopt markers of masculinity: the motorcycle.
(Photo: L. Muller)

Elle: I was always like a little boy, always in pants and T-shirts. I was always
a little tomboy.

These girls noted the masculinity of punk style and merely chose to adopt it:
"I just try to [wear] what is unisex" (Hallie). In constructing their punk mode
of self-presentation, these girls sacrificed sartorial markers of femininity.
They called this "androgyny," although it lacks the blending of gender characteristics that define the term. Rather, they were more likely to be unisex—
masculine—and to pass as males; thirty-one-year old Rudie, with her graying
mohawk and baggy clothes, said:

I've always strove for androgyny. Although my friends would make fun of me. They do. They're like, "Oh, you're such a girly-girl." They do! I like pretty flowers, man. I'd like to be able to really turn someone on by being a woman but, man, look at me. I usually have my collar buttoned up to my neck, I have two pairs of pants on almost all the time. You can't really tell. Especially with my hair . . . mostly I was mistaken for a guy most of my adolescent years.

In addition to constructing these "androgynous" identities through dress, girls described their personalities or mannerisms as being tomboyish:

Clara: I'm just a little tomboyish. . . . I consider myself feminine except that sometimes I have little, little [parts that are] tomboyish. For sure.

Girls who described themselves as tomboys tended to claim that they have always been this way:

Candace: I tend to be real tomboyish. I've always been a tomboy.

These girls recognized the mainstream construction of femininity, and may even have wished to attain it, as Rudie did, but were also constrained by their identification as punks. Anna, who works as an erotic dancer, also identified as "androgynous," contrasting two models of femininity:

[I'm] not particularly superfeminine. I'm not really butch or anything, but I have some friends that are dancers that are just the essence of female, and I don't really see myself quite so much as that. I'm a little more androgynous, or a little tougher, which I like. That's just the way I am. I'm kind of like an [androgynous singer] Annie Lennox, or something. I like to be myself more like that than a Madonna, I guess. But, no, not particularly feminine.

In constructing such tomboyish or "androgynous" (actually, unisex masculine) appearances, these girls abandoned any markers of feminine appearance, so much so that they reported often being mistaken for males. Even when they sought to construct very feminine self-presentations, the prevalent masculinity of punk style still led to this gender ambiguity:

Denise: I identify very much with being [feminine]. . . . I like to wear skirts, I like to wear small tight things. . . . I take pride . . . It offends me, because little kids are always going "Look at that guy!" And I'm like, "I'm wearing a *skirt*! Do I *look* like a guy?!" I identify very much with . . . I guess all the reasons that most women, other women would. Whatever that would be. . . . We all know what it is.

As in the mainstream femininity game, these punk girls defined their femininity in terms of their rejection of masculinity, but the masculinity of punk still overrode their feminine style.

For some punk girls, retaining a feminine identification was of paramount importance, even if that identification ran counter to the behavioral norms of punk, and even if it required them to reject the masculinity of punk behavior. Jessie, in her painted leather jacket and shaved head, proclaimed:

> I have manners. I don't know if that's really feminine or not . . . but there's a lot of people don't have them. I hate that. I know I, I know some, some people, some women they are, I don't know, I consider . . . I think the way I carry myself isn't very manly or anything. I'm very like, I'd rather be a lady. I don't want to be walking around bad, like, "I'm going to kick your ass." I don't do any of that shit.

Stone, a street punk whose style fluctuates between Goth and hardcore punk, sometimes including a mohawk hairstyle, adds:

> I'm always feminine in my way. I don't go around like, "Kiss my ass, motherfucker! Suck my cock!" . . . Well, I can be [like that] when I want to be, but yeah, I'm usually pretty feminine.

Another girl contrasted her retention of feminine behavior to the lack of it in other punk girls:

> Amalia: You've met, I'm sure you've met some girls that are like "arrrgh" all the time. I mean, I can get like that, but most of the time . . . If I'm really pissed off I get like that, but most of the time I'm feminine, I think. Not feminine like a "tee hee" that kind of way. But just, I'm a girl. I think I act feminine.

Like Denise, who countered the prevalence of punk masculinity by wearing skirts (the hardcore girl variant of the punk uniform), other girls maintained feminine identities by rejecting the masculine toughness of punk. By "acting feminine," they refused to engage in the type of confrontationalism that connotes some of the masculinity of the subculture. In doing this, these girls sought to maintain their femininity in direct contrast to the masculinity of the punk subculture. However, none of these girls used this opposition to masculinity as a way to accept all aspects of femininity, as all of these girls did adopt other aspects of punk style, such as shaved heads and leather jackets, which are coded as masculine within the subculture. Thus, their rejection of the aggressive, masculine behavior expected of punks was offset by their adoption of some of the more "hardcore" aspects of punk style. As a result, their rejection of femininity could only remain a partial one, as the masculinity of punk, either as sartorial or behavioral style, remained a component of their self-presentations. Thus, girls have little choice but to continue to negotiate between punk and femininity.

"I Have Girlish Qualities about Me": Being Somewhat Feminine

Punk girls must contend with the norms of femininity and punk masculinity in some manner. Although they may denounce femininity in some ways, this does not necessarily mean that they renounce their own femininity. Those punk girls who do not wholly drop out of the femininity game accept certain attributes while rejecting others. Like Susan Brownmiller's (1984) dissection of femininity into its constituent parts of "body," "hair," "clothes," "voice," "skin," "movement," "emotion," and "ambition," punk girls consider femininity not as a total package, but rather as a set of discrete aspects, such as physical appearance, attitudes, and roles. They may then choose to accept only certain attributes pertaining to appearance:

> Mina: I don't think that I'm very feminine in appearance. But I think that I have girlish qualities about me. . . . In my appearance, my hands, I wear a lot of jewelry.

Feminine grooming was a commonly noted way to attain this femininity:

> Basilisk: I bathe, I shave, I put on makeup, I do my hair. I don't go around well, what's unfeminine? That's basically, I guess, why I consider myself to be feminine.

> Ava: I'm definitely a girl. I paint my nails and wear skirts and fishnets. I'm pretty, pretty girly. But I don't really hang out with girls and stuff that much. Yeah, I'm pretty feminine, I think.

Femininity in appearance was also constructed through clothing and other ornamentation:

> Wanda: I think in a lot of ways I'm feminine. I like feminine shoes. . . . I like little pointed-toed shoes and stuff like that, I'm into that. And I like to wear a lot of skirts sometimes too. And hose. Yeah, I'm feminine, I believe. I don't like a lot of jewelry though.

Other girls extended their readings of femininity to include bodily appearance:

> LL: Do you consider yourself to be feminine?

> Andie: Not when I'm dressed like this. Other guys do. I don't think I am. . . . Because my tits aren't big enough. I'm being truthful! You asked!

For other girls, femininity was not necessarily constructed through the physical manifestations of dress, grooming, or body, but through less tangible measures of behavior. For Justine, femininity included mannerisms as well as appearance:

> Well, I have little polished nails. And sometimes when I talk I have little mannerisms. I should say little graceful mannerisms, but that's not at all the case.

> Cora: I wear skirts. I'm feminine. I'm not a tomboy, you know, in jeans. . . . I'm always wearing skirts and in little tight tops. . . . Look at my legs! My legs are crossed!

Mina described femininity as a behavioral convention:

> [I'm feminine in] the way that I act. Sometimes I'm giggly and . . . kind of stereotypical.

This feminine behavior also extended to encompass manners and mannerisms:

> Lola: I'm very, I'm *very* feminine. And that's made a point to me every single day, how feminine I am. [The other punks] make fun of how I eat. . . . I always sit with my legs crossed. And this is unconscious, but they're making fun of the way I drink, because of the way I drink and the way I eat. Because they were eating bread and they were tearing into it, and I was eating there, just holding it and eating and chewing. I was just sitting there and Agatha, all of them, they always tear into me. They always say I'm the most feminine person they've ever met. . . . Yeah, and, but I am extremely feminine.

Whether they accept or reject aspects of femininity, these girls retain the prerogative to rejoin the femininity game when it is situationally advantageous. This was explicit in Hallie's rejection of traditional femininity:

> Feminine? It's because I feel that it's somewhat of a front. You get a lot . . . you get a lot from people when you act more feminine. It can work to your advantage. But it's so sexist. It's so stereotypical that it just gets on my nerves. Because I see females, they're just batting their eyes, like, "Hee hee hee." I totally know they're not like that. I know they're not at all. And they're getting kick-downs [handouts] and other stuff like that, but I can get kick-downs and stuff like that just for being myself, so why would I have to act like that?

Other girls concurred with Hallie in describing femininity as situational, as roles they, or others, play:

> Carnie: Sometimes I can be [feminine]. Like when I'm schmoozing. I schmooze off of guys. Yeah, it's like, I get all sweet and stupid and I cross

my legs. I get real femmy. I'm pretty feminine, like when I'm around Agatha, because she's a girl, I feel more feminine. When I'm with a bunch of guys, I don't. It depends on who I'm around.

In creating androgynous, tomboyish, or unisex styles, these girls reject the norms of femininity, adopting, in their stead, the masculine sartorial and behavioral styles of punk. They then revert to the games of traditional femininity (Carnie's "I get all sweet and stupid") only when this is advantageous.

That these punk girls play some part of the femininity game does not preclude their identification with the punk subculture. Although the other punks may have mocked Lola's feminine mannerisms, they nonetheless accepted her within the subculture. This acceptance, however, was based on the girls' rejection of some forms of femininity, especially in their concern with the behavior expected of girls (Ava: "Girly-girls, they won't ever do anything fun. They won't go get drunk and fuck shit up, usually") and of their concern with very feminine appearances (Cathy: "Most girls think, 'I can't cut my hair because it's not girly,' or something"). Those girls who did describe themselves as feminine defined femininity as stereotypes governing appearance (makeup, clothing, hair) or behavior (mannerisms, manners, posture). They then accepted only certain aspects of that construct while rejecting others, controlling their place in the game by moderating their play. As a result, they became adept at challenging and changing the rules of the game.

"My Mohawk's Got Little Bangs": The Construction of Female Punk Style

The ways in which punk girls combine their punkness and their gender in changing the rules of the femininity game is best demonstrated by the punk female style of dress. In constructing style, punk girls subvert the norms of the mainstream culture, the feminine norms of both culture and subculture, and the norms of the punk subculture as well, creating a feminine style outside the confines of mainstream or punk culture. When constructing style, punk girls use the same techniques of appropriation and subversion as did the original punk "bricoleurs" described by Hebdige (1979). While some punk girls completely adopt the basic male punk uniform of combat boots, torn jeans, leather jacket, and shaved head, most combine female items with punk elements, in "a feminised interpretation of working-class male imagery" (Brake 1985:173). This has resulted in a female variation on the male punk uniform: many punk girls will combine the masculine symbols of Doc Marten army boots, spiked mohawk, oversize shirt, and leather jacket with more feminine clothes, such as ripped fishnet tights and mini-kilts.

Many girls spoke at length about constructing their femininity, in terms of their appearance, in keeping with the style of punk. They nevertheless maintained their own distinct vision of self-presentation. Carina, for one, was explicit about maintaining her femininity despite her participation in the street punk scene:

> I'll keep myself feminine. I don't want to look really rough, because it's not attractive to a guy for a girl to look rough. I'll keep my style, I'll try to have my style have a [feminine] appearance to it but also look the way I want it to.

The way that Carina maintained this femininity was specifically through constructing a feminine appearance, but, as with other punk girls who maintained some femininity, not a traditionally feminine look. Ava, another girl who maintained some femininity, also stated, "I don't like dressing in really girly-girly stuff." Like Ava, Carina avoided overly feminine clothing: "I don't want to wear a dress or anything, but I'll still have something in my dress." She then described that "something":

> I'll only wear certain jewelry. I like these spikes right here [homemade leather bracelet with three-quarter-inch nails as spikes] because they're just wild looking. They're not like the regular [store-bought chrome] spikes. Just have my own style. . . . Like, my boots. I mean, my boots aren't like, I haven't seen anybody else have my boots before, except this other girl.

Such distinctiveness in dress is a result of combining mainstream teen girl style with punk:

> Elle: I'm not like all the other little girls, with little kickers and little sweater and nice Levi's blue jeans. . . . I really like to wear jeans and a bodysuit sometimes. Except that my bodysuit is really weird and different. The body piece here is square, here it's all lace, here it's striped wine red and white. . . . I wear it frilly with pants and my bullet belt. I like it. It gives me a certain look—it's marginal. It's not like every other little girl who has a bodysuit like that.

> Jennie: Sometimes [I am feminine] by the clothes I wear. That way . . . Yeah, well, not high heels. No, never. Skirts, sometimes you have to go break out that emocore shirt, get from the sister those tight little shirts, stuff like that. I don't like wearing makeup or anything. Maybe sometimes I'll put on perfume or oils or something. Sometimes I do wear makeup but that's about it. . . . That's about as girly as we get.

Thus, punk girls combined elements of female dress (bodysuits, skirts) with punk accessories (bullet belt, emocore shirt) to create a distinctly female punk look that's "as girly" as they get.

These girls' constructions of femininity also extended to the creation of a punk version of makeup:

Carina: Sometimes I'll put black eyeliner on my lips and rub it in, just to make my lips stand out. I'll just do little things, just to make sure they know I'm a girl.

However, many girls such as Carina drew the line at some aspects of punk style, still seeking to maintain some traditional notions of femininity:

I couldn't shave my head. I just couldn't. I want my hair to get real long. That's another [feminine] thing that I'll keep is my hair.

Thus, in constructing punk style, these girls blended aspects of conventional femininity (makeup, perfume, styled hair) with those of punk (black eyeliner and lipstick, spiked bracelets), while rejecting more masculine aspects of punk behavior (confrontationalism, swearing).

The most striking way punk girls combine punk and femininity is by contrasting punk attributes of style or behavior with femininity. Some girls accomplish this subversion by juxtaposing punk dress and punk behavior. Rosie did this by constructing a specifically punk feminine appearance while maintaining a mode of confrontational punk behavior:

It's weird, because I guess in a way I dress superfeminine sometimes. I dress punk, but I dress with really feminine stuff. I'll wear big crinolines and stuff and lots of lace and lots of fishnet. I guess in a way I am feminine, but I think I'm much more raw than other girls. I'm much more like, when I walk into society, I'm rude and I want to beat the shit out of everybody. I just want everyone to go die. And I guess there's not that many girls that are like that. You don't see that many real hardcore girls. It doesn't really exist that much. . . . I think because a lot of them, it's hard to be a punk and be a girl.

Punk girls took pleasure in counterpoising traditional aspects feminine style with the behavioral and sartorial styles of punk, and vice-versa:

Lola: I enjoy, I like being a lady with attitude. There's nothing more fun than being all geared up and all, and then going and being so feminine. Or just looking feminine or something and everybody's like "Oh, yeah!" and then just beat the fuck out of someone.

These girls often sought to contrast punk masculinity and femininity by juxtaposing modes of dress with radically unexpected modes of behavior, playing off the expectations of femininity against those of punk. Some chose to present a very feminine sartorial image, and combine this with aggressiveness, a char-

_____ *Illustration 13* _____
Juxtaposing a feminine punk style with masculine roughhousing
(Photo: D. K. Rabel)

acteristically "masculine" trait. Others chose the option of dressing in a more masculine punk style, yet still behaved in the delicate and genteel ways recognized as being particularly feminine. In doing so, these girls drew on both the behavioral and sartorial codes denoting masculinity and femininity in constructing a third position.

"Fuck Cindy Crawford and the Normal Standards of Beauty": *Subversive Punk Femininity*

When joining the punk subculture, young women seek alternatives to the norms that dictate their position in mainstream society; chief among these are the norms of femininity. Punk girls reject conventional femininity by projecting these on mainstream female peers and denying their own participation in that mainstream femininity game. In order to resist the gender games of the dominant culture, punk girls turn to male models of subcultural rebellion and create or adopt forms of dress and behavior that subvert the norms of female propriety. These include adopting male dress, so as to efface gender distinctions, or combining elements of traditional female dress with those of the established, masculine, punk style. Punk girls also create such subversions by juxtaposing masculinity and femininity in both dress and behavior, and in discursively challenging the underlying norms of femininity. All of these result in a variety of positions between the masculine norms of punk and those of the female gender role.

Punk girls construct a wide spectrum of negotiated positions between the masculine norms of punk and those of the female gender role. In all their rejections or reconstructions of femininity, punk girls exhibit a reflexive position that is much more complex than that of their male peers. In "doing gender" in such a way that challenges the dominant cultural scripts of femininity, they create a position of what I call "trebled reflexivity": they challenge the norms of the dominant culture, as well as the feminine norms of both culture and subculture. As punks, they counter the sartorial, vocational, and behavioral norms of the mainstream culture; as female punks, they counter the norms of feminine propriety, beauty, and behavior; as punk girls, in combining the discourses of punk and femininity, the subvert the punk subversion, challenging the masculinist norms of the subculture. This trebled reflexivity uniquely positions punk girls as subversive actors within the structures of culture and subculture. In doing this, they create a third position outside the parameters of both the mainstream and the punk subculture. They are not merely girls, nor just punks, but punk girls.

Punk girls' blendings of punk and femininity subvert both the norms of the dominant culture and those of the subculture. Susan Willis notes such an instance of this female subversion in 1990s American punk: "Those girls who understand that equal opportunity in the military means the right to participate in capitalism's genocidal wars tend to degrade military style by feminizing it. They might sport a long wool army coat open to reveal a consummate punk ensemble: sheer black blouse, black sports bra, black lacy tights, cut-offs, and huge socks spilling over the top of a pair of Doc Martens" (1993:371). In combining feminine clothing with military style, punk girls affront the hard-edged masculinity of the military. In doing so within the punk subculture, which adopts the militaristic style, they also subvert the masculinity of punk style in order to convey their own antiauthoritarian messages.

Punk girls who adopt the feminized style construct a type of "sartorial terrorism" (Carter 1992) aimed at both mainstream and punk culture. To juxtapose full geisha-style makeup and a miniskirt with combat boots and a green mohawk is to create a statement of dissidence against traditional forms of beauty. It is, in essence, to state that the culturally dictated masks of fashion and makeup that define female beauty are as constructed as the subculturally celebrated hairstyle and footwear that define punk. On the other hand, it removes the male warrior mark from the combat boots and the mohawk hairstyle, which British punks originally adopted to emulate the Native American "savage." In constructing style, punk girls explicitly seek to simultaneously change both subcultural and cultural norms:

> Anna: I did wear some stuff that showed my breasts and stuff, but it was more to desexualize it. Because I think there's no reason why we shouldn't be able to go topless. In other countries, nudity is no big deal, so I thought, "My breasts are my breasts. Get over it." The body can be sexy when it needs to be, but also it's also, it's a nude body. There's been times where it's hot and I wish I could have been in the pit and took my top off and danced and stuff.

It is not only through the reinscription of the traditional feminine norms of appearance that femininity is inscribed into punk—rather, this requires a whole re-visioning of the meaning of femininity itself:

> Sue: Well, my mohawk's got little bangs and I wear it up like Pebbles Flintstone all the time. I just don't wear makeup. I don't wear "formfitting" clothing and everything. I'm not saying I have to dress like a girl to be feminine. I'm feminine in a lot of my speeches and actions, and everything. I'm not saying I'm feminine because I'm passive. I'm feminine because I'm trying not to give a militant point of view from the beginning.

Thus, punk girls' re-visioning of femininity extends not only to their subversion of traditional behavioral and sartorial constructions, but to the deeper meanings and norms (i.e., passivity) underlying these symbols.

Many girls reported that the punk subculture is the ideal place to carry out their subversions of femininity, not because the subculture is particularly supportive, but rather because its sartorial code has opened up a space for girls' self-expression:

> Elle: I think that the punk style looks better on girls than it does on guys. It's true. There are more clothes for girls than there are for guys in punk.

They have carved out a space between the mainstream norms of femininity and the masculinist expectations of punk, where they find the freedom for self-expression:

> Lisa: I like it because it doesn't really matter because it's such an open sort of situation as far as what you look like. Be it a formfitting suede dress or jeans and a ripped T-shirt or whatever . . . and also in behavior, the way you address people.

In punk, they can reconstruct both the behavioral and sartorial norms of femininity in ways which are in keeping with punk identities. Girls like Anna were very clear about making this rejection of femininity a statement:

> It would make me uncomfortable to have to wear pink lipstick and do my hair in a little mall hairdo and stuff. It's not fair to ask me to do that when everyone else, just because their choices happen to be accepted by the majority, can, they can get away with it.

Nikita was explicitly political about this rejection as well:

> A typical femininity would be like makeup, doing your hair. The thing that a lot of punk people don't seem to understand is that it's just as womanly or stereotypical girlish to put on black lipstick as to put on pink lipstick. . . . In a sense. It's primping. It's making yourself look beautiful to whatever your standards of beautiful are. And if that happens to be just big black circles around your eyes, or purple hair, blue hair, or bleaching your hair blonde and wearing pink lipstick and blue eye shadow, it's all the same. . . . Their standards of beautiful, in a way, I mean, they're also saying, "Fuck Cindy Crawford and the normal standards of beauty," which is a statement in itself, I guess. But they're also making themselves beautiful to themselves and to guys that they would want to attract, which would be punk guys. Punks.

In constructing their challenges to femininity using dress and makeup, punk girls create and maintain a unique aesthetic:

> Courtney: In high school, I never wore dresses, I wore a skirt and shirt, but dresses seem so feminine. . . . I acted really butchy, but I still felt feminine. I was totally butchy but I still . . . I was still very in touch with my feminine side. I didn't like try to make myself pretty or anything. To me I was sort of nice looking in a fucked-up kind of way.

This aesthetic sense leads them to have a bond with other punk girls:

> Cathy: I personally think it's very pretty. If I see girls with shaved heads or lip rings, I always think it's so beautiful. I think it's pretty. Why not wear it?

This aesthetic also provides punk girls with a stronger sense of self in the face of cultural proscriptions:

> Sue: I don't consider it defacing myself. I think I look a lot better like this. What the rest of the world thinks, "Damn, you woulda been purty with long hair, girl." I've seen some punk girls that just look like [vermiform *Star Wars* alien antagonist] Jabba the Hut, but I've seen pretty punks, it happens.

For punk girls, the possibilities of creating such a reinscription of femininity within the parameters of punk served as a form of empowerment, as Allie reported:

> I hate being treated like a girl. . . . I really don't like femininity at all. . . . I like to look like a girl. Women are beautiful. I'm attracted to women too. I think that women should look like women. Sometimes even if they don't they can still be attractive. But I don't try to hide the fact that I'm a girl, but I do not like to be treated like I'm less because I'm female. And I don't *act* less because I'm female. I try in every way possible to compete in a world where men are supposedly superior.

Punk girls reconstruct the discourses of both punk and femininity by stylistically, behaviorally, and discursively reconciling the contradiction in their acceptance of both sets of attributes. They do so by viewing femininity as a discourse with parameters they can re-define by inscribing feminine attributes into the style and ideology of punk. In combining attributes of punk masculinity with those of femininity, these girls are creating strong self-images. They are very like the white adolescent girls that Kathleen Wells (1980) studied, who combined the attributes of femininity (i.e., warmth, sensitivity) and masculinity (i.e., competitiveness, aggressiveness), and thus were better adjusted and scored higher on measures of self-esteem than did purely feminine girls. In negotiating their gender between mainstream femininity and the masculinity of punk, these girls are creating identities that draw on the strengths of both sets of characteristics.

As a reflexive subculture, the purpose of punk is to illuminate features of the dominant culture (Levine and Stumpf 1983). The trebled reflexivity of punk girls' positioning within the dominant culture and the punk subculture presents a manifold of such illuminations. The positions punk girls negotiate with female gender norms, be they of acceptance or strategies of rejection and subversion, offer valuable perspectives on the game of femininity. They suggest that a diversity of positionings vis-à-vis female gender norms is possible in the face of the omnipresent pressures of feminine socialization. In his examination of male-dominated youth subcultures, Mike Brake argues that "as yet no distinct models of femininity, which have broken from tradition, have evolved" within such youth subcultures, but that "this may well happen when female-dominated subcultures evolve" (1980:141). Brake fails to note the impact of subcultural participation upon femininity, instead claiming that "girls are present in male subcultures, but are contained within them, rather than using them to explore actively forms of female identity" (1985:167). I propose that girls within male-dominated youth subcultures are already developing alternatives to mainstream gender norms; they are showing us ways in which women can change the rules of the femininity game.

In her work on gender nonconformity, Wendy Chapkis notes that such rebellions may be politically and economically ineffective, but remain personally empowering: "Radically transforming one's appearance can be an exercise of personal power in a life that feels out of control. While it may not be possible for an individual to change the reality of high unemployment, housing shortages and poverty, it is possible to transform one's body into a visual shout: 'No, I do not accept the goodness of your goals and expectations. No, I will not help you feel secure in your choices. Do I look frightening? Do I look angry? Do I look dangerous? Do you still feel safe in thinking that the system works just fine? Think again'" (1986:83). Many of the punk girls I interviewed reported that joining the subculture indeed had a profoundly liberating effect, allowing them not only the means to express themselves aesthetically, but the freedom and strength to do so in the face of cultural proscriptions against creating rebellions to gender norms. As Lola put it:

> People think, if you're a female punk rocker that you're worthless and you're stupid and you're nasty, but we have more if not, equal if not more power to, to do things, to go places and to be, and to make kick-ass music, to open our own stores, to do our own thing, to like, to raise hell. We have, just because we *are* girls. Because we're women and we can, and we're strong women and I think, I think that's why we get looked down [on] a lot. . . . We're not afraid to say, "Fuck you, that's not right," and so they kind of laugh at us and stuff, but deep down inside, they want to be us. They do! . . . They do! They want to be us! Look at Donna Reed. Can you see Donna Reed in combat boots? In green liberty spikes, mopping a floor? "Get your own damn dinner!"

Such forms of subcultural resistance also have an important impact on mainstream gender norms. The concordance between cultural and subcultural gender norms implies that change brought about within one system impacts the norms of the other. Angela McRobbie notes the strong similarities in the nuances of punk-girl styles and feminist styles; both sport heavy boots and cropped hair, although the more extreme forms of punk-girl style may remain "unpalatable to many feminists" (1991:32). In constructing symbolic challenges to the discourse of femininity, which is, after all, a semiotic system, punk girls change the accepted parameters of the discourse. As the fashion industry repeatedly plunders street styles in the quest for new fashion, it brings aspects of punk style into the mainstream. Importing punk-girl style expands what is permissible in mainstream femininity. Dorothy Smith argues that the discourse of femininity is "continually undergoing elaboration, contradiction, reworking at the local level among women actively participating in it" (1988:55). When creating such challenges, punk girls contribute significantly to the deconstruction of oppressive gender norms. Imagine more girls saying, as Lola does, "I actually enjoy being, I like being a girl. It's cool. It's a fun thing to be. And getting away with shit. . . . I'll slap on my lipstick and then kick their ass." True, housewives may not soon sport combat boots and liberty spikes and refuse to serve dinners, and punk girls in mohawks and crinolines and mainstream girls sporting combat boots with their prom dresses may not topple the government, but they certainly do expand the parameters of what is permissible. They are changing the faces of femininity.

Six

"Oh, I Hope I Don't Catch Anything"

Punk Deviance and Public Harassment

Even before I became a punk, the popular kids in my high school, who hung out in the "upper foyer"—the only route from my locker to the library—routinely made disparaging remarks about me in my hearing. After my transformation, the kids at school left me alone, for the most part, but the world, which had until then failed to note my existence, seemed to turn against me. When I was fourteen, I narrowly avoided a garbage man's booted foot aimed at my mohawked head as he sped by clinging to the back of his truck. When I was fifteen, a tourist photographed me without my consent at McDonald's as I sat eating a hamburger—hardly a flattering pose (especially now that I've espoused vegetarianism). When I was sixteen, I was surrounded in the subway by a gang of young thugs who threatened to beat me up unless I erased the hammer and sickle stenciled to the toes of my hi-top sneakers (I refused, and they backed down). In those years, it became routine for store detectives to follow me, for people to stare openly at me, for pedestrians to cross the street to avoid me, for strangers to shout insults at me from moving vehicles, for children to taunt me with screams of "Mrs. T! Mrs. T!" and—twice—for people to physically attack me on the street without warning or provocation. In 1984, despite my perfect grades and an immaculate behavioral record, I was expelled from high school.

Eleven years later, undeterred, maybe even spurred on to attend graduate school by these events, I independently taught a college course for the first time: "The Sociology of Youth Subcultures." By then, I had let my hair grow back, adopted a somewhat more conservative style of dress, and had gradually reaccustomed myself to people's reactions to me, or, I should say, their

166

lack of reaction to me. Gone were the stares, the gratuitous insults, the suspicious looks. Then, one day, toward the end of the semester, in order to wrap up my course, I had (for sound pedagogical reasons, might I add) declared the last day of class to be "Come as Your Favorite Youth Subculture" day. I, of course, chose punk. Dressed in tatters, with my cranberry-colored hair in multiple braids, I sallied forth into what had become by then a largely indifferent world. Unfortunately, I also decided, that day, to book my airline tickets for my winter break vacation.

Despite the fact that I had been conducting research on this topic, despite the fact that I was writing this very chapter at that time, I was surprised and bewildered by the travel agent's reaction to me. I had forgotten what it was like to be the recipient of such disdain, to be subjected to suspicious glances, dubious looks, to be asked questions such as "And *how* will you be paying for this?" It was not until I produced my American Express gold card from my wallet that our transaction could proceed with any amount of civility. (Incidentally, I now take my business elsewhere.)

Today, with longer hair, university accreditation, and the approbation of an ever-increasing number of credit card issuers, I tend to pass through the world largely unnoticed and unmolested. Such advantages vouch for my character, I suppose, and I find that I am usually proffered the common decencies and civilities that should be the unquestioned right of every human being. But that day in the travel agency, I revisited the world of my youth, and once again had a taste of the phenomenology of punk. And I learned how far I had come, and how little the world had changed.

In resisting mainstream femininity, punk girls construct sartorial and behavioral challenges to conventional dress and mores. As they do so within the context of punk, perhaps the epitome of "spectacular subcultures" (Hebdige 1979) their challenges are highly visible. This visibility is heightened by their presence in public. Punk is a street-based subculture, often engaging the public in its construction of revolt and refusal. As well, in constructing style, punk draws on highly theatrical forms of deviance, with punks having cultivated an often-exaggerated reputation for antisocial behavior and unconventional values. With this image of deviance partly constructed by and largely diffused through the media, punk girls' engagements with nonpunks are heavily marked by public perceptions of punk "deviance." How does the mainstream public act upon these perceptions? How do punk girls perceive others' perceptions of them? How does this shape punk girls' interactions with nonpunks?

Punks, along with skinheads and gangstas, spearhead the current round of public fears concerning "America's youth." Considered to be the most threatening of adolescents, members of oppositional youth subcultures are often cast as "folk devils" (Cohen 1972) social deviants responsible for anything from rising crime rates to falling property values and urban decay. As a result, agents of social control are called upon to counter this "menace," news media routinely issue reports of the state of such measures, and young people suddenly find themselves bearing the brunt of public scorn and derision. In the face of popular consensus casting such adolescents as social problems, few look beyond the sensationalism of media reports to discover the version of events offered by the adolescents themselves. Critical sociological perspectives on deviance have taught us not to accept attributions of deviance at face value, but rather to investigate their origins and their effects. In this chapter, I examine how members of one oppositional youth subculture—punks, and especially punk girls—experience and counter such attributions. I begin by grounding my analysis in critical perspectives on deviance. Following this, drawing on both interviews with punk girls and observations of punk scenes, I explore how events of public harassment contribute to the construction and perpetuation of such deviant imputations. I conclude by focusing especially on the ways in which punks' reactions to and interpretations of incidents of public harassment challenge their being labeled as deviant.

Deviance as Social Problem and as Social Construct

Social problems are produced in the meeting of the powerful and the powerless. Simply put, in this interaction, the powerful create and implement normative standards, simultaneously inventing, pointing out, and sanctioning both normalcy and deviance. This occurs as the more powerful or numerous group designates itself as normal, and then describes smaller, less powerful groups as deviant. Efforts at social control soon follow these accusations of deviance. Using formal and informal sanctions, the powerful seek to control the powerless deviants. Howard Becker (1963), the originator of this critical perspective on deviance, argues that attributions of deviance and efforts at social control, as they arise from power differentials, must be regarded essentially as political conflicts. He argues that, rather than examine the causes of deviance, we should focus on the creation of deviant definitions and on social reactions to such definitions. Thus, the labeling perspective champions the underdog, being partial to the views of the labeled, rather than to those of the labeler.

In order to critically examine the process of deviant labeling and social control, it is crucial to examine interactions between the labelers and the labeled. This is especially important when the labeling process occurs between groups with great disparities in social power and when it has deleterious effects on disempowered individuals. This is the situation that confronts members of oppositional youth subcultures, who often lack access to conventional media sources, mainstream political processes, and legal protection. Because subcultures are embedded in mainstream culture, any subcultural study that ignores the relationship of members of youth subcultures to those of the mainstream public misses an important part of subcultural participation (Fine and Kleinman 1979). Outsiders to the subculture have an important impact on the subcultural experience. For example, in their hostility toward the subcultural members, mainstream outsiders may serve to consolidate subcultural identity.

As interactions with the general public play such an important role in consolidating a subculture, establishing its boundaries, and compelling its members' commitment, it is important that any study of youth subcultures examine their relation to the general public. In this chapter, I examine the ways punk girls experience public harassment by strangers.[1] Few researchers have closely examined the interactions that occur to directly reinforce imputations of deviance. I detail the ways punks encounter such harassment and the strategies they use to counter it. I conclude that critical examination of such acts of public harassment calls into question the designation of deviance.

Punks and Public Harassment

The primary way that the general public perceives the punk subculture is as a group of social undesirables, often as a result of inaccurate media depictions. The punks I interviewed are well aware of this reputation:

Alexea: Some people, some people really dig it and some people are disgusted by it. . . . A lot of people are disgusted by it, especially older people because they don't understand it. They think it's disgusting and they think you're an asshole. There's a lot of prejudice against it from people.

Arizona: I think society looks down on it. . . . Still people are really shocked when they walk by and see all the people, all these piercings and their earlobes with things that big in them.

Lyrics of punk songs also reflect this sensitivity to the deviant image of punk:

Rosie: There's a song that's called "There's No Room for You Around" or something, it's by Chaos UK and it's super old, and it talks about how punks, they're never let into anything, they're banned from everything, they can't find their niche in society because there's not really a niche in society for punks. Because if you want to be a punk, that's it. You can't be like the rest of society, because society just doesn't accept it. They just laugh at it. They think it's stupid.

Many punks view this image as a stereotype, a result of inaccurate media coverage and general misunderstanding about the ideology and style of the punk subculture. For some, this stereotypy is the most bothersome aspect of being a punk:

> Candace: I don't like being classified. I don't like the attention it brings automatically. I don't like the automatic, "Oh, you're a punk. Oh, you must be a drug addict. You must be hateful." I don't like that attitude. I don't like that. That's the main thing I don't like. And sometimes I just feel like I don't care. "Fuck you!" But a lot of times I don't like it, mainly since I had a kid, because it brings me a lot of trouble.

Punks therefore disputed this stereotypical view, speculating on some of the effects of such labeling:

> Joanie: I think a lot of people assume that you're a disrespectful person. And I really don't like that. And which in turn, when people do that, they project that on you and so that's what they're going to see.

The stereotype of deviance, delinquency, and danger dominated punks' interactions with nonpunks. The popular image of punks as violent, doped-up, and hateful comes most into play in punks' everyday interactions with members of the mainstream public. When encountering punks, nonpunks seek out "access information" with which to construct their public interaction with punks.[2] Having recourse to no other source of information, members of the general public often access only the deviant images available through the media and youth authorities. Consequently, punks' interactions with the public occur mainly as confrontations best described as "public harassment." Both sides claim harassment, with punks and community members accusing each other of behaving rudely without provocation. Tracie Randolph, manager of the Jackson Square Cafe in New Orleans, has this to say on gutter punks:

> You could walk a mile away and still smell them. . . . They harass people to get money. They pee in the hallways. I walked up one morning and right in my door they had started a fire to keep themselves warm. (quoted in Yardley 1996)

While a punk's experience may be like Anna's:

> It's people that don't know me and just go—when I haven't said a word to them, not being mean or copping attitude, or anything—and they'll just come up and say shit right to my face, or push me, or try and start a problem.

Accusations of public harassment are a contentious issue in punks' interactions with the mainstream public, and public harassment is the weapon used in their conflict over public presence.

In her germinal work such events, Carol Brooks Gardner defines public harassment as "that group of abuses, harryings, and annoyances characteristic of public places and uniquely facilitated by communication in public" (1995:4). Generally, the targets of public harassment, the "situationally disadvantaged," are marked as "open persons," approachable by virtue of the lower status of their gender, race, or other characteristics. In our adult-oriented culture, adolescence denotes low status, as adolescents occupy a social position analogous to that of the elided working class (Grossberg 1994). In addition, membership in an oppositional youth subculture opens adolescents to such incivilities.

Unfortunately, the vast majority of interactions between members of oppositional youth subcultures and the general public could be described as negative by both sides. Most often, the public perceives these people as threatening, or, as many punks panhandle, as annoying.[3] Opportunities for negative encounters abound, as the street and other public urban areas often serve as the primary location of social interaction in the punk subculture. Punks live out substantial portions of their subcultural participation on the streets. Of the forty girls I interviewed, nineteen reported living or having lived on the streets, and twenty-seven either reported having participated in, or were observed engaging in, some form of street-level economic activity such as panhandling, selling handmade jewelry, or busking. This lifestyle requires higher levels of interpersonal interaction than are usually found between strangers in public spaces. In addition, whether or not a punk has a permanent residence or engages the street economy, the street remains the primary locus of the punk scene.

In my months of field research, I had many occasions to both observe and experience interactions between punks and nonpunks. Most of the time, these took the form of public harassment. Punks did receive occasional compliments about their appearance:

> Jennie: And then you've got people that are really cool, that like, "Oh, yeah, check that out. That's rad." . . . More people come up to me and they'll be like, "I totally love what you do. I just can't do it myself. Keep your individuality." People love it.

They were also the recipients of curious questions:

> Cathy: I don't mind when people are curious, and they'll come up to me, like, "Did that [piercing] hurt?" or, "Why did you do that?" I don't mind that so much.

Denise: Usually it's more people being curious. . . . Most of the time, though . . . most people really like it, most people are like, "Oh, that looks so cool!" or, "How do you sleep [with a mohawk]?" and "How do you put it up?" But that's a lot more of the attention that I get than negative.

While these were not perceived as harassment, punks reported that they become annoying through repetition:

Hallie: Strangers usually come up and ask me stupid questions. . . . Happens at least twice a day. It's usually the same thing, like, "Did your tattoo hurt?" . . . I am so used to it. A lot of [punks] get really frustrated and feel it's really redundant. Yeah, it's really redundant but I don't really care. I'm just like, "Yeah, Yeah."

Sue: I've had people stop me in the mall while eating and play twenty questions. And I'm just like, "Look, you've got a hairpiece. You look far more ridiculous than I do. Just run along." And I've also given people lines about, "Well, if I looked normal, would you question my politics and learn something?" So, that's about the way I see it. I try not to be extremely rude because that gives punks an even worse name.

Some punks claimed that their style even deterred some harassment:

Andie: People don't harass you, they actually leave you alone. They leave you the fuck alone, that's it. They just don't want anything to do with you.

Hallie: It's cool when you're traveling far, because . . . people don't want to fuck with me, man, they don't want to fuck with you. . . . I find people don't want to fuck with me as much. Because I've traveled with really mainstream-looking people. It seems they get fucked with more than I do.

Despite these denials, both Andie and Hallie went on to describe incidents of public harassment. Others who were complimented or approached for their looks proved to be exceptions to the rule, for although many punks did receive positive responses to their subcultural identity, most received negative remarks as well: "Some people are like, 'Wow, that's nice.' There are some that are, 'Ick'" (Cora). Despite the number of positive or curious remarks addressed at some punks, most reported that harassing incidents far outweighed these. Even Jennie, who reported that most attention she received was positive, added: "People harass you all the time."

Public harassments are such common occurrences for punks that my questions about such incidents elicited responses such as vigorous nods, rolled eyes, "Yeah, definitely" (Ava), and "Oh, yeah, all the time" (Sheila). The punks I observed and with whom I interacted experienced this daily. The types of public harassment of punks ranged in severity from obtrusive gazing to physical assault, including instances of visual harassment, verbal harassment, and physical harassment.

"You're Illegal": Exclusion

One of the most flagrant types of public harassment is being excluded.[4] This includes being denied access to both public and semipublic places (such as streets, parks, shops, and restaurants); being subjected to surveillance, and being offered poor service if admitted. Members of "situationally disadvantaged" groups, such as women, racial minorities, gays, and lesbians are often denied taken-for-granted access to public space as a whole, to certain areas, or at certain times. As did the Jim Crow laws of the pre–civil rights South, such practices act as a type of discrimination, denying some citizens those rights that are accorded to others. In his research on antiblack discrimination, Joe Feagin (1991) documented such exclusionary practices against middle-class blacks. These were primarily subtle incidents involving receiving poor service rather than being refused access or service outright. Yet, while harassers may feel constrained by law to avoid overt discrimination in the form of refusing service in the case of African Americans, they clearly feel no such constraints when dealing with punks.

Exclusion from places of business, such as shops or restaurants, was a common experience for punks. Gutter punks especially (but not exclusively) reported having been refused entry into stores and restaurants. One girl who had only recently become a punk found this to be in stark contrast to shopkeepers' behavior toward her in her more conformist days:

> Carnie: Before, I could go into stores and stuff, and now people don't even want me to come in their store. The other day, I was going into a store with Lib . . . we were going into a store, and this guy was hanging in front of the door, and we're like, "Excuse me." He's like, "I don't want you street kids in my store." We were like, "We just want to look at something," and he was like, "I don't care." We were like, "We just want to see something. What if we have money to buy something?" And he was like, "I don't want your money. . . . Go away. You stink." And we were like, "Well that's illegal." And he was like, "Well, you're illegal." And we were just like, "Fuck." Before, I could have just gone to any store, and they wouldn't even come follow me around the store and nothing. They didn't care. So that's a lot different now.

Punks were not only blocked from entering businesses, but were also often ejected from stores and restaurants:

Rudie: We went to buy a cup of orange juice with a twenty dollar bill. . . . And they didn't want us in their store. They told us to get out. . . . they were like, "No, no juice." We're like, "Okay, how about a soda?" They said, "We don't have any." And they're standing in front of their refrigerator. They were like, "Just get out," And [my boyfriend] Cy just went berserk. He started spitting everywhere, on the walls and on the floor. He was like, "Fuck you! That's discrimination!" And then a cop walked in and took us back . . . and for the first time, a cop didn't arrest us. Instead, he didn't say anything and they had to give us the orange juice.

This type of discrimination was experienced not only by gutter punks such as Carnie and Rudie, nor was it exclusive to North America. Lydia is a thirty-seven-year-old photographer with a college degree who has been involved with the punk scene since the mid-1970s; she reported such an incident on a recent trip to Germany:

I don't think that even I look very extreme, but when I was in Heidelberg about two years ago, all that I was wearing [that was punk] was this . . . cap with skulls on it. And I tried to get service in a travel agency, try to book a flight to England. This woman paid no attention to me for fifteen minutes and then finally she turned to me and she started pushing me out the door and said, "People like you do heroin." I was just thinking, "Fucking hell," I was thinking, I was thirty-four by then, "Fuck, I'm thirty-four and this is going on still?"

In addition to these reported incidents, I repeatedly observed police and security guards telling punks (and me) to "move on" away from park benches, vacant lots, and stairways. Punks were told to circulate when sitting in public areas, and in extreme cases, were arrested for misdemeanors such as obstructing the sidewalk, criminal trespass and, in New Orleans, the offense of "leaning with intent to fall." As Clara noted:

If your hair is colored, you can't stay at the park . . . a little old lady can sit there, but not you.[5]

A more subtle type of exclusion occurs when businesses offer only poor service to such social undesirables. This happened in restaurants:

Lola: There's this great restaurant named Caesar's, and [the waiter] used to give me attitude at the beginning, this old Italian guy, and then he noticed, because this is when I was working and stuff, I'd be all torn and everything, duct-taped boots and everything . . . I'd get the shittiest service. Take the longest time. I remember sitting down, fifteen minutes, people, these people came in. They got served way before I even got served.

And in stores:

> Wanda: We went in to return something in K-Mart, me and my friend, and she had something that she was returning and I had something I was returning. And they returned her thing, and then I was behind her, and then I was returning my thing. And they were like, they asked me for picture ID and all this and all that. And this girl, my friend, was all, she was normal looking, and they didn't ask her that. And they gave me sort of a hard time about it and all that.

Offering poor service is a common way in which establishments discriminate against "undesirables." This is a much more subtle form of discrimination than refusing service, and punk girls such as Lola and Wanda were only assured of their assessments of the situations by comparing the treatment they received to that offered other patrons.

A more common and more subtle tactic used by businesses to discourage the presence of punks is surveillance. Because punks are perceived as delinquent, security guards and store employees often took it upon themselves to monitor punks' behavior in their shops:

> Hallie: There's this one store called Smartlook and I went in there one time looking at bras, and I realized that wherever I went, this chick was just straightening stuff, stuff that doesn't even need to be straightened, like, "Oh, this hangar is kind of like at a ninety degree angle, maybe I should turn it to a sixty," or some shit.

> Lola: I can't go into a store without being followed around. I've always noticed that I can't go through a store.

When asked if she was ever hassled, Chloe, a rather normal-looking twenty-year-old, immediately responded:

> When we go in grocery stores we have people running after us saying "Hey, hey! I saw you steal that!" And we don't steal things. We get some really foul looks too, believe it or not. I know I don't even look very bad. I've got some combat boots on, but you'd be surprised these days. Because I live next to [an upscale community], and they have these yuppies, they see you walking around in a leather jacket and combat boots or something and security guards, they'll follow you around.

As did Chloe, a few punks reported that being subjected to this type of surveillance usually preceded being accused of theft, whether such accusations were founded in reality or not.

Such exclusions serve to deprive punks of the rights and privileges accorded to citizens in public places. There is no justification for such discrimination, for despite popular and police opinion, there is no evidence to support the perception that punks are more likely to be shoplifters or petty criminals than are any other young people. (In fact, a criminal would be well advised to avoid sporting such conspicuous apparel.) Although access to public places is protected in the United States by the 1964 Civil Rights Act and in Canada by the Charter of Human Rights, such provisions apply only to discrimination based on race, color, religion, or national origin. It remains unclear whether business owners' actions to exclude punks are, indeed, illegal, as Carnie claimed. Certainly such exclusion from public places accepts the description of punks as deviant, and the punk parody of delinquency at face value, thereby enforcing discrimination against a group that enjoys little protection under the law.

"The Triple, Quadruple Take": Exploitation

When punks are accorded presence in public places, they become targets of further instances of harassment, in which their presence is exploited. Such exploitation occurs when individuals take unusual liberties with others, often intrusions that violate these persons' privacy and contravene norms of public courtesy (Gardner 1995). These behaviors include staring, foul looks, photography, threats, and attacks.

The visual harassment of the intrusive stare is the most common single form of harassment punks encounter. Indeed, this can be called the quintessential punk experience; a newspaper article once advised parents to dissuade their children from becoming punks by asking them: "Is your dress style interfering with your life, do people look at you and roll their eyes?" (Kogan 1991). Such attention extends much beyond the ways in which strangers look at each other in public:

> Sue: I get it daily if I leave the house. And not even verbal harassment, just kind of the triple, quadruple take.

Strangers' scrutiny is the most immediate and noted effect that follows the construction of a punk identity:

> Stone: The only thing it really changed was the way certain people looked at me.

Members of the mainstream public treat punks as a type of ludic display, a sideshow of sorts, as Lola noted:

They go out of their way to fucking go look to where we're at, to walk by and look, and they kind of stare and everything. They go out of their way, just to pay attention.

Beyond staring, punks are often the recipients of foul looks, including looks of disgust, prolonged and intent staring, eye rolling, and being "looked down" upon:

Sloopy: They treat you like shit. . . . They just give you looks of disgust.

Carina: Another thing that pisses me off is we'll all be walking down the street and we'll get looked down upon. That sickens me, because you don't know who I am. How can you look down on me like that or roll your eyes or snicker your nose? That disgusts me.

Overall, punks found that such staring was intrusive, bothersome, and completely undeserved.

A more intrusive form of visual harassment punks frequently experience is unwanted photography. Many punks undergo this at least once in their subcultural career, so much so that it is one of the common experiences which punks discuss among themselves. Gardner (1995:79) notes that such intrusive photography appears to serve the purpose of confirming that an unconventional appearance is indeed real. Persons with cameras become amateur anthropologists, photographically documenting the unusual:

Rudie: [My boyfriend] Cy and I, when we go to Central Park . . . he usually has blue hair, I usually have purple . . . but we get our pictures taken.

Punks are positioned in this way as tourist sights:

Lola: People take pictures and stuff. Like, "I've got a little eight-year-old boy at home." Click.

The intrusiveness and nuisance of this practice is exacerbated by the fact that, realizing people's interest in their image, punks occasionally capitalize on their photogeneity:

Courtney: There's so many [college graduates] who have me in their photographs, because I'm watching the [graduations] and I'm like, "Five dollars for a picture and I'll put my arm around you. . . . Give me five dollars. Oh, okay. Happy graduation." Or just, they like clicking pictures of you. If I don't get money, if I'm in a good mood, then I don't mind. But if I get money, "Do what you want." I've chased people for their cameras and stuff. I threatened them.

I observed a similar incident as I waited to meet with a girl I interviewed: as Emily's boyfriend crossed the street, a well-dressed yuppie took a camera out of his Volvo and snapped a couple of frames. Fortunately, the punk did not notice, for, as Emily assured me, her boyfriend would have sought to retrieve the camera or the film. Permitting photography of oneself as a source of income is common among punks, making unwanted photography an even greater source of annoyance. Such photography is also offensive because these photographs have been widely marketed to the tourist trade as postcards, an economic practice that does not benefit punks though capitalizing on their image. Thus, unsolicited and unremunerated photography is a common practice which many punks find offensive. Beyond that, however, unwanted photography, like staring, is a practice which punks find annoying simply because it brings undue attention to their "deviance" from the mainstream public.

In addition to staring, foul looks, and photography, punks experience more serious exploitations—pushing and shoving. Such incidents occur when punks are threatened or even attacked without provocation:

> Anna: I had a mohawk and dressed full jacket and all the shit a couple of years ago, and I had a lot of people . . . they couldn't tell if I was a guy or a girl, and so you'd have people come up and try and pick fights with you, "If you're a guy, I'm going to kick your ass." Stuff like that. I've had a lot of very violent problems with people just coming up for no reason and shoving on you or trying to cause a fight and stuff. You have to deal with it. It's scary.

These forms of public harassment can be very threatening and even escalate to the point of physical abuse:

> Alexea: I've gotten my ass kicked for looking punk. In different parts, different states like Idaho and shit, they're really intolerant of me. They don't think it's so cool.

Such threats and attacks were not exclusive to small towns:

> Ava: Sometimes girls try to rip out my lip ring on the bus. . . . That was scary. . . . Because she didn't like it. . . . She was like this big gangsta chick and she didn't like my lip ring and she was talking shit to me, "How can you do that to your face?" And I was like, "Does it matter to you? Do you care?" Are you going to go get one done?" And she was just like, "I'm going to rip that thing out of your face!" And she starting going towards me and I was like, "Fuck this!" and got off the bus.

Thus, in some instances, punks experience more than discrimination or scrutiny; they may experience outright attack, based solely on their membership in this "deviant" subcultural group.

"Look at the Peacock": Evaluation

Punks are also subjected to a vast amount of evaluative harassment, such as indirect but derogatory comments, unsolicited advisory remarks, verbal attacks, and physical acts intended to communicate derision, such as spitting or avoidance. The most common of these is verbal harassment through remarks that are evaluative or advisory. In her research on the harassment of women, Gardner (1995) found that street remarks directed toward women usually pertained to their physical attractiveness. While punks do receive compliments about their appearance, the majority of remarks directed toward them can be characterized as insulting and confrontational. As Lisa reported, such harassment can come from a number of sources:

> Actually, it ranges from grumpy old men to brash young little kids, actually. Just, just people who aren't happy with themselves. Mainly it's after you walk by. Which is always nice.

This type of verbal harassment can take many forms. Most often it is directly addressed to the punk, but it can also occur as remarks that are deliberately uttered to be overheard. This is also one of the more remarkable changes that occur upon assuming a punk style of self-presentation, as Carnie discovered:

> The way older people look at you changed. Because I used to dress really nice and look pretty, and now it's like, "Look at that dirty white kid."

The content of such harassment was not usually very confrontational, but it was nonetheless rude:

> Stone: They just freak out, like, "Omigod, look at that!"

This type of harassment also includes laughing:

> Lola: I put on this pair of silver Mary Janes . . . and I put on these really funky tights—they're red with flowers all over them—and this green minidress and I was dressed really funny and my hair was, my hair was red, this really flaming red, and I was walking down the street. And these rednecks come out to their porch, dragging their family, laughing at me, and it really, it really irked me . . . because they were like, "Come here and look. Look at her!" And they were laughing, and I got so pissed off, I'm like, "Yeah, it's funny, isn't it?" And that whole night, that whole night all I could think of, I was sitting there, I was thinking about just taking my shoe and just crashing their door out.

Such remarks and laughter, made in passing, allow the harasser to evaluate the target while incurring little risk of retaliation, as social norms dictate against replying to the overheard content of private conversations. Some punks do use this norm to their advantage in their response, laughing off harassment: "I just sit there and laugh at them. I can, I can sit there and laugh in their faces and they can't do shit about it" (Stone).

Remarks that are uttered deliberately to be overheard are some of the more benign forms of verbal harassment punks experience. More overt types of verbal harassment occur as direct-address verbalizations, either as attacks or assessments, which punks can hardly ignore. Children are often told that words can never hurt them, but such verbal assaults are actually "weapons of the street . . . ammunition in the hands of powerful groups . . . capable of inflicting injury, since they serve to define, demean, and even destroy" (Rogers and Buffalo 1975:102–103). One type of such verbal harassment is the advisory comment. Harassers routinely comment on punks' appearance, most often with negative evaluations. These are often couched as advisory comments, which constitute very overt pressures toward conforming to mainstream norms of appearance and lifestyle.

In the case of punk girls, such advisory comments are not-so-subtle evaluations of unattractiveness, as well as overt pressure to construct a more conventionally feminine style. These occur in startlingly consistent language, as Sue stated in an exaggerated redneck drawl: "Damn, you woulda been purty with long hair, girl." Mina, who has prescription glasses, reported that she was harassed in this way mostly by male yuppies two or three times a week:

> The other day I had a guy say, "Oh, you would be so pretty if you just grew out your hair and took that [silver ring] out of your nose," and, "Why do you have to shave your head and wear those ugly glasses?" and stuff like that.

Other girls reported a similar form of advisement from a variety of sources:

> Ava: Everyone's always tried to tell me, "Why don't you grow your hair out? Why don't you look like the other girls?" And it's just made me not want to do it. At all. And I never will now. [Sarcastically:] I really want to look like that. Like, real cute.

> Jennie: I've had a few guys, "Why don't you grow long hair?" I'll be like, "No. Why? To make you happy? No, I'm not doing that."

> Stone: The big snobs and shit. Come up like, "Why are you dressed like that? Why do you have your hair like that? Why can't you wear more makeup?" It's, well, because I don't fucking feel like it. That's about it.

While harassers' overt intentions may be to pressure punk girls into construct-ing appearances more in keeping with mainstream norms of femininity, punk girls interpreted such comments as "you would be so pretty" as confrontational and insulting.

In addition to being told to let their hair grow, female punks are often ad-vised, as are their male counterparts, to get a haircut. (When I had a mohawk, I was always extremely amused by people telling me to get a haircut—how much shorter could I go?) In addition, strangers advise punks about employ-ment practices, with the phrase "get a haircut" often immediately followed by "get a job." Anna, who sports green and black hair and works as an erotic dancer, was frequently harassed by "anywhere from children to old people," with the majority being "lower-middle-class or upper-lower-class Southern middle-aged couples—rednecks, mostly"; she was often advised to "Just fucking dye your hair and go get a real job." Amalia, a crusty punk, added: "Just, ev-ery once in a while, normal average people freak out and go, 'Ooh, ooh, why don't you get a job? Blah blah blah blah blah blah. How can you do this when you don't wash?'" I once again found myself the target of such a comment dur-ing my field research, when a young middle-class white couple Justine had just "spare changed" looked at me, as I sat on my concrete block taking field notes, and exhorted me to get a job (little knowing that this *was* my job). In fact, the phrases "get a haircut" and "get a job" are so often directed toward punks that they have become a subcultural catchphrase: A common punk joke is for one mohawked punk to yell this to another. In their unsolicited evaluations of punks, harassers often combine insults with what are meant to be perceived as more positively intentioned advisory remarks ("get a job"; "you would be so pretty"); clearly, if a punk were to heed the harasser's advice, the harasser would have succeeded in eradicating one little patch of "deviance."

Beyond being treated to advisory comments, punks also report being sub-jected to verbal attacks that are deliberately insulting, confrontational, and com-pletely lacking the veneer of advisement. Jennie reported that this includes name-calling: "Look at the peacock! Look at the butch walking down the street!" Denise also experienced some drive-by harassment:

You'll get people go by and go "Nyah, you're so, what the hell happened to you?" ... Lots of rednecks who drive by ... Mostly, mostly I'd say, I think mostly guys over ... what I picture is pickup trucks driving by, just people in it, going, "Nyah, nyah, look at that!"

Some punks also found that such confrontational comments were not always made in an expected form or place:

Cathy: Recently I went to visit my mom. We went to a casino to go gamble . . . I'm just walking around the casino, minding my own business, spending my little quarters. Some man was standing in a little aisle, started to back up, so he stepped on my foot. And he's like, "Excuse me, oh, excuse me. [pause] Oh. Oh I hope I don't catch anything." Just made this big huge scene in the middle of the casino.

Despite punks' cultivation of a tough and menacing image, rather than maintain their distance, strangers would occasionally simply and inexplicably approach a punk and begin provoking her:

Lola: A lot of people are totally freaked out and scared by it and think you're stupid and they're like, "Why are you, you're fucking your life up," and "You're so stupid and you're going to . . . " and "How can you do this?" and, "How can you do that?" and, "How can you work?" and all this . . . So people are always like, "You're messing your life up. You're trash," and all this.

Sloopy: This old lady comes up and goes, "This is my city, my town, my right!" So she's like, "You freaks! Blah blah blah." She went and got the police and stuff and we were like, we weren't doing anything at all. He was saying, "Please don't make [trouble]." Because she was crazy, she went and phoned the police and went, "I don't have to listen to you."

Connie: Me and this other girl, this guy came up to us. Me and my fucking buddies are sitting there, and he was like, he just sat there and looked at us for like, this was, he just sat there for the longest time, and we were just giggling and kept looking at him. And he, and he said, "What planet are you guys from?" We're like, "Mars, man." Totally, man, they totally ask you what . . . planet you're from. . . . They just, they have crazy stuff to say to you.

In addition to being verbally attacked, punks are routinely subjected to acts that communicate a derogatory message, such as spitting. To Rosie, this was just one instance in a string of harassment:

Well, sometimes they laugh, sometimes, they spit, sometimes they'll say I'm a junkie, sometimes they'll say a bunch of stuff. A lot of people are really, really shocked.

Lydia also found such unexpected harassment when she started to look punk:

The day I cut my hair, Tea cut my hair, I was walking down [the street]. . . . And this guy spat on the ground in front of me. . . . Actually, I had forgotten that I had done that to my hair. I thought, "What the fuck is he doing that for?" And then I realized.

Suspicion and avoidance also communicate their message of vilification. Clara described an instance where nonpunks exhibited fear of mugging when they encountered punks:

> Old ladies, when they go by here, they hold on to their purses really tight.

Rudie and her sister, who is also a punk, found that people avoided them in the street:

> There we are, walking down the street, me and her, and she had a mohawk, I had something else and our faces all pierced and stuff and she's pretty heavily tattooed and she has short sleeves on. Me too. And she has a rat on her back and she had her dog and I had my dog, and man, people were clearing the sidewalk for us. They weren't jumping us, but they were clearing the sidewalk for us.

Some punks may have found these instances humorous, but others found that such avoidance and suspicion is bothersome:

> Cathy: I hate when people just stare at me and then people will pull their children away from me, like I'm going to kidnap their child or something. That's the part that bothers me. . . . I have that happen to me all the time.

Such acts as spitting, avoidance, and suspicion (clutching purses, pulling children away) communicate, without words, that punks are objects of scorn, fear, and disgust.

The harassment punks experience hinges on the public perception of punks as pathologically deviant—they are often assumed to be delinquents, drug addicts, or otherwise dangerous individuals. Such harassments appear to function as acts of labeling, whether overt, as in calling punks "junkies," "trash," and "freaks," or covert, through the use of derogatory acts and other forms of indirect insults. This harassment can also serve as a form of informal social control. This is especially apparent in store owners', police officers', and security guards' use of exclusionary tactics such as poor service, surveillance, and refusal of access to both public and semipublic places. More informally, such attempts at social control appear in advisory comments, such as those directing punk girls to be more feminine, or directing punks to get jobs. However, such attempts to "straighten out" punks through overt discrimination or advisement often fail. Rather than obey such injunctions, punks, in keeping with their rejection of mainstream social norms, construct a number of strategies to counter and reverse such imputations of deviance.

Responses to Public Harassment

The targets of harassment often have very little recourse to formal protections against events milder than outright assault. Women who are harassed may turn to police, and members of racial or ethnic minorities may have recourse to community or personal economic resources, but punks lack the opportunities to retreat or escape from such harassment.[6] Instead, punks use informal responses to harassment.

By far the most common punk response to harassment is to ignore or block the incident, a response I call "the whatever strategy":

> Lisa: [I] just ignore it, because these people have obviously nothing to offer me, so . . . I don't think it a, I don't have any point to make, really, other than, "Well, whatever."

Punks not only pretend that nothing is happening, but in many cases, fail to notice harassment at all, especially in cases of staring or indirect verbal comments. For most punks, being stared at is such a common occurrence that it has become normalized. Thus, most do not even attempt to counter this behavior:

> Nikita: I've become oblivious to it, to the stares. I don't even notice it, and somebody will point it out to me: "Everyone in the room is looking at you." I'm like, "What?"

> Hallie: When I go into a small town, right? And people are staring at me and I'm with a friend who's mainstream looking or whatever, they freak out about how much people are staring at me and making comments. I don't even notice until they point it out.

> Lisa: I don't know if I'm oblivious. I tend not to notice it unless it's sort of obvious, because I'll walk down the street with friends and they'll just say, "Oh, did you see how that person looked at you?" or "Did you see blah blah blah?" And I won't even notice.

Such attention had become so habitual that some reported noticing its absence when they temporarily looked more mainstream:

> Anna: You get used to that and that becomes a norm for you, people making comments and noticing you and seeing you, and yeah, the times where I just had a black bob or something, just a could-be-conservative haircut, people just walked on by, and it was weird. You're kind of like, "Hey, aren't you going to say something to me? What's the matter?" It's weird.

Others anticipated missing it:

Arizona: I have tunnel vision, usually, when I walk down the street. I don't pay attention to no one because I've got my destination. I don't care if they're staring at me. . . . Whenever I get normal, I'll be going around like, "Why is this weird?"

Although punks experience a vast amount of staring and other harassment, it does not dominate their public interactions:

Rosie: It takes a while, at first it's hard. But eventually you get used to it, the looks from people, the comments, the stuff. Eventually, you're just so used to it that you don't care anymore.

Punks quickly become adept at blocking out scrutiny and indirect comments. However, even when they do notice harassment, their most common response is to ignore the attention. Much of the time, punks ignore even very insulting remarks:

Elle: Sometimes there are people, "Look at her, she looks like a clown, She's so ugly." . . . I don't care. I just walk right by. I stay indifferent. Well, I can't stop living just because people don't like the way I am.

Why would punks, who are reputed to be confrontational, ignore so much of the harassment they experience? Leslie Kennedy and Stephen Baron (1993) noted that the group of punks they studied (which was predominantly male) used few retaliatory strategies when verbally harassed. Although the punks claimed to be unperturbed by such harassment, Kennedy and Baron argued that failure to respond may be due to situational factors limiting the possibility of violent retaliation, to the absence of other punks, or to fear. Only two girls I interviewed cited fear as a reason to ignore or withdraw from harassment:

Ava: If they're really big and mean looking, I won't say anything and I'll just grumble at them or something. But if they're stupid pieces of shit I usually just flip them off and scream at them, "Fuck you! You motherfucker, arrrgh, arrrgh, arrrgh." Anything that pops out at the time.

Jennie: It just depends what kind of mood I'm in. And who it is. If it's some big gangster guy, I'll be like, "Okay. It's wrong. You're right. I'm lame. Okay. I'll change for you." But it's like, someone else, it just depends who the person is. I just walk away from the type who are into conflict, or I'll be like, "Hey, I'm not going to take this."

Punks may ignore or block harassment because they fail to notice it or because they have become immune to it. Punks then become pragmatic about the attention they receive:

Lola: One time last year . . . I had purple hair and I was, I had on my combat boots and fishnets and an old woman's fifties dress on, and this jacket, and I was walking down to this corner—waiting to cross the street, and these old people walked by and this man goes, "What the hell is that?" And that's the way it is.

It may be that the sheer volume of harassment precludes individual response. Given the vast amount of public harassment which punks experience, ignoring such occurrences is necessary. Responding to all instances of verbal harassment, for example, could become rather time-consuming:

Chloe: I was walking around in this damned grocery store the other day, and I hear about eight choruses of "Did you see what that girl was wearing?" I swear, and you know what was weird? Older people were looking at us and ignoring us, and it was younger people that were freaking out over us. That was what surprised us. You'd think that young people would think it's cool, but the older people would just not take notice, and it was their daughters and their kids that were grabbing them and going, "Did you see what that girl was wearing?"

Punks also ignored harassment if they were unprepared. Despite the volume of harassment they experienced, specific instances of verbal attack could catch punks off guard, robbing them of their ability to respond:

Allie: A bus driver told me that I was . . . just taking advantage of everybody and I was just, I was sucking everybody dry. He didn't even know me, just started saying, made all these accusations, because I said something about that I was going to the welfare office and he was like, "Arrrgh, arrrgh, you're just, what are you going to do? Take off every, everything you can get from everybody? Take advantage of us?" And I was like, "Wow, man." . . . That guy was really in my face. But at the time I didn't have any comebacks. I didn't say anything. I was just like, "Whatever, man." . . . Well, I'm late. I think of stuff later because when somebody's yelling me, I'm just like, "Duh." . . . It takes me a while to comprehend what they, exactly what they're saying. I don't want to start talking back to people because I have to think out clearly what I'm saying and I can't just come out with something brilliant off the top of my head because it just doesn't happen like that. Sometimes. But rarely.

Punks lose the opportunity to respond by taking the time to process the information they receive, deciding whether to respond, and then devising an appropriate response.

Finally, some punks' failure to respond to even the most egregious insults is a result of their socialization. This was especially apparent in the case of Denise:

> This guy walked up to us, when I was out with a friend last night, actually, the [tattoo artist] I'm apprenticing with. This guy walks over and he says to Paul, "Do you date this thing?" And I was just like, "Excuse me?" I'm like, "Pardon me, wait, whoa." I can't just take that. Paul's like, "First of all, this is a very lovely young woman. And no, I don't date her." The guy was like, "Oh, I was just saying . . . " I'm like, "Just get the hell out." My problem is that I have a really hard time being rude to people. I was so deeply offended, I really was, but for some reason I just cannot be rude to people.

It may simply be the case that, ironically, some punks are just too polite to respond to such incidents.

When punks fail to respond to harassment, others may intervene, as did Denise's friend. Cathy, who was insulted in a casino, reported that her mother, a sheriff, came to her defense: "My mom's right there and she's like, 'Don't worry about him. He's just a jerk.' I was like, 'Yay!' She's saying all these mean things about him. 'That's right mom, kick his butt!'"

Punks did not always ignore harassment. Many reported using a number of more confrontational tactics in responding to harassment, such as talking back or acting back:

> Amalia: What do I do? Yell back at them and tell them what's up. Basically . . . I just tell them off. Tell them off. I've never beat anybody up over it. I just tell them off, tell them to get away from me.

Some punks used this tactic to address verbal harassment, even when such speech was not addressed directly to them:

> Carina: The other day, me and Wattie went to the bathroom . . . and [this man's] wife was in the bathroom and as we were walking down the stairs, the man was waiting out there and he was talking to another man and said, "Well, I don't know. I was just told I needed to wait out here because there were some people around here that my wife wouldn't be safe with." I talked to him about it. I was like, "That's ridiculous! It's totally ridiculous." I couldn't believe it. We just laughed and walked away.

Punks tend to use this strategy to educate the public, explaining to strangers, even those using more confrontational and insulting forms of harassment, that punk is a subculture of protest:

> Rosie: I went to the welfare office to bring some of my friend's papers there,

and this guy started with me, and he goes to me, "Jesus Christ, you look cheap," and all this stuff. I said to myself, "Who the fuck do you think you are?" He goes to me, "Oh, you're never going to be able to find a job like that." I said, "I don't want one in a society like this anyways. I really don't want your stupid jobs."

Tori: If they get in my face, then I'll start throwing stuff out at them and I'll say, "Just listen to me. Talk to me. Don't just sit there and scream at me. Talk to me." And if they don't want to talk to me, I'll just walk away, but if they do want to talk to me, we'll sit there and we'll battle it out, until whatever. Neither one of us is going to agree with the other person, but at least we stopped to listen to the other person. If someone comes up to me that I don't like what they're doing, which I don't care what anybody else is doing, but corporates or something like that, if they've got time to sit down and talk to me and tell me why they're doing what they're doing, wonderful. Look, I'll sit down and talk to you. Just listen to what I've got to say. That's, I'm more into rationalization, just having, just educating people on why certain kids are out here. Definitely.

Other punks attempted to dispel the myth that all punks are dropouts and losers:

Denise: People, I know, look at me and go, "Yeah, she's some schmuck, she's going to live on the street." And, as a matter of fact, it's like, "No, I graduated from college." . . . It's become sort of a personal mission to get people past my hair and get past my . . . look at me like a person, not just like hair standing up. . . . If somebody comes up to me in a bar and I'm not feeling . . . Half the time, I do get, I mean, I'm always nice to people because I know that people are just curious and if I'm rude to them, then that's sort of like, it's a stereotype, even though I get asked the same questions four million times a day, but I still, I don't want to be rude, but sometimes I'll just totally go off and I'll just be like, "Okay, this is what I do, this is what I believe, this is why I do it. You need to understand that this isn't all, the appearance isn't all of it, there's a lot more to it than that." And I think sometimes people will just be like, "Yeah." But then I feel like sometimes I really get through to people. I think that's really important. Get people to get past certain things, because that's a big problem in this society, I think. This country anyway. It's just, people are so obsessed with how you look, what kind of car you drive, how "That's not socially acceptable." Who cares?

It is especially in response to verbal harassment that punks will attempt more clearly to articulate the purposes and norms of the subculture and thus reinterpret what it is to be a punk.

Typically, it is only in the most egregiously confrontational cases that some punks resort to self-defense or to what is commonly believed to be typical, aggressive punk behavior:

> Wanda: Me and a friend of mine were going to the grocery store, and we pulled in and we were getting out and there were these redneck guys standing on this restaurant, yelling all these obnoxious comments. And I was just like, "Oh god, shut the, shut up!" We went in . . . And so we came back out and he started, he was still out there and he was yelling again. And I told my friend, I said, "Pull up over there." And so she pulled up, in the car, right beside this guy, and I rolled down my window, and I go, "Come here." And he comes over there and he leaned down and I spit on him. Right between his eyes. I hit him right about here. And his friend started laughing. And I started laughing and then my friend started laughing and just drove off. I just, my temper was shot. I was just tired of listening to him, so I was just . . . I couldn't help it. I was like, "Leave me alone."

Punks resort to confrontational tactics only with great provocation and only as a defensive tactic. However, given that punks are stereotyped as confrontational, such behavior is likely to being interpreted as typical of such "deviant" adolescents. For this reason, even in cases of extreme rudeness, some punks choose to let the harasser get away rather than risk further confrontation.

Punks only reported using the ultimate form of self-defense, physical confrontation, when the assault was initiated by the harasser, as did Stone:

> I've had people come up to me and start hitting me. It happens. Then, usually I get them back. I'll hit them back.

Even then, punk girls' use of violence was occasional and tentative:

> Carina: Sometimes, when I'm in a bad mood, and they shove me to get out of the way, I'll shove them back. I don't want to give them the wrong idea, but . . .

However, this self-defense can have negative consequences, as Anna reported,

> I've had an assault charge. I will fight back when I get pushed. I try to avoid [those] situations, and I'll ignore most. . . . If someone comes right up to my face, depending on how hard they want to push it, I will fight back. But most of the time it's, "Fuck you," and walk on. You have to, you get it too much to get in a fight every single time.

Not only do such responses further reinforce stereotyped perceptions of punks as violent, but as Anna and a number of other punks found, defending oneself physically occasionally led to further difficulty, as police typically assumed that the punk initiated the altercation:

LL: So what do you do when people get in your face about shit?

Sheila: Usually get the cops called on me. For fucking telling them to fuck off or whatever. And the cops look at me, look at them, they're like, "All right."

In addition to ignoring the harassment or confronting the harasser, punks also devised responses that demonstrate a good amount of humor and imagination. Often, these both turned the tables on the harasser and made a subtle point about stereotyping. For example, Lola, who received poor service in a restaurant, reprimanded her waiter:

I pulled out a hundred dollar bill and left no tip. I just started frequenting, just to piss them off. And then they learned, and then I got my respect. Then they were okay. When I get poor service, I just make an ass of myself and I'll make it known. I'm like, "This sucks."

Lola reminded the waiter, through refusing to tip, that appearances are deceptive. Continuing patronage, and thus "getting respect" by demonstrating that not all punks are broke or rude is consistent with many punks' efforts to educate the public that punk is a subculture of protest, rather than one of delinquency.

Other punks' attempts to educate the public may not have made the point so clearly. Thus, in response to shopkeepers' surveillance, Hallie led one pursuer on a chase, and then parodied the punk stereotype by feigning theft:

I'd make them go in circles until they realized that we were walking in circles. And then go the other way. We're going one way and just totally fuck with them. I like fucking with people like that. Or pretend that I'm stealing stuff, make it really obvious, then sneakily put it back. And they search me, they took my jacket off, they can't find anything.

This incident plays on a complex set of expectations: the store clerk following Hallie expected her to steal, so she played into the situation by obviously shoplifting. Hallie then rightly expected to be stopped and searched, and so covertly restored the merchandise. By elaborately staging her compliance with expectations, she redefined the situation, challenging popular expectations with regard to punk delinquency. This reversal, however clever, entertaining, and psychologically rewarding it may have been, may not have had the intended effect, as it is doubtful whether the security guards who detained Hallie understood her parody.

These types of parodies and reversals are characteristic of many of the strategies punks use to counter harassment. Many punks, who are accustomed to attracting a great deal of attention, have no qualms about acting out scenes or acting up in public in response to harassment. One girl turned to the culture of celebrity in developing and implementing her strategy to counter visual harassment:

> Sue: I just usually smile, wave. I've offered autographs before, just to be bitchy.

Others resorted to acting up and to citing rules of etiquette:

> Emily: Depends on what mood I'm in. If I'm in a passive mood, I'll just ignore it. But if I'm in a mood, kind of rambunctious, I like to do things like just stare at them, like really big. I'll stick my tongue out at them. Talk really loud, like, "Gee, it sure is RUDE when people stare." Stuff like that. It's fun because they get really embarrassed, they're like "Oh, go away." They look away real quick or something. It's funny.

> Cathy: Usually I end up telling them something to make them realize how rude they are. If people were just staring at me—I had this happen, especially old people, they always, just, they stare—and I don't, when you look back at them, they don't look away, they just keep staring. Most people will hurry up and turn their head. I'm like, "Didn't your mother ever tell you it's not polite to stare?" And then they'll turn away, because they realize, "Oh, that's not real nice." Or if somebody says something really snide to me, I don't want to say something snide back, because I don't want to fight. . . . Usually I just say, "You're rude," or something. Just tell them, "Go away."

By dramatically using sarcastic comments, or by "reminding" harassers of common rules of etiquette governing public behavior (the impropriety of staring), these punks inverted their social positioning, placing the harasser as the deviant norm-breaker. In remarking that the harassers were contravening the rules of public interaction by breaking norms of public courtesy and reserve, these punks discursively reversed the attribution of deviance.

Thus, punks construct such strategic responses to public harassment to resist the imputation of deviance, and indeed, to reverse the attribution of deviant labels. Rather than accept reprimands for their unconventional style, punks turn the table on harassers, becoming themselves the enforcers of the rules of social behavior. In seeking to educate the public or in citing rules of etiquette, some punks argued that their condemnation was a product of intolerance:

> Sophie: People judge me, "Ha ha, look at that going by," but really, I'm a person like everybody else. It doesn't matter.

LL: You said that people say "Look at that." Does that bug you?

Sophie: I don't care. Let them talk. They're just talking to themselves. I have a friend who limps. I don't care if he limps. I just let live.

Other punks simply viewed this harassment as the product of a profound ignorance they do not deign to counter:

Rosie: What do I do? I don't say anything. I just walk right by them. I have. Personally? I really don't care. Let them think about it. They're just scared of difference. They don't know what they're talking about. They don't want to be accepting, then let them not be accepting. If they're like that, they're not going to change. They're always going to be like that.

In ignoring harassment, punks saw themselves exhibiting the live-and-let-live attitude they would like to find in others:

Basilisk: I've been called horrible, but there's nothing wrong with it. They're just standing at the outside looking in, and looking at all the bad things, stuff they've heard about us. Because they hear, "Oh, they do drugs." But that's everybody's own choice. Whether or not they want to do drugs, whether or not they want to drink. It's not like you have to be a punk and you have to drink.

Joanie: If they were really uncomfortable with the situation, I'll be like, "Okay, I'm going to leave because you obviously can't handle my outer appearance. So I hope someday you'll know better." I'm still nice to them, I'm just like, "I'm sorry that you're not happy." That's what I usually say, "I'm sorry that you're not happy. Because I am. Have a good day."

In condemning them, these punks argue, their condemners are condemning themselves:

Camille: I try to show people, "You see the way that I am dressed. I have blue Docs. I am in black." When people see black, they say, "That's bad." But when they see black, they say, "That's bad. That's not me." But in the end, it's them. When someone says "yuck," he is saying "yuck" to himself. Because he is society. . . . I laugh. Because when they say "yuck" they see me. They say "yuck" to themselves. Because I reflect the ugliness of society. Everything that they have that is evil, I have it on me. But what I have inside me is pure. It's to show them, "You judge what I am, but you don't take the time to understand what is in yourselves. . . . In the end, when I dress like this, it's to show people how they are ugly, and at the same time it's to say to them, "Look at me. I am beautiful, but I am showing you what you want to see. You want to see that you are ugly. Look. You are ugly. If you look deeper, You will see that you are beautiful. Everyone is beautiful, but everyone is ugly." Like yin and yang. Life in death, death in life. There is always evil in good and good in evil.

Punks thereby reversed the judgments that others make of them. Some, like Chloe, viewed their tolerance of others as evidence of punks' moral superiority:

I get off on it a little bit. Sometimes I just, I do a real evil grin at somebody if I see them looking at me, just sort of like, "Yes, you look stupid too." Just because I think I think it's really ridiculous that somebody can look at some-body and freak out over what they were wearing when it's so superficial. . . . They look at you like, "Wow, you really stand out." And I'm looking that them and I'm like, "Yeah, you really blend in." . . . If I'm in a grocery store in [a nice neighborhood] or something and the yuppies are looking at me because I dress trashy or something, in a way I'm doing them a public service, be-cause once in a while, you need to see somebody that doesn't look like you.

Punks repeatedly characterized their harassers as being ignorant of punk ide-ology, of treating them in an undeserved manner, and of accepting and acting on stereotypes. Rather than respond to such labels and attempts at social con-trol by modifying their behavior (either through increasing or decreasing their "deviance"), they resorted to a third tactic: denying the validity of the label.

This refusal highlights the disparity between the behavior of supposedly deviant punks and that of ostensibly benign mainstream strangers. When punks were involved in incidents of public harassment that they did not provoke, they were likely to reverse the imputation of deviance:

Basilisk: This guy from the radio station interviewed us [a group of gutter punks] Saturday and he said, "How do you all feel that—a lot of tourists were saying that we were harassing them—and how do you feel about that?" . . . I started thinking, they, a lot of times, they harass us. The cameras, taking pictures of us, all right, that's no big deal, but it's still annoying, because they want to take a picture but they don't want to help you out. They take a pic-ture, then you go up and ask for change and they go, "No! Omigod!" And they run off. . . . I think they do harass us the same, and I don't go up to people and just start stuff. But if they do start, I'm not going to back down.

Punks thus discursively reverse the typical view of social deviance: it is not they who harass others, but others who are themselves deviant in harassing them through the exclusionary, exploitative, and evaluative practices of public harassment.

Deviance and Discrimination: Conclusion

The public harassment directed at punks serves as a form of informal social control. Whereas punks may adopt the subcultural style for self-expression, the popular misconception that punks are delinquent, deviant, or otherwise dangerous leads to an inordinate amount of public harassment. Using humor and irony, punks turn the tables on harassers, and discursively reverse the process of deviant labeling. In keeping with the reflexivity of the subculture, punks mirror social rejection and refuse, even when confronted and affronted, to accept the attribution of deviance offered by harassers. Punks' responses to public harassment return a critical perspective to the consequences of such labeling. Their challenges to such labels are more in keeping with Becker's (1963) original formulation of deviance as the outcome of a political conflict between groups with power differentials. In constructing challenges to harassment, punks not only highlight the social construction of these attributions of deviance, but question who it is, the "deviant" punk or the "normal" harasser, who is most flagrantly violating social norms governing public presence.

Beyond serving as a form of deviant labeling, public harassment is a form of discrimination, whether it is directed at gays and lesbians, at people of color, at persons with disabilities, or at members of youth subcultures. Punks argued that harassers' repeated treatment of them in demeaning ways dehumanized them:

Stone: I'm a human being. Don't treat me like shit. Don't ignore me. That's all I want. I want the same respect that you want from everybody else, because I have that right. I have the right to be here, and as for being out here and getting fucked with all the time, fuck it. If I could get a, people are always telling me, "Get a job." Give me a fucking job and I'll take it. I'll take the goddamn job. I'm not going to turn it down. People think that we came out here just because, oh hell, it's easier. Fuck you. It's not fucking easier. I'd like to see them try it. They wouldn't survive. They would not survive.

When women and black men are harassed, they are denied the rights and privileges accorded to white men, and when punks are harassed, their right to public presence is likewise challenged. Although many such forms of discrimination are illegal when directed at disempowered groups such as women, persons with disabilities, members of ethnic, religious, and racial minorities, and, increasingly, gays and lesbians, punks enjoy no such protection under the law.

When I present this research, it is often pointed out to me that punks are somewhat different from these other targets of harassment. Unlike other groups that experience such discrimination, punks have consciously created their modes of self-presentation. The means by which to modify their modes of self-presentation are not only readily available, but greatly encouraged. Punks are well aware that their style gives rise to such negative responses, and for some punks, receiving such responses may be enjoyable. However, none of the punks I interviewed reported that they constructed their style primarily in order to receive such abuses. Instead, they maintained that their style is an expression of their dissatisfaction with the political, vocational, and sartorial norms of mainstream society. As style is an aspect of their political ideology, punks argued that it is their right to express themselves through unconventional dress.

Does the fact that punks create their self-presentation, and even the interpretation of this presentation as deviant, excuse harassment? Should punks cease "whining" and adopt a more mainstream style if they dislike the harassment they experience? If so, does this not mean that blacks should attempt to be more "white," or that gays and lesbians should always pass as straight when in public? Not so, as punks would argue; it should be everyone's right, whether "different" by choice or by birth, to enjoy their full civil rights in a public environment that is free of discrimination and harassment.

Seven

"I Bet a Steel-Capped Boot Could Shut You Up"

Resistance to Public Sexual Harassment

Justine and I sit on the concrete blocks bordering the vacant lot next to the McDonald's at the corner of Ste.-Catherine and St.-Laurent streets in downtown Montreal. Despite the humid heat of the July afternoon, Justine is dressed head-to-toe in black leather: tall Doc Marten boots, a miniskirt, a bustier, a motorcycle jacket, topped by a black leather fisherman's cap on her lavender-blue hair. For the past twenty minutes or so, I have watched her wheedling pocket change out of passers-by with a string of fast-paced banter. Now, however, she is sharing her block with a man, a well-dressed individual in his mid-thirties. He is speaking to her in a low voice, in English, apparently oblivious to the fact that she doesn't understand a word he says.

She turns to me and requests: *"Demandes-lui ce qu'il veut"* (Ask him what he wants). He replies that he'll give her fifty dollars if she'll "go" with him. *"Dis-lui que je vend pas mon corps"* (Tell him I don't sell my body). "She's not a prostitute," I tell him, "she's panhandling. She's not going anywhere with you." He remains seated, mumbling repeated requests. I hesitate to interfere any further. Justine continues to sit next to him.

Just then, Johnny shows up. Johnny's about six feet tall, but seems bigger due to the foot-long mohawk upright on his head. He asks me what's going on, so I tell him. He approaches the man. "All she wants is your spare change." He looks at the man, who has stood up and is beginning to move away. By now, the man has disappeared around the corner. Johnny and his friend Greg run after him.

"Qu'est-ce qu'ils vont faire?" (What are they going to do?) asks Justine. *"J'sais pas"* (I'm not sure), I reply. Fifteen minutes later, Johnny and Greg reappear,

without the stranger, but with fast food bags full of burgers and fries. "That's the guy that was harassing Rosie yesterday," Johnny tells me. "We explained to him that what he was doing was fucking stupid. He said he was an Iranian terrorist," Johnny laughs, "but he ended up not being so tough." Justine seems neither grateful nor perturbed. We eat our lunches.

When punks of all stripes experience and resist public harassment, they encounter and deflect attributions of deviance. These types of harassment are common, shared experiences among punks, events that complicate both males' and females' participation in the subculture. Punks' resistant responses to harassment, their use of rebuttals and turnabouts, fit into the constellation of general punk resistance. In denying these attributions of deviance and in decrying this discrimination, punk girls employ the reflexivity or social commentary of the subculture to resist mainstream social pressure. In this, they construct resistance in much the same way as their male peers.

Such forms of punk resistance are usually attributed to males in the punk scene. This led one researcher, Stephen Baron (1989a, 1989b) to argue that female punks are "less resistant" than their male counterparts. However, his description of resistance ignores forms of oppression that affect only punk girls, and thus elides forms of resistance that are particular to them. For, in addition to encountering and resisting the public harassment that both male and female punks experience, punk girls encounter gender-specific discrimination: public sexual harassment. In these instances, they experience a form of oppression with which male punks do not have to contend, and construct forms of resistance that are unique to their gender.

Women and girls experience sexual harassment in a wide variety of settings. In the past three decades, as women's roles have expanded and brought us further into the public realm, we have increasingly encountered sexual threats in both traditionally public and semipublic areas. In the past two decades, feminist scholars and lawyers have created increasingly detailed analyses of, and strategies to combat, sexual harassment in workplaces, in public housing, and on campuses. Yet, despite the attention that sexual harassment in such semipublic settings has garnered, other forms of harassment, as well as strategies of resistance to that harassment, remain invisible in public discourse. Women in public areas are especially subject to "nondiscriminatory" and largely unexplored forms of sexual harassment. These forms of harassment are rarely documented. In this chapter, I refer to such forms of harassment as "public sexual harassment," and explore how punk girls experience and resist this form of sexual harassment.

In the previous chapter, I examined the type of public harassment punks encounter and argued that such forms of harassment serve as a mechanism of informal social control of perceived punk "deviance." I argued that punk girls discursively reverse such imputations of deviance by pointing out that such harassment in itself contravenes social norms. In chapter 4, I described the types of sexual harassment punk girls experience from male punks, and, when discussing male punks' protectiveness, alluded to the type of sexual harassment they experience from nonpunks. In this chapter, I focus more specifically on the public sexual harassment to which punk girls are subjected by strangers, again in order to detail their strategies of resistance. I proceed by first discussing definitions of sexual harassment and then briefly sketch legal provisions prohibiting sexual harassment as sex discrimination in both Canada and the United States. Following this, I propose a definition of "public sexual harassment" and present informal strategies used to combat sexual harassment. Finally, I explore punk girls' experiences of, and strategies of resistance to, public sexual harassment. I argue that in many cases punk girls' strategies of resistance to public sexual harassment demonstrate the variety and effectiveness of these in deflecting the sexual threats that they encounter. Thus, these girls' accounts offer useful (albeit occasionally extreme) cases that can be used by other women in our struggles against the same threatening and harassing behaviors.

Defining Sexual Harassment

Feminist analyses of, and strategies to combat, sexual harassment originated in studies of women's workplace experiences, which led to the definition of sexual harassment primarily as an interaction within a semipublic setting and involving formal power relationships. This led the creation of legal definitions that treat sexual harassment as a form of gender discrimination, rather than as sexual violence. In one of the earliest scholarly explorations of sexual harassment, Catharine MacKinnon (1979) defined this phenomenon, broadly, as "the unwanted imposition of sexual requirements in the context of a relationship of unequal power" (1), but amended this definition to refer specifically to workplace harassment: "Sexual harassment may occur as a single encounter or as a series of incidents *at work*. It may place a sexual condition upon employment opportunities at a clearly defined threshold, such as hiring, retention, or advancement; or it may occur as a pervasive or continuing condition of the work environment" (2; emphasis added). The Working Women United Institute, who MacKinnon credits with first using the term "sexual harassment" to describe this phenomenon, offered the following as examples of harassment: "verbal sexual suggestions and jokes, constant leering or ogling, brushing against your body 'accidentally,' a friendly pat, squeeze, pinch or arm against you, catching you alone for a quick kiss, the indecent propositions *backed by the threat of losing your job*" (quoted in MacKinnon:2; emphasis added). Such definitions constructed a view of sexual harassment that was restricted to a set of very specific interactions involving formal power relationships.

Within the context of the workplace, housing, and campus, discriminatory sexual harassment is divided into two categories: quid pro quo sexual harassment and sexual harassment as a condition of work, also known as "hostile environment" harassment. Quid pro quo ("this for that") sexual harassment is a "more or less explicit exchange: the woman must comply sexually or give up an employment benefit" (MacKinnon:32). This type of harassment includes sexual bribery, with rewards promised for the delivery of sexual favors, and sexual coercion, with threats or sanctions used to extort sexual favors. Hostile environment harassment does not include such explicit exchange. Rather, it describes sexual harassment that is prevalent throughout the workplace, such as lewd jokes, comments, and posting pornographic pinups. Such harassment is more diffuse and creates a "poison" atmosphere that interferes with women's ability to work.

In the decade following the identification of sexual harassment as a workplace phenomenon, this primary definition of sexual harassment was adapted to settings with similar characteristics, such as public housing and both high school and college campuses.[1] These permutations of workplace definitions of sexual harassment share the notion that sexual harassment is a phenomenon that takes place within the confines of a specific semipublic setting (work, housing, or school); involves formal power relationships (such as between superiors and subordinates); is often repeatedly targeted at the same victim, and has deleterious effects on women and girls in their roles as workers, as residents, or as students. Sexual harassment in these settings therefore is primarily identified and treated as a form of gender discrimination.

In both Canada and the United States, various levels of government create and enforce formal provisions to combat sexual harassment, including legislation and campus, housing, and workplace regulations. In the United States, legislation against sexual harassment as a form of sex discrimination in the workplace includes Title VII of the Civil Rights Act of 1964 at the federal level, and Fair Employment Practices statutes at the state level. Title IX (added in 1972) covers such discrimination in education. Title VIII, the federal Fair Housing Act, prohibits sex discrimination and sexual harassment in housing. In Canada, provincial and federal human rights statutes and the Canada Labor Code prohibit sexual harassment (Aggarwal 1992). These statutes extend only to harassment within the purview of the workplace. In the United States, a number of civil tort laws, such as those pertaining to intentional infliction of emotional distress and to defamation, can and have been used to fight sexual harassment in the workplace, in housing, and on campus. As a result of this narrow definition of sexual harassment, it is assumed to occur only within formal power relations and only in such semipublic settings. Thus, manuals detailing strategies to combat sexual harassment focus primarily on discriminatory harassment in the workplace and analogous settings (see, for example, Blackhouse and Cohen 1981; Bravo and Cassedy 1992; Farley 1978; Gutek 1985; McCann and McGinn 1992; Wagner 1992). Both analyses of and strategies to combat sexual harassment neglect other settings in which harassment occurs.

Public Sexual Harassment

Until the massive influx of women into the labor force in the twentieth century, the now semipublic areas of campuses and workplaces remained explicitly male terrain. Additionally, semipublic and private recreational areas such as clubs and bars enforced regulations designed specifically to exclude women. Although these overt forms of gender discrimination have been largely overturned, public space retains a masculine imprint. Today, public areas such as streets and parks remain male territory. Most of these areas are "governed" by males, as males make more frequent and freer use of public areas (Kissling and Kramarae 1991). Writing in the *New York Times*, journalist Katha Pollitt describes women's and men's differential uses of public space: "On the subways, men sit with their knees apart, claiming public space; women sit with their knees pressed together, ceding it. And there's the male sense of entitlement—on the street, men march boldly down the middle of the sidewalk, swinging their arms and looking ahead, swerving neither to left nor right for oncoming pedestrians. Women scurry along, clutching their shoulder bags, head down, weaving a zigzag path through the crowd while murmuring 'Excuse me'" (1985:C2). Regulations excluding women from public and semipublic areas may have been deemed unconstitutional, women may be increasingly present in formerly male-dominated occupations, but normative standards still exclude women from full public participation. Thus, writing in *Mademoiselle*, a women's magazine, Gwenda Blair colorfully concludes: "Women might be more welcome these days in offices or boardrooms or even on assembly lines, but down in the streets, they weren't being taken the least bit seriously; there, it was still men who were in charge of the show. It was their turf, the place where they belonged. Perhaps they hadn't actually pissed at all the crosswalks like territorial tomcats, but then they didn't have to. After all, who was going to challenge their domain?" (1984:184). The masculinity of the streets extends into the iconography of popular music videos, where, as Lisa Lewis (1990) notes, the street is depicted as the site of male adolescent leisure, camaraderie, and sexual adventure. Streets thus remain coded as sites of masculine presence and feminine absence.

In many ways, women's exclusion from public areas, and especially from streets, is encoded in normative standards of "safety." In the name of safety, women are instructed to take precautionary measures when venturing into public areas, measures from which men are mostly exempt. These measures also misrepresent the true magnitude and nature of violence against women: that 80 percent of crimes against women take place in the home. Nonetheless, women are taught that to dress "provocatively" or to have an "unusual" mode of self-presentation (be it being disabled or of color or sporting an unusual hairstyle) almost inevitably leads to negative attention and harassment. Women are often advised not to venture into public areas at night, or to do so only when accompanied by able guardians. It is the often unquestioned assumptions that men control interaction within these public areas and that women must conform to this social order that dictate these constraints.[2] In this sense, implicit sexual threats have replaced explicit regulations in order to exclude women from public life.

Public sexual harassment is a significant factor in the delineation of public space as male territory. This is the type of sexual harassment most commonly experienced by women (Langelan 1993) yet, paradoxically, it is that which is the least recognized in academic and feminist literature and least countered in law and public discourse. Behavior that is legally actionable or criminal in a workplace, housing, or campus setting remains largely ignored or tacitly approved in the streets. Like other forms of sexual harassment, public sexual harassment will remain unrecognized until labeled as such; until then, it will not be acknowledged as a social problem.[3] I refer to this behavior as "public sexual harassment." I label it "public" in order to differentiate it from the type of discriminatory harassment that occurs in semipublic areas, such as workplaces, homes, and schools. This label explicitly refers to a variety of public settings, including streets, parks, taxis, subways, and bus stops. I refer to it as "sexual harassment" in order to differentiate it from harassment based on other characteristics, such as age, ability, or ethnicity (or in the case of punks, self-presentation), and also to align it with more recognized forms of sexual harassment. Naming these behaviors "sexual harassment" allows us to recognize their importance and common practice. This in turn allows us to consider them to be "limiting, oppressive, and ethically wrong *political* behaviors because they attempt to disempower us" (Wise and Stanley 1987:114; emphasis in original). Thus, in describing these behaviors as "public sexual harassment," I argue that they fit into already-established categories of sexual harassment.

Public sexual harassment consists mainly of nondiscriminatory harassment akin to the hostile environment harassment that occurs in formal settings. Because the harasser and target are not in a recognized power relationship, there is little incidence of quid pro quo harassment.[4] Unlike discriminatory harassment, public sexual harassment is occasional, often does not involve multiple repetitions from the harasser to the same victim, does not involve formal power relationships, and ostensibly does not deprive the target of any benefits. As do other forms, public sexual harassment consists of "deliberate or repeated unsolicited verbal comments, gestures, or physical contact of a sexual nature which are unwelcome" (U.S. House of Representatives 1980:8). Anthropologist Michaela di Leonardo describes such harassment incidents as "when one or more strange men accost one or more women whom they perceive as heterosexual in a public place which is not the woman's/women's worksite. Through looks, words, or gestures, the man asserts his right to intrude on the woman's attention, defining her as a sexual object, and forcing her to interact with him" (1981:51–52). In her recent book on public harassment, Carol Gardner (1995) describes a variety of tactics used by harassers, including staring, touching, commenting, and following. Whatever the technique employed, public sexual harassment consists of an unsolicited, sexualized intrusion upon a woman's private space within a public setting.

There is a wide degree of variation in the forms of public sexual harassment. Harassing behaviors can range from wolf whistles to explicit sexual threats. Consequently, there is a great deal of difference in women's (and men's) identification of behaviors as sexual harassment (Gratz 1995) and thus, many options in responding to this harassment. Some women may perceive the more mild forms of "street remarks" and wolf whistling to be complimentary (Blakely 1982; Kissling 1991), while the more threatening and vulgar forms can be quite menacing. Often, however, a woman's failure to respond to a "complimentary" street remark, or her negative response, results in the revelation of a more menacing tone and intent (Gardner 1995). Thus, the difference between "street compliments" and incidents of public sexual harassment may be not a matter of kind, but rather a matter of degree.

Although we have little statistical data on the frequency or severity of such incidents, this type of harassment is perhaps the most commonly experienced form of sexual harassment. Di Leonardo (1981) argues that both the rate and incidence of public sexual harassment are increasing. The augmented rate is due to women's increased presence in the public arena as workers and as participants in public leisure activities. In addition, the ongoing growth of urbanization leads to a concomitant increase in the incidence of street harassment, as the majority of this harassment occurs between strangers in urban areas. Thus, as social and economic changes affect both urbanization and women's presence in public areas, they also indirectly affect the rate and incidence of sexual harassment in these areas. Despite such increases, there remains very little research on strategies designed specifically to combat this form of sexual harassment. Observational and interview studies attest to its existence, but few examine the strategies women employ in response.[5]

Even though it is often labeled "nondiscriminatory," the effects of public sexual harassment can be quite serious. The implicit sexual threat of public sexual harassment operates on several levels. First, it consists of an intrusion upon women's personal privacy. Second, it can be (sometimes correctly) perceived as presenting a threat of further sexual assault and rape; such incidents have been documented as part of rapists' repertoire of tactics to identify potential victims (Bowman 1993; di Leonardo 1981; Kissling and Kramarae 1991). Public sexual harassment is thus a form of "sexual terrorism" that functions as one aspect of the social control of women (Martin 1989). Such harassment can thus be considered the most widespread and under-reported form of sexual assault. Public sexual harassment, and the threat of harassment and further victimization, serve to severely limit women's participation in the public arena. Women who experience or who fear harassment or its implicit threat of rape may subsequently restrict their passage through public spaces, or take precautions to avoid certain areas. Thus, such harassment is an infringement of women's civil liberties, as strategies to avoid harassment preclude women's use and enjoyment of public areas. Third, the principal effect of public sexual harassment is to reinforce a form of covert gender discrimination. In the name of safety, sexual harassment and assault restrict women's right to full participation in the public domain. Spatial segregation, such as the maintenance of separate spheres in men's and women's lives, is an important mechanism in the maintenance of gender segregation, and hence, of unequal power relations (Spain 1992). Thus, public sexual harassment relies upon and reifies *informal* power distinctions between women and men. Clearly, then, although labeled "nondiscriminatory," this form of sexual harassment contributes to sex discrimination at a broad societal level.

Punk, Girls, and Public Sexual Harassment

The street and other public urban areas often serve as the primary location of social interaction in the punk subculture. However, because streets are male terrain, public areas contain dangers for punk girls, in the forms of sexual assault and sexual harassment, that are largely absent from the boys' daily concerns. As a result, punk girls may be subject to more public sexual harassment than are most girls. In addition, given the nature of their street-based lifestyle, they may have fewer options to retreat or escape from such harassment. Finally, given the often adversarial relationship between police and punks, punk girls may have fewer sources of protection from such harassment and threats.

In addition to their presence on the street, punk girls' experiences of harassment are exacerbated by their mode of dress.[6] Versions of female punk style that some of these girls adopted contain elements of bondage or fetishized sexual wear. Since the British punks of the 1970s, girls have appropriated bondage gear, adopting and displaying fetishized objects such as bondage collars and handcuffs in order to parody or subvert their original meanings. Most punks of both genders often wear the black leather and studs appropriated from bondage wear as jackets, boots, belts, and jewelry. In addition to this, female punks also occasionally wear short leather skirts and bustiers, as well as traditionally sexualized apparel such as (torn) fishnet stockings and lace clothing, which are dominant cultural markers of availability in women. Punk girls wear items of apparel that, in the context of the subculture, carry meanings opposed to those of the mainstream culture. In constructing stylistic parodies of traditional female sexuality, punk girls express their dissatisfaction with current norms of femininity. This choice of apparel is constructed as a subversive act. As Anna said of wearing a revealing top: "My breasts are my breasts, get over it."

However, the notion that punk girls wear sexually provocative clothing for the purposes of self-expression, parody, mockery, or subversion of conventional norms is a point that is often lost on the general public, as Wanda noted:

> Sometimes people have a stereotype that if you're a female and all different that you're just a slut or something. I think that's a stereotype.

Rosie added:

> You walk down the street and guys, just because you're wearing leather and lace because you're a punk, they'll ask you to do prostitution and stuff like that. I guess a lot of people have images of what a punk woman is supposed to be, how she's supposed to be slutty and she's supposed to be free and all that stuff in that way, because she's anarchy. But it's not true. It's just people misunderstand it.

Punk girls may wear conventionally sexualized apparel, but they invest these items with very different meanings. As Hallie noted:

> I guess you look exotic . . . bondage gear and stuff like that. I guess it turns some guys on, I don't know. For me, bondage gear is bondage gear.

In the absence of access to such subcultural meanings, nonpunks usually

_____ *Illustration 14* _____
Punk girls just wanna have fun—in black leather bondage collars.
(Photo: D. K. Rabel)

interpret such objects in their original, rather than subcultural, context. By interpreting such parodies as invitations to sexual solicitation, the harassers fail to comprehend the parodic, extremist elements of punk style, but instead, accept them at face value. Without understanding the punk parody, harassers assume that punk girls are intending to project the original meaning, as one harasser explicitly revealed:

> Carnie: My first five minutes [in this city], I had a [leather bondage] collar on, one with rings. And [this guy] grabbed me by, and he's like, "Do you mind if I follow you for a while?" And I was like, "Yeah," and I pushed him off me. And he's like, "Yeah, I watched this porno this other night and this guy, this lady was wearing one of those and she was into giving head and da da da." And I was just like, "Whatever."

Clearly, this harasser conflated Carnie's punk apparel with similar gear he had seen in a film. What renders this interaction more complex, however, is that it is doubtful that he drew other parallels between the two women, as Carnie's self-presentation as a crusty punk would negate any of the sexually provocative signals of her collar. Nonetheless, this harasser at some level interpreted Carnie's apparel as a direct sexual solicitation.

Punk girls' youth, their lower social status, their street-based lifestyle, their mode of dress, and their "deviant" status all contribute to harassers' selection of punk girls as targets for the intimidation of harassment. It is hardly surprising that punk girls report a great deal of public sexual harassment. Justine claimed that, in her life on the streets,

> I'm *always* being harassed by men . . . Even in the gay village. I'm in the gay village and I've got guys propositioning me, who harass me . . . It's everywhere. I went to [a nice part of town] yesterday, and some guy wanted to attack me. Men are really annoying.

In many cases, punk girls report being harassed by members of other street populations—as Lola put it, "bums and stuff like that and workmen." Andie, a fourteen-year-old gutter punk, stated that:

> The only problem [with being a punk] is the drunks in the Square. They are like, "Oh baby, come over here." And they whistle at people. Like, "Ooh, I'd like to get you into bed."

Tori remarked that she was harassed

> Mostly by crackheads. Just because, they just, a punk white girl, they just want a punk white girl.

Alexea, an eighteen-year-old gutter punk, interpreted such harassment as a fundamental clash of subcultural values. When asked whether she experienced harassment, she replied,

> Mostly by gangstas and homies and shit. They just fucking think they can come up and take whatever they want because they treat their "bitches" different. I don't think so.[7]

Besides being harassed by members of other street populations, punk girls are targeted by more mainstream males. The majority of instances of harassment I observed and that punk girls reported to me involved mainstream strangers, usually tourists,

> Basilisk: I'll be walking down the street, minding my own business and these drunk asshole tourists start fucking yelling at me and shit . . . about my hair, about, "Ooh baby, blah blah blah blah blah." Or about my tits or something.

Or young men:

> Lola: I was walking down the street . . . I was yawning or something and I was walking by and [my friend] Agatha noticed, god, this yuppie guy just

stared at my breasts and just followed them all the way around. And he's like, "Ooh!" I get all this shit.

Thus, punk girls are exposed to sexual threats not only from male punks and from members of other "deviant" street populations, but from members of the mainstream general public as well.

These girls reported that public sexual harassment is commonplace. Of the forty girls I interviewed, twenty reported being sexually harassed frequently; while only four reported never being sexually harassed, with two of these adding that it happened frequently to their friends. I suspect that most punk girls do experience this harassment, but, as in the general population, there is variation in girls' definitions of sexual harassment. As do nonpunk women, some girls may view verbal harassment as complimentary or nonthreatening:

> Allie: I consider sexual harassment to be, has to be physical. People say anything they want to me. They touch me, they're going to get touched back. I just don't feel a lot of harassment at all. Well, people can talk.

Girls and women such as Allie may not view such interactions as problematic. Most girls who did report experiencing public sexual harassment and who did consider this to be an important problem in their daily lives defined sexual harassment as verbal rather than physical. These girls indicated that it was such a frequent event that they usually answered my questions about sexual harassment by nodding vigorously or shrugging matter-of-factly as they said "yeah." Some reported that they were so often subjected to such encounters that they had no specific incidents to relate, as none stood out as particularly exceptional.

Initially to my astonishment, many of these girls reported being "mistaken" for prostitutes by male strangers:

> Justine: [Men say things] like, "Do you want to make some quick cash?"

> Hallie: I get asked if I want to sell my body a lot, though. . . . They're just like that. I haven't had to resort to that yet. I don't think I ever will.

Sue reported that even police officers are not above conflating punk with prostitution:

> I had a cop trying to tell me I was a prostitute in front of a club because I was wearing fishnets and had my hair green.

Again, it is odd that this officer conflated Sue's punk apparel with that of a prostitute; after all, not many sex workers would sport green hair in constructing a sexually provocative appearance.

Despite the popular assumption that punk girls, especially those who live in the streets, engage in prostitution, only one of the forty girls I interviewed confessed to having been a prostitute. Opportunities to engage in prostitution were quite common, especially for street punks:

> Justine: There's lots of recruiting going on around here. Lots and lots around here. There was one guy who was after me for three months. Him too, I thought he was one of my friends. But he was a guy who worked for the bikers. He started telling me, "Get yourself some sexy clothes and I'll make you some money." I caught on right away and I went to see his best friend and I said, "Hey. Tell me what's going on." He said, "Spider talked to me about it. He wants you to work for him." I don't think so. Now he's in jail for a year.

Two other girls worked as exotic dancers, and one had just left a job because of the expectation she would prostitute herself:

> Candace: I just switched bars, because the place where I was working was really gypping me on money. I'd go and I'd do three private dances and the bartender got forty [dollars] out of that and I got five out of each. And I was like, "No way." And basically it was because it was a real small seedy bar and most of the girls would prostitute themselves whereas I wouldn't. And [the bartender] figured, "Well, she's going to go back there and make a hundred and fifty dollars," whereas I was going back there and making nothing but the five dollars she gave me. That's what did it.

Punk girls denounce the assumption that they engage in prostitution, and many dislike girls who engage in sexual activity for money:

> Carnie: [Rona's] the type of women that don't need to be around. The women that go out on Bourbon [Street, New Orleans] and show their tits for a dollar to make money to do what they gotta do. I'd rather sit on the sidewalk and ask every person who walks by for a quarter than go out and show any part . . .

Even those girls who live on the streets refuse to engage in selling sex, relying instead on panhandling, dumpster diving, soup kitchens, and sharing to acquire food and money.

Nevertheless, due to their presence in the street and their self-presentation, punk girls are often accused of prostitution or solicited. It should be noted that such assumptions of solicitation are hardly particular to punk girls. In her research on gender interaction in public settings, Carol Gardner likewise notes that women's presence in public areas often leads to their misidentification as sex workers, and thus, as sexually accessible (1995:125). Thus, although punk girls may attract some of this attention through their sartorial style, the prevalence of this form of sexual harassment among non-punks lends it other interpretations. In soliciting punk girls, these harassers are reinforcing the notion that a woman on the street is necessarily a streetwalker.

Strategies of Resistance to Public Sexual Harassment

The legal provisions that apply to workplace, housing, and campus sexual harassment have little applicability in cases of public sexual harassment. However, women have turned to a number of alternate legal remedies against such harassment. In cases where the harassment involves physical contact, women may have recourse to criminal charges of sexual assault, usually by resorting to misdemeanor statutes concerning sexual battery. Some women have also turned to existing laws that pertain to obscene and abusive language; many states and communities have statutes that forbid, in some cases, the use of "fighting words" or of lewd and obscene gestures and language in public places (Bowman 1993). However, such statutes were not originally constructed to address women's concerns, and often, women who have recourse to such laws find it difficult to demonstrate that such ubiquitous incidents of harassment should be addressed by the courts. Women have also sought to prosecute harassers under a variety of civil laws such as torts of assault, infliction of emotional distress, and invasion of privacy (Bowman 1993). Resorting to such formal approaches, however, involves a variety of complications. In the case of public sexual harassment, identifying or naming the perpetrator may be problematic, as would be obtaining proof and finding corroborating witnesses. In addition, proving intent, finding and paying for legal representation, and having the legal system realize the severity of the incident provide further blocks to prosecution (Langelan 1993). Finally, the legal definition of *fighting words,* as well as legal definitions of sexual harassment in some jurisdictions, are judged according to a "reasonable man" standard. These statutes are therefore difficult to apply to public sexual harassment because much of the content of harassing gestures and language are not judged to be offensive by men.

As legal remedies fail us, women continue to draw on informal remedies or strategies of resistance to fight harassment. Feminists devise educational strategies such as speak-outs, Take Back the Night events, and workshops in order to raise public awareness concerning the prevalence and severity of public sexual harassment. Recently, feminists have begun to examine direct-address, informal defensive strategies such as reporting on-the-job harassers (such as construction workers) to their supervisors. In *Back Off!,* a defense manual that addresses a variety of forms of sexual harassment, former Washington, D.C., rape crisis center director Martha Langelan (1993) details strategies of single-person and group confrontations of harassers as tools that all women can use in these situations. Such informal strategies continue to prove less expensive, more effective in stopping harassment, and more empowering for women and girls.

For many women, such common and repeated experiences of harassment would lead to increased fear and to such measures as avoidance of certain areas (Gardner 1995). Punk girls did not report feeling afraid or employing any such measures. However, this is not to say that such instances of harassment had no effect. Experiences of harassment and the threat of sexual abuse may lead some punk girls to an increased dependency on punk males (see chapter 4). Punk girls become habituated to public sexual harassment and devise a variety of strategies that they use when encountering it. I characterize these as "strategies of resistance," where resistance is conceptualized as action (thoughts, words, or deeds) intended to counter a recognized form of oppression. With punk girls' chronicles of sexual harassment as subjective accounts of oppression, and of their desire to counter this, I argue that the strategies I present below, whether effective or not, are instances of their resistance to the type of harassment they experience. While none of these strategies is completely unproblematic, as I discuss below, some may be more effective in deterring further harassment than are others.

"Not Many Jocks Try to Pick Up on Me Anymore": Avoidance

Avoidance, one of the most commonly used tactics women and girls use to counter harassment, is more deterrent than reactive. Women and girls are routinely taught to avoid areas where harassment is likely (i.e., construction sites) or to venture about accompanied by such harassment deterrents as friends, husbands, or babies (Gardner 1995). To this, punk girls add another tactic. Some girls reported that adopting a punk appearance, although it can serve to attract the attention of most people, could also deflect that of others. Sue, with her green mohawk, said, "When I was a little pixie model, people didn't look at me, they were staring at my ass." When asked what she liked about being a punk, she stated that since she became a punk, "Not many jocks try to pick up on me anymore . . . I've managed to get [rid of] the scum that I've tried to eliminate by [dressing like this]. In constructing an appearance that satisfies her aesthetic sense, but which she realizes runs counter to mainstream notions of beauty, Sue feels she has managed to avoid or deflect some sexual attention, despite the amount of public harassment which she still experiences. Likewise, Connie, who has self-executed facial scarification, noted a dramatic decrease in harassment:

I used to [get sexually harassed a lot] when I first started living on the streets.

But now I have scars on my face, so they don't like that. [Sarcastically:] I guess I used to be cuter or something.

This deflection was one of punk's major attractions to Lydia:

> I think a lot of it was because I really hated—I was raped by a businessman in L.A. that time—and I hated the fact that, with my long hair, these guys were always trying to hit on me. And this way I found that I could control who was going to hit on me. It was going to be people I wanted. . . . So I just found it was a way of cutting out all the fucking businessmen and the straight people I really didn't want to deal with. . . . I like that I could exclude a lot of idiots, as far as I was concerned, out of my life. It did empower me because, yeah, people were afraid of me, and I'm sorry to say it, I sort of, yeah, I had some sort of vicious power, love of this, that I could make them afraid. It was just such a joke. Afraid of me. I've never hit anyone in my life. It was just like, all I had to do is just wear my hair really fucked up.

In constructing their punk styles, these girls found that they thereby had the power to deflect unwanted sexual attentions.

Although facial scarification, odd hairstyles, punk clothes, and head shaving may not be appealing alternatives to more mainstream women, these girls' tactics are analogous to those employed by women who feel they must dress plainly in order not to receive any undue attention when in public.[8] However, these girls constructed such appearances from their own aesthetic sense, rather than with the sole intent to deflect harassment. Nevertheless, although they did not deliberately seek to avoid such harassment, their experiences attest to the efficacy of such a strategy.

Police and Punk Protection: Ignoring the Harassment

Other tactics women and girls use to counter harassment are more reactive. The most common response to public sexual harassment is for the target to ignore, or to pretend to ignore, the offending behavior (Bowman 1993; Langelan 1993). There are many reasons why a woman would choose ignore harassing behavior: she may interpret the harassment as complimentary (and thus not define it as unwanted behavior—de facto, not as harassment); she may fear escalated retaliation to her responses; she may feel powerless; she may be unwilling to overstep cultural taboos on females' expression in public areas, or she may simply be unwilling to dignify such behavior with a response. Such unresponsiveness does little to deter further harassment. Furthermore, this option merely inculcates the passivity that is an aspect of feminine socialization. As well, given that public sexual harassment may be a tactic occasionally employed by criminals as a technique to select potential targets of sexual assault, letting it pass may prove to be not only an unproductive tactic, but a dangerous one as well.

Ignoring harassment is the most common response to public sexual harassment among women in general, and ignoring the incident is the tactic punks use most frequently in response to general harassment. Contrary to popular conceptions of punks as aggressive and confrontational, some girls did report resorting to this option when harassed. Many respond to the harasser by saying "whatever," thus passing off the incident without confrontation.

In some of these cases, others, such as friends or police officers, would intervene. The incident involving Justine, which I described above, is one such instance. In another instance during my field research, a number of male punks badly beat a homeless youth who had allegedly attempted to molest girls who were too inebriated to fend him off (see chapter 6). Girls sometimes actively seek out the assistance of male punks, who have somewhat of a tough reputation:

> Tori: Sometimes if I feel like, if it can't be possible, if [some guy]'s pushing himself too far on me and I can't advance, if I can't get out of it, then all's I've got to do is go up to a punk boy and just walk with him and then everybody just clears out. Because a lot of people think, even the government thinks that anarchists, say the punks, are this big militia [anti] government movement.

In requesting such intervention, girls let the harassment pass by not directly confronting the harasser, and allow male punks to "rescue" them. While this strategy may be effective in stopping harassment, it also perpetuates girls' subordinate position within the punk subculture.

When punk friends are unavailable, others may intervene. Sue reported a successful defense on her behalf on the part of a police officer: "I got stuck in Panama City over spring break. I got harassed so much that this cop finally gave this guy a seventy-dollar ticket for screaming stuff at me about my sexuality and cussing me out and stuff." Strangely enough, this incident was reported by the same young woman who had been accused of prostitution by another police officer.

In these cases, by allowing or requesting men to defend them, these girls avoided resorting to actions that would run counter to female socialization. As a result, men—punks and police—took it upon themselves to protect the girls from sexual predators—other men. As "chivalrous" as this may seem, such a response merely reinforces females' dependency upon males, either punks or other bystanders. Furthermore, when the harassment occurs without others to assist, these girls may find themselves without any recourse at all. Although letting the harassment pass may allow girls and women to preserve their dignity or maintain their femininity, it is ultimately an accommodation to the harasser, as it does little to respond to, halt, or prevent the harassment.

"Do You Want Me to Knock Your Teeth In?": Confrontation

A more proactive alternative to ignoring harassment involves responding to the harasser in kind, or confronting him. Some women may find this option unacceptable, as responding to harassing behavior with any form of confrontation further contradicts women's feminine socialization. Furthermore, some fear that this may escalate the situation while also alienating possibly helpful passers-by. However, this was by far the most common strategy employed by punk girls.

Some girls who experienced sexual harassment reported using patently aggressive speech, threats, and violent acts to counter these threats. Some girls immediately resorted to confrontational tactics, usually including obscenity:

> Lola: Usually I just tell them to fuck off or something . . . I was walking down the street . . . and I'm walking past these two college guys and one of them comes up and puts his arm around me. I'm like, "Get away from me."

> Alexea: I'm just rude. I'm rude as fuck. Like I said, I stop it before it starts. If I'm up front to them from the start, they don't want to talk to me. They just talk shit and say I'm a bitch.

Justine, whose repertoire of tactics included ignoring harassers, did confront on occasion:

> I'm not the kind of girl to make trouble. I try to defend myself [verbally]. Only once did I almost get in a fight with a guy who was three times my size. I was panhandling, and the guy gives me his empty bag of chips. He gave me this look like he was pissed. I said, "Fuck you!" And he said, "Suck my dick." So I followed him, I was walking behind him wearing my boots with the big steel caps and I was stepping on his heels. So I was like, "Do you want me to knock your teeth in?" I was really aggressive that night. Strange, because that's not me. I'm really peaceable.[9]

Only one punk girl reacted to verbal harassment with physical self-defense:

> Courtney: One time, it was a—this was when I was dressing more . . . grew my hair out a bit, well, I had a flat-top—and some black guy said something to Priscilla, actually, and [I] fucking was like, "What?" And she was like, "Pardon me?" And just, a fucking street scuffle, just fucking, I was like . . . they said something to her about her being sexy . . .

These types of aggressive verbal or physical response are problematic in that they may escalate the situation, either by angering the harasser or by drawing negative attention to the harassed. For example, Connie reported that such a tactic had created difficulties for her:

> "Hey baby." It was like I had *prostitute* written on my forehead. I was in jail in Denver for that. Because this guy was just like, "Hey baby, what do you like? What do you want?" And I was like, "I'm fine motherfucker." I got all up in his face. And he thought he was treating me like I said, like I had a "prostitute" sign on my forehead. Cops went and put me in jail for a week. They said I was drunk in public. I was like, "That guy fucking started it." . . . I talked to them, I told them, I said, "That motherfucker just propositioned me and blah blah blah," and they were like, "Well, whatever."

Given the possibility of negative sanctions, responding to the harasser in such a way, whether through escalating the encounter to a brawl or getting "all up in his face," can hardly be advocated as a positive response to harassment. Nor are these confrontations the type advocated by feminist activists.

Feminist activists do, however, recommend the use of structured confrontational tactics. This type of confrontation typically involves engaging the harasser in dialogue and making him accountable for his behavior (Langelan 1993). None of the girls I interviewed appeared to be familiar with such tactics as are described in feminist literature. However, some reported resorting to a similar type of plain speech and direct address to deflect such unwanted attention:

> Lola: I'm pretty used to it, but I just either ignore it or I'll tell them, if they get too lewd or whatever, I'll put them in their place.

> Hallie: The first day I was here . . . we were at this street corner . . . and this guy came up to me and said, "Twenty-five dollars to have sex with me," or, "I'll give you twenty-five dollars to have sex with me." I'm like, "No. I'm not a prostitute." He's like, "Damn. OK, baby, fifty bucks. Fifty bucks for a blow job." I'm like, "I'm not a prostitute! I don't sell my body!" And he was like, "Really? How about if I give you fifty dollars now and I come back later?" "I'll be gone with it," I straight out told him. I was like, "I'll be gone." . . . I'm just like, I'll laugh at him for a little bit, but I'm like, "I'm sorry, but I'm not a prostitute. Keep your money." Just stuff like that.

Sue, who reported being accused of solicitation by a police officer, responded by replying to his accusations:

> No. No, sorry. I'm pretty selective about who I date in general. I am not a prostitute.

In these cases, the girls responded in ways that did not escalate the situation, yet effectively communicated that such attentions were unwanted.

"I Bet a Steel-Capped Boot Could Shut You Up": Humor

Finally, some punk girls resorted to humorous tactics, not playing along with the harasser, but rather mirroring the harasser's behavior in order to defuse it. These girls reported that such a strategy worked extremely well in deterring further harassment. In her work on women's humor, Regina Barreca argues that "a battery of humorous responses you can cultivate like a beautiful and slightly poisonous garden" (1991:98) can be the most effective tool in combating sexual harassment. This is particularly true when the retort mirrors the form of the harasser's comment. Thus, Justine, who was asked "Do you want to make some quick cash?" reported that:

> When it happens I say, "Yeah, for twenty bucks, I'll punch your face in." Or [men ask] "Do you do blow-jobs?" And I say, "The day I've got your dick in my mouth it'll be to bite it." I defend myself the best I can.

Sue also reported the effectiveness of such a humorous mirroring technique:

> The worst line I've gotten since I've been into the punk thing was, "I bet a punk rock girl can give you a rough ride." And I'm like, "I bet a steel-capped boot could shut you up."

These girls found that such humorous, sarcastic retorts were quite effective in ending harassment. In another instance linking punk appearance to sexual provocation, Arizona related:

> Guys, with my piercings, they'll ask me what it feels like, do guys like blow jobs with my piercings? And stuff like that. I don't even answer them, just like, "Whatever." [Sarcastically:] "Sure. Come here, let me show you!" That's about it. They'll just use my piercings [to get at me]. Guys are like, especially when they're drunk, they'll have the nerve to come up and ask me.

Candace, who works as an erotic dancer in order to support herself and her three-year-old daughter, tells of her sarcastic response to solicitation:

> I get sexually harassed a lot. Especially coming home after, or even walking to a bar after work, walking down [the] street, I'll still have my high heels and sometimes my fishnets on, but I'll have on, a lot of times I walk home in pants or a long dress, or walk to a bar, and guys will be like, "Hey, how much you charge?" Stuff like that, and that really bothers me. I say, "Too much for you!"

Girls who used such humorous techniques found them to be effective in ending the harassment, without escalating a potentially threatening situation. Furthermore, these humorous strategies allowed girls to take the upper hand in
the confrontation, getting the better of the harasser through mirroring or sarcastic retorts.

"Keep Your Shit in Your Pants": Conclusion

Punk girls create a broad range of strategic responses to sexual harassment As do other women, they do not limit themselves to one type of defense, but rather use the gamut of strategies situationally:

> Nikita: Different circumstances lead to different [responses]. . . . If they get
> physical, I'll do something to them. If not, usually I ignore them or whatever,
> "Keep your shit in your pants," or, "Go jack off. Get it out somehow. Don't
> come to me."

While none of these cases provides entirely effective strategies, some do
present satisfying remedies to incidents of public sexual harassment. Clearly,
not all of these strategies appeal to all women; engaging in street brawls or
dressing in a punk style will be unacceptable to many. Nevertheless, these cases
present but a sampling of the breadth of options which women may choose to
adapt or adopt.

Yet such forms of resistance to public sexual harassment remain merely
transitional strategies. Such responses are still problematic, because they occur within the context of an unequal power relationship, a discourse initiated
and controlled by male harassers, one that is unsought and unwanted by female targets. No matter how effective the tactic, strategies of resistance to
sexual harassment remain accommodative, reactionary acts that empower
women only when we are assailed. No matter how effective the response, harassers continue to target women. Ending this type of sexual harassment will
not result from adding statutes to the legal system, as Bowman (1993) is at-
tempting. Although criminalization of this behavior may lead to its increased
recognition as a social problem, creating statutes may actually accomplish little
more than increasing the power held by judicial authorities rather than protecting women.

The problem of public sexual harassment lies in the unequal distribution
of power by gender. The solution therefore lies in re-visioning cultural notions
of gender and power. In the interim prior to such a thoroughgoing cultural revolution, or perhaps even as a condition of it, individual women have been creating effective strategies to combat this harassment in everyday life. Public sexual
harassment is a common and growing social problem. Until it can be elimi-

nated, it is imperative that women recognize this behavior, name it, and share the creative and original strategies that we have used to combat it effectively.

These strategies of resistance to harassment are yet another tactic punk girls use to challenge the prevailing gender norms of late twentieth-century North American culture. In becoming punk, they counter mainstream cultural norms of propriety, but pay the price of accommodating male punks' abuses and domination. In dressing punk, they resist mainstream norms of femininity, but become targets of forms of harassment which further require their forms of resistance. In encountering and fighting sexual harassment, punk girls construct forms of resistance unique to their gender. This slice of punk experience has remained invisible to their male peers, sociologists, and the public that surrounds the subculture.

Eight

"Girls Kick Ass"

Nonacademic Conclusions

My version of events is that becoming a punk made me rebellious. My dad's version is that I had always been that way, and that becoming a punk merely released and expressed my innate rebelliousness. Not that he was terribly pleased about it, but there it was.

Mind you, he didn't tell me this until fairly late in my punk career. My relationship with my dad had always been somewhat distant. At various points in my childhood, he had worked two jobs, including the night shift at the truck factory, so he would come home in the morning, have supper while the rest of the family had breakfast, and go to bed. In the afternoons, when my brother and I came back from school, we would have to play very quietly so as not to wake him up. When he was around, he was usually occupied with trying to get my brother, who was more interested in reading, to help him fix cars, chop wood—the myriad tasks of manhood. My interests in these things were discouraged, because it wasn't my place as a girl.

The strain in our relationship only increased as we both grew older. The problems with our relationship evolved from distance to difficulty. I did not know this at the time, but when I was spending all my time in full punk drag, my dad's brothers, and one of my uncles in particular, lit into him: "How can you let your daughter walk around like that?" "She's going to turn out a junkie or a slut." "If she were my daughter, I'd beat her ass and never let her out of the house." My dad never resorted to physical violence, but he did give me a hard time. I gave him a hard time back.

Then, when I turned eighteen, something changed in our relationship. A tide had turned and our reconciliation began. On my eighteenth birthday, my dad told me this story:

"When you were three years old, I drove the family up to Manitoba to visit your uncle. We were staying in a motel, and when it came time to go, we couldn't find you. We looked and looked and when we finally found you—There was a little boy, he must have been five or six, and he had been throwing small rocks at you all day—When we found you, you were behind the motel with this little boy. You had wrestled him to the ground and you were on top of him, with a handful of gravel, hitting him in the face. I knew then that you'd never let people walk all over you. I knew then you'd be a fighter. You were only three." He told me this story like he was proud of me.

Thanks, Dad. I hope that we can make this happen for other girls too.

Girls pay a heavy price for becoming punks, for refusing to play the femininity game, for trying to change the rules. They experience public harassment from strangers and sexual harassment from men. They are sometimes expelled from school, rejected by their parents, and hassled by police. Within the subculture, they are constrained by the masculinity of punk norms and contained by the judgment and behavior of male punks. I began this work by quoting Sue, who stated:

> The punk guys will really overpower what the punk girls have to say. I think the punk girl thing is a very aggressive scene, and very assertive and aggressive girls tend to get into it. I don't know many passive, timid little girls who are going to shave their heads and look like a freak, take harassment from everybody all the time, and then fight off the guys in the scene.

Listening to her, I asked myself why such an articulate, thoughtful girl would shave off most of her hair, dye the remainder green, and glue it into a mohawk upright on her head. I wanted to know who were the "assertive and aggressive" girls she described. I wanted to find out why such girls chose to contravene conventional norms of female beauty so as to "look like a freak," when their only reward is that they must not only "take harassment from everybody all the time," but then also be forced to "fight off the guys in the [punk] scene." I asked: What attracts these girls to male-dominated youth subcultures such as punk? What are girls' roles within the subculture? What role does the subculture play in their perceptions of themselves, and in their self-esteem? How do girls reconcile a subcultural identity that is deliberately coded as "masculine" with the demands of femininity?

I discovered that girls use the punk subculture to resist the prescriptions of femininity, to carve out a space where they can define their own sense of self. I found that girls turn to punk for a variety of reasons: as a rebellion against their parents; as political rebellion; as a survival network. Within the subculture, they not only encounter a masculinist ideology, but suffer its enforcement through the expectations and behavior of their male peers. In order to retain their positions within the punk scene, girls must accommodate the harassment and abuse they receive within the subculture. As a result, they distance themselves from what might possibly be their best source of support: other girls. They pay this price so that they can continue to access the resources of punk, which allow them to shape their gendered identities by drawing on the rhetoric of punk rebellion and its support for such rebellion. They thus draw on the subculture to create feminine identities that contravene the norms of mainstream adolescent femininity. When they encounter social sanctions—harassment—from outsiders for that rebellion, they again draw on the resources of the subculture to buttress their sense of identity.

The one question that I have left to address directly is the following: What role does the subculture play in their perceptions of themselves and in their self-esteem? Throughout these girls' narratives and accounts, we have heard intimations of their resourcefulness, glimmers of their inner strength. When I interviewed girls, I would ask them, "Did anything change in your life after you encountered punk?" Sometimes, they would tell me that the way in which people—their parents or teachers, the police—treated them changed, but sometimes, they would also tell me more personal accounts of their own development.

For Carina, becoming a punk offered a way to assert her sense of self against the expectations of her father:

> My dad had me being a prep[py], right? And he wouldn't let me out of the house unless I dressed like one and everything. And I was just so unhappy. I could not relate to them. They were just, "Oh, I don't want to get my hands dirty. I gotta fix my hair." I can't stand that.

In contrast to the conservative philosophies and behaviors of her father and of the preppies he wanted her to befriend and emulate, Carina sought out a more relaxed social group, one with fewer expectations of her:

> Just have fun, who cares? And then finally I met some really good friends and I just said "Fuck you" to my dad and, and I finally found some girls that didn't care and we were just, we weren't, I don't know what you would label us. We were just girls and we always hung out with these guys. Because all the girls up there are just preps, really stuck on themselves, "we don't care about you" people, and so all we would do is hang out with guys, because they're, they're more fun to hang out with.

Punk girls repeatedly asserted that their punk peer group helped them overcome their feelings of depression and isolation:

> Carina: They made me really happy. That was when I started coming out of my shell and not caring what my dad said to me anymore. Because after thirteen years—well, it was about fifteen years that—I couldn't handle him anymore. I had to find out who I was. And the day I left him to go live with my mom, I told him, "You never knew me, and you never will know me." Because all what I was was what he wanted me to be. I really don't care to see him again ever, or let him know who I really am, because I don't think he deserves to.

Many girls cast their involvement in the punk scene as their emergence from a shell or a cocoon, as did Justine:

> I started hanging out with other punks, it's when . . . Up until the age of thirteen, I was hypersolitary. I had one of these shells that was impossible to— it was like "tap tap tap," you could have knocked on it. I wouldn't have looked. I didn't want to know anything, really nothing. Really, really antisocial. I started having friends when I was around thirteen. Before, there were people I knew that I'd hang out with and talk to, but I started hanging out with punks when I was thirteen.

Despite being characterized as a subculture of individualism and confrontationalism, and despite the isolation they experience from other girls, punk girls found that punk gave them the resources to become more social. Lisa noted the irony of this:

> This is so funny, because everybody thinks punk people are really anti-social and mad at the world, but I think it really got me to come out of my cocoon, because for a while I was very unsure of myself, la la. So, and I just didn't think people were all that much a big deal, just from elementary and beginning of high school experience. It just didn't really turn my crank so I think that getting out somewhere where you meet people and a lot of them are nice. Obviously, it made a big effect on me, I guess.

The reason that punk offers them this freedom, that it helped them overcome their feelings of social isolation, punk girls explained, is that it is a much more liberal and accepting subculture than is any other scene:

> Carina: You don't have to be afraid to be yourself in front of these people. I had real low self-esteem and I was real afraid to do anything in front of anybody, but they, they kind of woke me up. And so that makes me really happy

that someone could do that for me. Because, you have to be something good to do that for me. Because I was just all messed up.

Girls like Carina repeatedly told me that becoming a punk had released or realized their inner resources, strengths that they had not possessed, or known that they possessed:

> Joanie: It made me assertive. . . . It was just inspiring to see other people that had done what they felt like doing. Express[ed] what they felt like expressing. And it was, it was all right and my mom's not that way. I wasn't raised that way, so it was just like, wow!

Despite the harassment they experience both within and outside the boundaries of the subculture, these girls had found punk to provide a supportive environment in which they could develop qualities of assertiveness, to become the "assertive and aggressive" girls that Sue described.

Personal fulfillment and happiness were recurring themes in girls' summations of their experiences as punks and the way in which punk has affected their lives. Carina noted: "To tell you the truth, I'm more happier. I really am." Stone expanded on the happiness she found in the punk scene:

> I see so many people with these good jobs, big fucking houses and all this money, and these big families, and yet they're not smiling. They ain't smiling because they're dissatisfied with their, their lives because they haven't found that part of them that they need so much, the happiness. They just haven't been able to dig deep enough into themselves and into the world. And they, it just makes me so sad. I'm always trying to make people laugh. I'm trying to make people smile. I may bitch a lot, but I smile all the time too.

Anna considered the lingering effects of her involvement in the punk subculture to be personal growth and strength:

> I'm glad I wasn't popular in high school, because it's very easy when you have a group of people telling you what to do, how to dress, how to think, and you don't really take time to know yourself or have, be forced to come up with things for yourself. . . . Since I wasn't popular in school, that allowed me the freedom to be whatever the hell I wanted.

Cathy, who comes from a middle-class background, added that punk provides the challenges that lead to growth:

> It's easy to live a cheerleader lifestyle and stay in a sorority house and drive a BMW. It's just too easy. It's harder this way. You learn a lot more things

about life, and about other people. You see things, I think, differently. Instead of looking down on everyone, you're at the same eye level. . . . It's just seeing things in a different way.

Anna added that the self-reliance and self-expression fostered in punk helped her develop other inner strengths, more so than a conventional adolescent life course would have:

And I'm glad for that, because it, I think it makes you a stronger person. And you're more, I think we probably know ourselves better than any of these little people that grow up, from high school go straight to a fraternity or sorority and then they freak out once that's over, because then they don't have that group holding their hand and telling them what to do and taking them everywhere.

These girls thus saw punk as a resource to facilitate personal growth and self-esteem, to grow up differently than they would have had they adhered to a more conventional adolescent lifestyle.

Having discovered the possibility of rebellion and self-realization within the punk subculture, girls tried to carry the message out to their peers:

Allie: I want to show other women that they can be strong too. Like my girlfriends up at [home], they think that have to be this way, they have to do this, and I just, more than anything, I want to be proof to them that they can do whatever they want. Because I'm a dreamer. I'm living out my dreams. That means a lot. I don't care about reality at all. . . . Reality's going to affect me whether I like it or not, but I'm living out my dreams and if it doesn't work out the way I wanted it to, I'm going to accept the fate.

Girls like Sue saw punk as an agent for girls' liberation from the confining stereotypes of adolescent femininity:

I think more girls should get into punk and tell these guys that are trying to shy them off just so it can be an elite punk men's thing to fuck off. And get involved, who cares. It's like, do whatever you want with yourself. It doesn't matter how attractive you are to the boy next door. If you don't like yourself, nobody else is [going to]. They might, but I doubt it. You gotta be happy with yourself, you're going to be around with yourself for a long damn time. So if you want to do something outrageous, do it. Mom and Dad aren't going to be there to bother you.

Finally, Rosie summed up both the challenges and the benefits of growing up punk:

Everyone has to eventually realize either they can live their life the way they want and be happy with what they're doing, or instead just follow what everyone else says and live up to everyone else's expectations. But I think that like truly, somebody who does that, inside is really self-insecure. I think someone who does what they want and knows what they want to do and are happy with it, that's someone who has security at least. Even though some other people might think they're insecure and fucked up, they still live their life. And that's really cool, I think, people that have the strength to do that, because it takes a lot of guts. Trust me, it does, really.

Despite the difficulties of becoming punks, despite the harassments they experience, these girls repeatedly told me that they would remain committed to the values, if not necessarily to the styles, of punk throughout their lives. They described these values as being rebellion, individuality, assertiveness, aggressiveness, and freedom. They did not find these in pure forms within punk, for they experienced constraints on a number of levels. However, they found that punk not only provided them with strength and resources to follow these goals, but released the strength and resources that were already within them.

Learning and Saying

What can we learn from these girls' experiences? What do they have to say to us? Throughout this text, I have attempted as much as possible to bring out the voices of punk girls, to allow them to address you in their multitude of accounts and narratives. I have tried to remain true to their words and to respect their perspectives and realities. Even in moments of discomfort and difficulty throughout my fieldwork and analysis, I attempted to remain somewhat objective and to avoid condemnations, even of those who behave in condescending and abusive ways to punk girls. A professor once told me to "write like a punk," but, save for the brief introduction to my preface, I have restrained much of my anger and impatience with ignorance and deprecation. I will do so no longer.

Soon after I had finished my field research, I met with ethnographer Carol Stack, whose assistance was invaluable in ordering the chapters. She asked me two questions: "What have *you* learned? What do *you* want to say?" I will address the first question by considering a number of perspectives that have informed this research: subculture theory, socialization theory, and feminist methodology. Following this, I will tell you what I want to say to parents, teachers, and youth authorities, as well as what I have to say to punk girls.

A Note on Subculture Theory

Whether in male-dominated youth subcultures, in schools, in the workplace, or in their communities, women's and girls' experiences have been largely ignored and their voices silenced. It is hardly surprising, then, that within the world of sociology, our experiences have been discounted as sources of knowing, our lives have not been the subject of research, and our perspectives have not contributed to the development of theory. Given the paucity of sociological research on women until recently, the absence of girls in sociological research is unexceptional. As we know that women have been ignored in mainstream sociological theorizing, we know that such theories often cannot apply to the full discovery and explanation of women's and girls' lives and experiences.

While it may seem banal to continue to harp upon this theme of exclusion, its importance to the enterprise of sociology should never be discounted. We know that girls suffer from lower self-esteem than do their male peers. We know that girls and women experience eating disorders and depression at higher rates than males. We know that girls and women are sexually abused every day and yet fail to raise their voices to cry out for cessation or for help. We also know that girls join gangs, commit crimes, adopt unconventional lifestyles, and rebel against authority. When sociologists have studied boys' forms of rebellion and resistance to authority, they have done so in laudatory ways, envying the masculinity of gangstas, expounding poetically on the "sartorial terrorism" of Mods and punks, discussing how such rebellion enhances males' self-esteem. Girls adopting the same modes of self-expression as their male peers have been described as marginal, girls in subcultures have been described as sluts and victims, and girls' contributions to the creation of subcultures and style have been elided. Girls in subcultures have been discounted as groupies, as detractions from pure male rebellion, and as bimbos and playthings. Most importantly for subculture theory, girls' roles within the social structure have been ignored, so that their adoptions of subcultural lifestyles have remained unexplained, not because they are inexplicable, but because they are deemed unimportant.

Subculture theories carry an explicit tag of masculinity, and even though they purport to apply broadly, they have sought only to explain a limited number of cases, within a limited framework of research on males. Attempts to "add gender" to such theories—rare as they are—fail because they do not begin by inquiring whether such theories are applicable to girls, and whether their additions hold up under empirical scrutiny. Can these theories apply to girls? Why has no one ever tried to apply these theories to them? True, subcultures are male-generated and male-dominated, but does this mean that girls are not attracted to them? Some girls may find such subcultures to be alienating, but others, such as those who become punks, find that the masculinity of punk is indeed an attractive alternative to the more feminine identities that are offered them.

The key to girls' subcultural participation, I believe, is resistance. This resistance against gender roles must be considered when we examine girls' deviance. While it may be true that males use subcultures to celebrate and explore masculinity, it is also the case that some females use subcultures to repudiate or reconstruct femininity. These are the tough girls and macho chicks, the "assertive and aggressive girls." They may not necessarily approach the subculture with these qualities already manifest, but are certainly forced to develop them throughout their often-rocky tenure. Their adoption of these traditionally masculine qualities enhances their self-esteem, allowing them to become expressive in various ways, and to reconstruct their femininity using the variety of behavioral, stylistic, and discursive resources offered by the punk subculture.

Further research into women's and girls' roles in male-dominated subcultures should continue to explore the ways women and girls articulate gender within the confines of delinquent gangs, criminal subcultures, and otherwise "deviant" groups. Work such as Anne Campbell's (1984) and Karen Joe and Meda Chesney-Lind's (1994) research on gang girls and Eleanor Miller's (1986) and Chesney-Lind's (1989) explorations of prostitutes and "street women" expand our knowledge of women's and girls' motivations for engaging in such activities. Beyond describing the victimization of these girls and women (although they document this as well), they argue that girls and women use such deviant groups and activities to construct alternatives to the traditional traps of conventional femininity. Girls' and women's participation in such groups is not without cost, and their forms of resistance are tempered by the accommodations they make to the masculinity and male domination of their chosen surroundings. Nevertheless, their use of these resources calls for further exploration, and their constructions of strength through resistance must be acknowledged and celebrated.

Thus, I propose that subculture theory and research further conceptualize femininity not as an absolute construct which women and girls carry with them into any circumstance, but rather as a discourse with fluid boundaries. In this way, we can continue to investigate not only the effects of female gender on subcultural participation, but the obverse as well: the effect of subcultural participation on the construction of female gender. There is a long tradition in sociological and cultural research on youth subcultures that celebrates young men's rebellions against authority; let us now move forward to exploring and lauding girls' complementary resistances as well.

A Note to Socialization Theorists

The concept of gender as a discourse likewise impacts theories of socialization. I have not, in this work, explored myriad ways in which gender-role socialization occurs. I interviewed these girls at adolescence (for the most part), when their gender identities were long set, and so any exploration of the mechanisms by which such early socialization occurred was outside the scope of this research. However, I had opportunities to note that such socialization continues over the life course, and that the ways in which these girls described their participation in the punk subculture pointed to important ruptures in their thinking about their roles as daughters and young women. As they became punks, they learned to "do gender" differently.

Again, the idea of gender as discourse has important repercussions for the ongoing exploration of gender role socialization. With this discursive construct, the possibility of resisting gender, even after primary socialization has occurred, becomes feasible. As I read much of the literature of girls and self-esteem, I encountered two prevailing themes. First, such writings are highly critical of the content of gender norms that North American culture and society imparts to girls. The emphasis on beauty over brains, the downplaying of assertiveness in favor of pliability, and the media's responsibility for promoting images of slimness over health are prevailing themes in such writing. Researchers have found that girls who internalize such a normative femininity exhibit low self-esteem, both from their inability to approximate that ideal, and from the way in which that ideal itself is devalued when compared to the positive attributes of masculinity. Second, writings on self-esteem often conclude with ways teachers, parents, and others can work to counter the influence of these images, or on ways that such media images can be challenged and changed. These include the promotion of healthy self-images, the production and distribution of alternatives to girls' magazines that promote beauty over other attributes, and school- and home-based programs to boost self-esteem.

While all of these initiatives are important in reducing the damaging messages girls receive and internalize, what they ignore is the role of girls themselves in their socialization process. By this I mean that a child is not a tabula rasa, a blank slate onto which the distorting contents of female gender-role socialization are writ large. Rather, girls continually struggle with these precepts, accepting some aspects while resisting, and even sometimes managing to reject, others. This agentic view of girls' socialization is absent from much of the work on girls and self-esteem. Instead, we encounter page after page of victimized females, girls with eating disorders, suicidal girls, girls with low self-esteem. Very few researchers follow the work of Lyn Mikel Brown and her colleagues (Rogers, Brown, and Tappan 1994) in recognizing girls' unique developmental patterns as forms of resistance to their socialization. These forms of resistance must be recognized so that they can be further elaborated and explored. As a society, we must learn to identify this struggle in our daughters so that we can learn to nurture, rather than punish, their forms of resistance to the debilitating messages we teach them. The only people who can lead us in this exploratory journey are girls themselves.

A Note to Feminist Researchers

As a participant in the 1996 National Women's Studies Association conference at Skidmore College, I found myself acting out conflicting roles. As a researcher into girls' lives, I was present to participate in an embedded conference on female adolescent development, to learn about, teach, and explore the topic of girls' maturation with other scholars. As a young woman, I was sympathetic to the concerns of the girls present, who not only objected to the exclusion of their voices from the planning of the conference, but who objected as well to its cosponsorship by a psychiatric hospital that allegedly engages in the psychological abuse of young lesbians and other girls. I attended meetings at which these issues were discussed, and was heartened by many older women's willingness to include girls in women's studies. I was further delighted by the articulateness and passion of the girls who attended the conference and who raised their voices in protest.

However, I have been disappointed by the failure of the feminist and academic communities to build on this promising start. The amount of sound sociological research on girls remains pitiful, and the exploration of girls' culture continues to advance in very small increments. At the close of the century, I still find little interest in what girls have to say, both among feminists and other scholars. I still find girls' voices silenced, ignored, or devalued in favor of academic discourses. Despite the recent spate of scholarly and popular research on girls and self-esteem, I still find girls struggling to be heard, acknowledged and respected. If we continue to silence girls and fail to explore their forms of resistance, how can we learn what their lives are like, what they need from us? As feminist researchers and sociologists, we have written, taught, and practiced doing sociology *for* women. Let us begin a sociology that is about girls, for girls, and practiced *with* girls. Let us solicit and respect their voices.

A Note to Parents and Youth Authorities

As I conducted my fieldwork, I encountered tale after tale of parents' and schools' intolerance toward these punk girls' styles. Girls told me that their parents accused them of being prostitutes and junkies, simply because their mode of self-presentation differed from the norm. Girls told me that their parents refused to hear their protests of innocence, their explanations that the style carried layers of meaning. Girls told me that their parents threw out their punk clothes, destroyed their tapes of punk music, and burned their punk posters. Many told how schools expelled them for breaking sometimes fictitious dress codes, for "distracting" other students with their hairstyles, their tattoos, or their clothes. Others explained that police targeted them for selective enforcement of arcane and ridiculous laws, solely on the perception of their deviance.

I have written about attempts in the mid-1980s to institutionalize such repressive measures, through the efforts of the Back in Control Training Center in southern California. I have written about the attempts of groups such as Parents of Punkers to cast punk as a pathological form of deviance. I have reported on Rosenbaum and Prinsky's (1991) research that showed that some psychiatric hospitals viewed the simple construction and display of punk style as a form of mental illness treatable by institutionalization. Some of the girls I interviewed spoke of being institutionalized, and one pointed out that she believed her hospitalization was precipitated in part by her preference for a punk look over a more conventional feminine style. I have reported on public perceptions of punk, about media portrayals, and about how all of these result in ongoing maltreatment of these young girls.

When I conducted my fieldwork in Montreal, girls who lived or had lived in foster care repeatedly told me that the group homes that sheltered them from abusive families confiscated their spiked bracelets and combat boots, made them wash out their spiked hairstyles, and decreed all punk apparel and paraphernalia taboo. I wanted to discover why group homes undertake such repressive measures. Visiting the central office, Les Centres jeunesse de Montreal, I came away with a handful of pamphlets about group homes and the services offered there. In none of this literature did I find specific dress codes, merely vague references to the aims of the centers, to "reduce the negative aspects of [an adolescent's] behavior" (Governement du Québec 1990:13).[1] A report dated October 1988 by Le Comité pour les droits des jeunes en centres d'accueil (Committee for the Rights of Youths in Group Homes) found that the rights of adolescents in group homes were ill defined and poorly explained to the adolescents and to their parents. The report concluded that young people's rights were continually violated, and that they had no recourse to any remedy or representation.

While there, I also had the opportunity to informally interview a youth counselor, who requested anonymity. He agreed with me as I set forth the premise that adolescents, and especially girls, may view their style and lifestyle choice as a source of strength and self-esteem. When I inquired why adolescents were then still denied the opportunity to express themselves through their clothing, he replied that the role of the youth center was to re-integrate the adolescents into society. Removing traces of "moroseness" (such as heavy metal band T-shirts or spiked bracelets) from the youth was one way, he argued, in which youth authorities achieve this goal. That this type of repression was not only probably illegal, but also prompted some girls to run away and live in the streets, seemed beside the point. Conformity was all that mattered.

This counselor's viewpoint contrasted sharply with that of Tommy Ross, who runs the Project Home drop-in center for New Orleans's homeless young people. Funded by the New Orleans AIDS (NO/AIDS) Task Force, Ross coordinates outreach activities, bringing condoms and AIDS peer education to homeless kids. As well, the center provides homeless squatters with showers, laundry facilities, an air-conditioned place to spend their summer days, a place to store their gear, food (thanks to the Hari Krishnas), counseling, and various programs and groups. In conversation, Ross argues that attempts to "convert" these kids to more mainstream lifestyles, be it by forcing the runaways to return to their families or foster homes, by arresting them, or by applying pressure to them, are bound to fail. He is more concerned with their health than with their lifestyle, not urging them to conform, but rather asking them to protect themselves in whatever activities they choose to undertake. The kids respond to Ross's concern, returning daily to the center, sometimes taking condoms from the coffee jar on the counter, and offering him the respect that they accord no other authority figure.

Ross's attitude of acceptance wins adolescents' confidence and encourages their return and openness. I have written about parents' reactions to their daughters' assumptions of punk style and lifestyle, and documented that most of these are, initially, negative. Parents who managed to maintain good relationships with their children were not those who used "tough love" measures like those of the Back in Control Center; these parents succeeded only in alienating their children and sending them out into the streets. Those who were accepting, who allowed their daughters to express their individuality and resistance, salvaged their relationships, and encouraged their children always to return to them. Those who encouraged their daughters' ambitions, no matter how bizarre in their eyes, found that their daughters respected them and acceded to their larger aspirations for them by remaining at home or in school. By overlooking minor transgressions of their rules, by exhibiting flexibility and understanding, they had forged close bonds to their punk children. Parents must learn to be proud of their daughters' originality, individuality, and strength in the face of adversity.

In punishing punk girls' attempts to redefine femininity, in rejecting their daughters, in removing the symbols of resistance and subcultural identity from these adolescents, some parents and youth authorities rob these girls of sources of self-expression, strength, and self-esteem. In expelling them from school, in arresting them for minor misdemeanors, some school authorities and police remove opportunities for girls to continue to try to engage in further growth and learning. Girls' adopting of punk styles is not a cry for help, nor a symptom of some psychological disorder, but rather their way of using whatever resources they have in order to make sense of the conflicting messages they receive: Be passive, but don't make yourself a victim. Be pretty so boys will find you attractive, but don't be a bimbo. Be sexy, but don't be a slut. Be intelligent, but don't let it show. Be strong, but don't be assertive. Be a girl, even if this means that you have to be less than what you are. In opting out of this game, in resisting these messages of feminine inferiority, punk girls try to construct sane identities in an insane world. For the love of these girls, don't punish them for it.

A Note to Punk Girls

I have not much to add in my address to punk girls, save to reflect to you what you said to me. Over and over, girls talked about unity, about how the punk subculture used to have more unity, and about how you wish that this unity would once again arise. Over and over, you talked about your isolation from other girls and about your dependency (whether you realize it or not) on males for companionship and protection. And so I combine these concerns to call for unity among punk girls. Your resistance to the harassments to which outsiders subject you shows your strength. Your use of punk style in creating alternative femininities demonstrates your creativity. If united, that strength and creativity could transform the punk subculture from a declining "working-class bohemian" protest movement to a revolutionary force in reconceptualizing social and cultural ideas about youth and gender. Make punk your own. Take heart from the words of one of your peers, Jennie: "Girls can do whatever guys can do, but girls can do it better, because girls kick ass!"

Appendix A: Punk Glossary

anarchy: The overall political ideology of punks.

bihawk: A variation of the mohawk haircut, featuring a shaved head, save for two strips of hair running from the forehead to the nape of the neck. Unlike the mohawk, the bihawk has a shaved strip along the center part, dividing the hair into two distinct rows.

bondage collar: A black leather collar featuring chrome rings affixed to it for the purposes of restraint.

bondage gear: Clothing and accessories usually made of rubber, leather, and/or metal, and designed to be used in sadomasochistic sex. Adopted by early punks as street wear.

Bromley contingent: Early group of fans of the Sex Pistols, named for the area of Britain in which they lived. Members included Siouxsie Sioux and Billy Idol.

Chelsea cut: Feminine version of the skinhead hairstyle, in which hair is buzz cut save for bangs and a fringe about the hairline. Adopted by punk girls in the 1980s.

combat boots: Black military boots favored by punks. These are usually inexpensive when purchased second hand at army surplus stores. Have been somewhat superseded in popularity by the Doc Marten boot.

couch surfing: Moving from the home of one acquaintance to that of another, usually sleeping on their sofas. Sometimes an alternative to squatting.

crusty punk: Variation of gutter punk. Crusty punks take pride in their lack of hygiene.

DIY: "Do it yourself," the prevailing ethic of artistic production in the punk subculture. Also extends to an overall philosophy, leading to such lifestyle choices as squatting and panhandling.

Doc Martens: A type of boot originally favored by skinheads, but now also worn by punks. These resemble combat boots, but they are available in a variety of colors and heights, and feature orthopedic "Air Wair" soles. Also referred to as "DMs" or "Docs."

dog collar: A leather strip worn around the neck, typically adorned with spikes. Usually ornamental, but can also prevent police from gaining a chokehold.

dumpster diving: Reclaiming discarded food and sellable or usable goods from the trash.

emocore: An offshoot of punk spearheaded by bands espousing straight edge, animal rights, and, on occasion, Christianity. Characterized by less cynicism than hardcore music.

fin: Another designation for **mohawk**.

goth: A subculture often associated with punk, which actually emerged as an offshoot in the late 1970s and early 1980s through Siouxsie and the Banshees. Goth centers around romantic, dramatic notions of death and decay.

gutter punk: A punk who lives on the street or in squats, or who travels. Gutter punks are typically unwashed and support themselves by spare-changing. Also known as street punks.

hardcore: A type of punk music that emerged in the early 1980s, characterized by more aggressive rhythms and a faster tempo than early punk music. Also refers to a type of punk who adheres to the punk style associated with this music. Can also refer to the level of one's commitment to the punk subculture.

hippie: An adherent of the peace-and-love ethic which characterized the counterculture of the late 1960s and early 1970s. Usually despised by punks.

house punk: Derogatory term used by gutter punks to designate punks who have jobs, live with their parents, or have their own apartments. Gutter punks perceive house punks to be less than true punks.

liberty spikes: A style of punk haircut; the hair is left longer and sculpted into spikes with the use of gel, hairspray, glue, eggs, or gelatin. Names for its resemblance to the headgear on the Statue of Liberty. One variation of this haircut features shaved areas around the spikes.

McLaren, Malcolm: Punk svengali. Owner of the original punk shop, Sex, and manager of the Sex Pistols.

mohawk: The most popular and recognizable punk haircut. The sides of the head are shaved, leaving a strip of hair from forehead to nape. This is usually worn upright, but can also be left down or worn in spikes.

mosh: Another term for **thrash** or **slam dance**. This term is associated most closely with the grunge subculture.

new school: An expression designating a punk who entered the subculture after its heyday in the late 1970s and early 1980s. Can also refer to hardcore punks.

New Wave: A movement that tones down early punk music and style for popular consumption.

old school: An expression designating an original punk from the late 1970s and early 1980s. Can also refer to new punks adhering to the older style, such as Spirit of '77 punks.

panhandle: To beg for spare change from passers-by.

piercing: A form of body modification involving puncturing the ear, lip, nose, cheek, or other body part with safety pins or specially designed jewelry.

pit: The area directly in front of the stage at a punk show reserved for thrashing.

pogo: A style of dance reportedly invented by Sex Pistols bassist Sid Vicious. Involves jumping up and down in place and facilitates seeing the band when standing at the back of a crowd.

poseur: A derogatory term used by punks to designate hangers-on or wanna-bes, for example, people who adopt the punk style merely as a fashion.

preppy: A fashionable, upper-middle-class young person, usually dressed in Benetton clothes and Lacoste (alligator) polo shirts. Despised by punks. Also known as "preps."

punk rocker: Generic designation for nongutter punks.

Quincy punk: A derogatory term for (a) depictions of punks on police dramas—as junkies, petty criminals, or other bad influences; or (b) new school punks who emulate television punks, without realizing the importance of punk ideology (substance) over punk dress (style).

safety punk: Another term for **house punk**.

scene: The local punk subculture of any city. Designates the totality of the local punks, plus the shows, record stores, clubs, and other areas they frequent.

Sex Pistols: Band that emerged in London in 1976, generally lauded as the original punk band. Members included Sid Vicious and Johnny Rotten. Hit songs included "God Save the Queen" and "Anarchy in the U.K."

show: Any musical event featuring punk bands.

Sid and Nancy: Sid Vicious and Nancy Spungen, a legendary couple of the early London punk scene, who exemplified mutual destructiveness. After allegedly murdering his American girlfriend, Sex Pistols bassist Sid Vicious later died of a heroin overdose. Their relationship was immortalized in the Alex Cox film *Sid and Nancy* (its original, working title was "Love Kills").

skater: A subculture that presents an urban version of the surfer subculture of the 1950s. Occupying the same subcultural turf, skaters have close links with punks.

skinhead: A subculture predating British punk but that arrived in North America at the same time as punk. Renowned for being white supremacists, skinheads sometimes affiliate with the punk subculture and sometimes prey on the local punk scene. Also includes a faction called SHARP (SkinHeads Against Racial Prejudice).

slam dance: The original name for thrashing or moshing. This style of dance involves many people moving around rhythmically in a circle in the pit, with dancers slamming into each other's bodies in a ritual form of violence, to the tune of hardcore music. If performed correctly, does not result in severe injury.

softcore: A designation for nonhardcore punks. May indicate commitment to the original punk style (Spirit of '77 punks). May also indicate a lesser commitment to the punk subculture than that of the hardcore punks.

spare-change: Another term for **panhandling**.

spikes: May refer to a hairstyle, where the hair is sculpted into upright cone shapes using various means (see **liberty spikes**). Also refers to metal studs or nails and screws used to ornament bracelets, dog collars, or leather jackets.

Spirit of '77 punks: Punks who adhere to the musical and sartorial style of the original London punk scene.

squat: An abandoned building housing gutter punks and others (called "squatters"). Squats range from houses creatively restored by committed squatters to garbage-strewn, bug-infested, urine-smelling disposable housing. As a verb, also refers to the act of occupying an abandoned building.

stage dive: The act of jumping off the stage at a show and into the pit, where the audience will break the stage diver's fall. An integral part of the slam dance.

straight edge: A form of punk that emerged on the East Coast of the United States during the early 1980s. Straight edgers do not drink, smoke, or take drugs. In some cases, they do not engage in "illicit" sex and refrain from eating meat or using animal products.

street punk: Another term for **gutter punk**.

thrash: The style of dance also called **slam dancing** or **moshing**. The musical style this accompanies is sometimes called "thrashcore."

'zine: A homemade publication featuring rudimentary graphics and a cut-and-paste aesthetic, arising from the DIY aesthetic of the punk subculture. The primary form of intra- and inter-scene communication, 'zines such as *Punk* and *Search and Destroy* in the United States and *Sniffin' Glue* in the United Kingdom started the trend, institutionalized in such larger publications as *Maximum Rock 'n' Roll*.

Appendix B: Punk Girl Biographies

In order to maintain anonymity, pseudonyms are used and some details of physical appearance have been altered.

Alexea (17) is a hardcore crusty gutter punk. Very heavyset, she dresses in baggy patched khaki, gray, and black clothes, green tights, and black boots. She sports a brunette bihawk (a double-rowed mohawk) which usually lies flat on her head. She has multiple facial piercings, including a safety pin through her eyebrow; she also wears many necklaces (some made of hose clamps), rings, and bracelets. She highlights her large, dark eyes with heavy black eyeliner. Alexea exudes strength of character and street smarts; she speaks very frankly, is not at all shy about expressing liking or displeasure on any topic, and is quite smart and funny. She currently squats, where she sometimes runs into her parents, who are also homeless. She is considering a number of options for the future, including learning to tattoo and going to college.

Allie (20) wears her dyed-black hair up in "Sid Vicious"–type spikes, ornamented with plastic barrettes. She typically dresses in a grimy T-shirt, a black "hoodie" (hooded sweatshirt), baggy black jeans, and ancient Adidas sneakers. She also wears a variety of necklaces and bracelets and, most notably, multiple earrings in each piercing in her ears. Her mother is a waitress and her father is a transient; her parents are divorced and Allie has spent time in foster care. A genuinely nice girl, she describes herself as down-to-earth, frugal, and adventurous. She has spent the last couple of years traveling, squatting, and couch surfing. She is content with this lifestyle and has not yet formulated plans for her future, describing herself as "pretty much down-to-earth. And I know what I want. I just try to get by on necessities. Just looking for adventure and a different way of life. Just the never-ending kid."

Amalia (17) described herself as "drunk and belligerent"; she was actually quite slow speaking and thoughtful. Of medium height and build, she very much looks the gutter punk; dressed in baggy clothes in the regulation black, khaki, and muted colors of that scene, she has, like many others, ornamented her clothes with chrome lighter tabs (metal pulled from disposable lighters and attached to the edges of clothing). She usually wears a green knit cap on her straggly blue hair and has gray eyes and lip piercings. Her mother works as a dental receptionist and her father is an electrical salesman; she doesn't get along with either of them. Amalia currently travels and squats, and admits to no future aspirations.

Andie (14) is petite and delicate, with small hands and ears, a self-described cross between a hippie and a gutter punk. When we met, she was rather grubby, and admitted that she had not washed properly in two weeks. She has brownish-black hair with blonde roots, which she wears long on top and shaved along the sides and back. In the summers, she lives mostly on the street with friends, supporting herself by playing the violin. In the winter, she lives with her widowed father and her sister while she attends an alternative high school. Her father works as a drapery installer. She participates in poetry readings and other subcultural and arty events. Although the subject at which she excels in school is math, she would like to continue her musical career. She is quite popular with her peers, and somewhat of a mascot of the punk scene where she lives.

Anna (24) is tall and graceful and moves in a very self-assured manner. She wears her long hair loose; it is dyed green along four inches of roots and black at the ends. For the interview, she wore baggy black jeans, a shirt with a whiskey company's logo, and a pair of black Doc Marten boots. She has a B.F.A. in photography, but currently works as an erotic dancer, in the hope of earning enough money to continue her education. Articulate and curious, Anna originally came from a small town. Her parents are still married, and her mother is now a teacher and her father a genetic biologist. Anna currently lives in a rented house with her boyfriend and two roommates.

Arizona (23) is tall and articulate and possesses a forceful presence, describing herself as "very strong-minded. I don't let people intimidate me. Free-willed, open-minded, and just be myself as much as I can." A street punk, she dresses in predominantly black or muted colors, in loose, baggy clothes. She also wears a variety of ornaments, such as leather thongs, bondage bracelets, chains and locks, hose clamps, and safety pins as jewelry. She has extensive facial piercings, including three in her lower lip; she wears her dyed black hair long on top and shaved along the sides and back. Arizona's father is deceased and her mother is a surgical nurse. She plans to continue traveling and squatting, although she hopes to settle down some day, be in a band, and perhaps marry and have children.

Ava (18) describes herself as "crazy": "I guess I'm not very responsible and I'm honest. I'm a good friend, but I'm just not very responsible. I watch out for my friends." An enthusiastic and good-humored girl, she wears her wavy violet hair short, with longer sidelocks. Ava's mother is a college secretary and her father is a drug and alcohol counselor; they are divorced and, although she gets along with them, Ava has spent much of her life since the age of thirteen living in foster care. She wore ripped fishnet tights, black baggy shorts, a Misfits T-shirt and khaki hi-tops to the interview. She has multiple facial piercings and a wonderfully detailed tattoo of a spider. She shares an apartment with her boyfriend and is currently unemployed. She has not yet decided what to do in the future, but is determined that she will move to another country.

Basilisk (19) is tall and lanky, with sky blue hair tied into fluffy spikes with multicolored elastic bands. She ornaments this hairstyle with various metallic objects, such as nail files, screws, nail clippers, tweezers, bells, and utensils. She often dresses in baggy black clothes, with black boots and purple laces. She has some facial piercings, tattoos, and a number of scars on her forearms. When she goes out at night, she wears dramatic makeup, with dark eyeshadow and lipstick. Basilisk's father is deceased; she does not get along with her mother and has spent the last few years in and out of hospitals. Although she has been traveling and squatting, Basilisk, pregnant at the time of our interview, is planning to settle down and get a job and an apartment. When she isn't out scrounging for food, she is rarely seen without a book. She describes herself as "quiet. I think a lot of stuff is funny and I've got a good sense of humor."

Camille (16) is a striking figure, with a black-and-blue mohawk and black bondage wear. Her large, almond-shaped, green eyes dwarf her delicate face, an effect made eerie by the red eyeliner she wears. Camille recently quit high school in the tenth grade and currently works in a warehouse. She lives with her divorced mother, a media buyer, when she is not undergoing psychiatric treatment for what she describes as a personality disorder. Camille is a very intense listener and speaks in a very precise and focused manner. She views her participation in the punk subculture as an integral part of her search for religious truth.

Candace (21) has been on her own since the age of fourteen; she now has a small child, lives in an apartment with friends, and supports herself and her daughter by working as an erotic dancer. Her parents are still together; her mother is in marketing and her father is a heating and air-conditioning repairman. She does not get along with either of them, although this has been changing slowly since the birth of her child. Candace has short, blonde hair, styled in an all-over buzz cut except for two longer "pigtails" on either side of her head. She favors one particular blue dress, which shows her scarred legs. She describes herself as an unconventional individualist; she is a vegetarian and practices holistic medicine: "I don't follow any sort of norm, as far as what society says. I eat the way I want. I'm a vegetarian. I also kind of disagree with conventional health care and I rely mainly on herbs. I'm just kind of myself. I don't take on anybody else. I'm definitely influenced by the world around me, but I try to keep myself as sacred as possible. Because if you don't have yourself, then you don't really have anything." She plans to return to school at the same time as her daughter, and perhaps to have more children.

Carina (16) is quiet and soft spoken, although neither shy nor reticent. She says, "I wish I could say I was carefree. I hate to worry, but I do it a lot. I can stay pretty happy most of the time. I try to be real nice to people, no matter who you are, even if you do piss me off, but I'll only take it so far. I won't let you walk all over me. I don't like to be a bitch, but sometimes I am." She has only recently become part of the street punk scene via the skater subculture. She is short and petite, and wears baggy, worn, and ripped clothes in muted colors, most remarkably a pair of overalls that would probably be baggy on a 300–pound person. Her facial features are sharp and well defined, and she has large, almond-shaped, brown eyes. She wears her long, curly hair loose, streaked in shades of auburn, brown, and black. Her parents are divorced; her mother is a casino worker, and her father, with whom she does not get along, is a (usually unemployed) painter. Carina squats and travels, and is uncertain as to what her future aspirations are.

Carnie (16) is a self-described crusty punk; under a veneer of grime, she is pretty, with large hazel eyes and a short blonde Chelsea haircut with brunette bangs. She often wears an eclectic outfit consisting of tweed cut-off trousers, fishnet knee-high stockings, and a black undershirt. Carnie was raised by her mother, an architectural designer, and never knew her father. She squats and travels, and eventually hopes to live in a survivalist commune in the country. She describes herself as a "flibbertigibbet": "I talk a lot and I'm really happy and it's annoying. To myself and to all my friends. I'm kind of flighty. It's okay."

Cathy (21) is short, plump, and extremely good humored. She says, "people tell me that I look like I'm twelve and act like I'm eleven. I think that's great. I'd rather be that way than have people tell me, 'You act like you're forty.' I'm silly and young. Clumsy. Generally always in a good mood." She wears her burgundy hair in a Chelsea cut, buzz-cut all over, with long bangs framing her face. She is "on hiatus" from college, where she was in between her junior and senior years, training to be a high school social studies teacher. She has an apartment and sometimes lives with her mother, a sheriff's deputy. Her parents are divorced and her father works in wholesale food marketing. Both of her parents have some college education. She is not currently working, just "hanging out" until she decides to return to school. She is a very open person, with an engaging personality, an easy laugh, and a certain air of frivolity and gaiety.

Chloe (20) is "just your average pissed-off person. I'm not bitter or anything, but I think I've had my eyes opened to the world for a while." She is small and slight, but a forceful presence nonetheless. She came to the interview wearing a purple flowered "hillbilly" dress, white longjohns, combat boots, and a painted motorcycle jacket. She is extremely self-assured, and spoke at length, and quite fast, on many subjects. Chloe dropped out of high school despite her standing in the gifted program. Originally from England, where she first encountered the punk subculture through her older sister, she now lives in a rented house with her fiancé and is not close to her family. Her parents are divorced and her mother works in her father's small electronics store; her father received training in electronics while in the army. She reads a lot and plans to write a book that she hopes will be published within the next five years.

Clara (15) is tall and rail thin, with dark eyes and dark hair cut in a choppy, spiky 'do. She can be picked out easily in a crowd, as she always wears knee-high Doc Marten boots that she has painted yellow. Clara is still in high school, but recently ran away from the group home where she was staying and is living in the streets. She lives on handouts and is half-heartedly looking for work. Her parents are divorced; she has no contact with her father and her mother receives welfare. Clara is outspoken and vivacious. She is considering attending a technical school and training as an electrician. A former occupant of a group home, she says, "The government runs my life. And that's why I ran away. It's the government that tells me what time to get up, what time to go to bed, what time to piss. No, I can't take it. It seems to me I didn't choose to be born, so it seems to me that I have the right to take life as I please."

Connie (20) sports self-made facial scarification, which makes her stand out even among the punk crowd. A crusty punk, she wears baggy black and brown clothes and keeps her black hair scruffy looking. Of herself she says, "I feel like a wingnut sometimes." Her mother is a lawyer and her father is deceased; as she does not get along with her mother, she has spent much of her time since the age of eleven living in foster care as a ward of the state. Connie, who reports having already married and divorced, currently travels and squats.

Cora (15) is small and quite shy and quiet, despite her large blue mohawk and black leather clothes. She is a high school dropout and has just returned to her parents' home from the group home where she had been staying. Her parents are still married; her mother is a nurse. She is somewhat unsure of where she stands now, and of what she envisions for her future, although she is looking forward to having children someday. She describes herself as "a good person."

Courtney (25) is tall and thin, with curly, dyed hair and brown eyes. She describes herself as "easygoing, ambitious. Easygoing. Ambitious." She is very soft-spoken, although quite articulate and thoughtful. She is no longer in school, and has some years of college education in psychology and drama. She first became a punk at the age of fifteen; although she has been distancing herself from the scene, she still attends shows and maintains contact with her friends from that time. However, because she is now working at an investment firm and training to be a broker, she has toned down her appearance. She lives in an apartment with her boyfriend. A second-generation German immigrant, she maintains close ties to her widowed mother, a housewife; prior to his death, her father owned a plastics manufacturing company. She hopes one day to live in Europe, marry her boyfriend, raise a large family, and work out of her home.

Denise (20) sports a large purple mohawk (approximately six inches long), which she wears upright on her head. She describes herself as "pretty driven.

When I see something I want, I'll go for it. Try to do it until I can do it. Probably the biggest element of me that most people would just never see, and people don't believe me when I tell them [, is] that I'm shy." Friendly and curious, she is in her junior year of college, where she studies sociology. She lives on campus and is close to both of her parents, who are still married; her mother, who has a college degree, is a homemaker and her father, who holds a Ph.D. in political science, is a vice president of a corporation. Denise is very engaged in the punk scene; she is especially interested in original, older, punk bands and in the philosophy of the subculture. She is currently apprenticing to be a tattoo artist, and will marry her fiancé when she completes her college degree.

Elle (14) is a true child of the streets; she is small, painfully skinny, sports track marks, and is missing one front tooth. She wears her hair in a mohawk, with multicolored strands handing around her face. She recently quit school and lives on the street, squatting and supporting herself by panhandling. She states that she left home at the age of twelve to escape an abusive situation. Her parents are divorced, and her mother works in a hotel. Although small and scruffy, Elle is intense and engaging. She would really like to become a coroner and perform autopsies; however, she foresees that she will wind up on welfare.

Emily (19) is tall and slim, with brown eyes and short green dreadlocks. Her manner of speaking is somewhat guarded and thoughtful, but as she becomes comfortable with someone, she becomes more forthcoming. Emily has a high school education and currently lives in a converted warehouse apartment with her boyfriend; both are artists. Her widowed mother is a social worker and has a college degree; her father was a scientist. Emily supports herself by working part-time as a waitress, but is hoping to get a full-time job in a condom store. For the future, she hopes to become self-employed, travel, and name her first child Ichabod ("Ick" for short). She says, "I do things that make me happy. The basis of my life is to be happy and to be happy with my surroundings. My beliefs make me happy, I suppose."

Hallie (19) is of medium height and very thin and angular. Her hair is short, spiky, and streaked with black; she has dyed her bangs in varying shades of blue, indigo, and purple, cut them in different lengths and ornamented them with beads, wire, and ivory skulls. Hallie attends an alternative high school; she very much enjoys the original teaching methods and their relevance to her everyday life. On occasion she lives with her divorced mother and she has lived in group homes and squats. Her mother is a state clerical employee and her stepfather transports toxic waste. She spare-changes for money and spends much of her time outside school hours traveling around the country. For now, she plans to continue doing so indefinitely. She describes herself as "a go-with-the-flow kind of person. I consider myself to be intelligent. I'm outgoing. I give a lot of my stuff away, even though I have nothing."

Jennie (19) has a short green and orange mohawk, with longer, blue bangs, brown eyes, and facial piercings. She says: "I'm outgoing. I can be a bitch. I can be quite happy. I try to help everyone out as much as I can. If I give something to a person, I hope that maybe two days down the road they can help me. I'm always there for my friends. I'm outgoing. I just kick ass." She is somewhat of a caretaker, often getting her friends out of trouble, although she admits that she can also be a troublemaker. Jennie lives with her mother, who owns a local newspaper, and works full-time in a fast-food outlet. A recent high school graduate, she is considering attending college, and vehemently opposes any notion of getting married or having children.

Jessie (21) is small, shy, and somewhat uncertain of herself. She has shaved off her hair, save for spiky bangs and a thin Hare Krishna-like braid, both of which are dyed green. She can often be seen wearing an ancient painted leather jacket with chrome spikes. Jessie currently attends art school; she already holds an associate's degree and continues her education in graphic design. She is close to her parents; her mother works in advertising and her father works for the government and both have college degrees. She lives in an apartment with a roommate and just quit her job in order to dedicate herself to her studies. She plans to have a child by the time she is twenty-five and does not plan to marry. Although shy and timid, she is a curious person, and once she is comfortable, becomes quite outgoing.

Joanie (22) is a college dropout, but continues to educate herself from books she dredges out of the dumpsters behind bookstores. She describes herself as "constantly trying to be honest to myself and other people at the same time. It's a hard job. It's really difficult." She works part-time as a medical health assistant in a youth center. Joanie's green dreadlocks match her green eyes; she also has many facial piercings, including many in her nose. Her parents are divorced; her mother is a pediatric nurse and her father is a salesman. Joanie tends to be quite guarded. She lives in her own apartment, and plans to leave the United States some day and have children.

Justine (18) is tall and solidly built. Her purple hair is styled in a choppy cut, and she can often be found dressed head-to-toe in black, with her trademark leather vest, spiked dog collar, and tall Doc Marten boots. Justine has a high school diploma and, although she was admitted to college to study visual arts, she does not plan to attend any further schooling. She has recently moved into her first apartment and out of the group home where she lived for the past five years. She collects welfare and supplements this by panhandling and by working in government-funded "back to work" youth projects. Her parents are divorced; her mother works in a greenhouse and her father is a teacher. Both live outside the city; she could live with neither due to disagreements with both her step-parents. She says, "I would describe myself as someone who has a very big heart, who can't be mean. If I saw my worst enemy lying on the ground, I'd grab him and say, 'Hey, get up.' A person who is generous, who really likes to share, but without being taken advantage of. Someone who's calm. I consider myself to be someone who is really sociable. Someone who doesn't really have problems talking to people. A human being among so many others." Articulate, outgoing, and intelligent, Justine hopes that her future will include either a career in the arts or further work in humanitarian causes.

Lisa (20) is small, compact, and very energetic. She describes herself as "fairly well-balanced, while at other times I can be quite sensitive. I'm not a very linear thinker, but that has its advantage. Even though I'm not the most logical person, I think I'm pretty well at assessing the situation and doing the best thing. Fairly self-confident and fairly intelligent." She wears her shoulder-length hair loose; it is dyed black, with fire-engine red bangs. She quit college after one year, but hopes to return to more practical studies, such as at a polytechnic institute. She lives in a co-op apartment complex with her mother, who edits a trade magazine; although her parents are separated, her father, who has been diagnosed as depressive and collects a disability pension, lives in the same co-op. She currently works at a government-funded center for aboriginal film and video. She plans to continue in that area and perhaps to move into publishing and broadcasting; she does not plan to marry or have children.

Lola (20) describes herself as "open-minded, just very spontaneous, and creative." She is short, with a voluptuous figure. Lola wears her thick hair in a bob, dyed a reddish purple, and with the sides and back shaved. She wears baggy clothes, green hi-top sneakers, and astonishingly brightly colored blouses. Her large brown eyes are quite expressive and add to her general animation when she speaks. Lola was raised by her mother, who is a cook in a restaurant, and has no contact with her father. She currently travels and squats and would like to save up enough money to move to Scotland, where she hopes to work doing theatrical makeup.

Lydia (37) is tall and elegant. She originally encountered the punk scene at its inception, when she was eighteen. Her first involvement in the subculture was through her studies in film and video; she often documented the punk scene for her college assignments. She believes that this orientation, along with her experimental aesthetics, contributed to her suspension from the fine arts program she was in. She has continued her involvement in the punk subculture and, though she now supports herself and her son with government arts grants, she retains her punk appearance. Lydia wears her dyed-black hair loose around her face and shoulders; at the time of the interview, she wore a long black skirt and a leather jacket ornamented with chains. She is a warm, friendly person as well as an engaging and entertaining speaker. When asked to describe herself, she says, "I don't subscribe to any religions, but I believe in the sanctity of life. I have my own version of events in terms of what I think is the meaning of life and the meaning of existence on this planet. I don't have any political affiliations that are very distinct either, but I think I have been politically active though. I choose my own little causes."

Mina (18) is small, but carries herself with some presence; she is also quiet and almost taciturn: "I'm not shy, but I'm not loud and obnoxious either. I try to keep to myself and try to keep in my own business, pretty much." She sports a short green mohawk with fuschia sidelocks; she often wears black-rimmed Buddy Holly–type glasses over her dark eyes. Her baggy clothes, large black boots and oversize leather jacket make her appear smaller than she is. Mina has just finished high school. She currently lives in an apartment with her boyfriend and a roommate. Her parents are divorced; her mother works with airplanes and her father is an artist and "househusband." Her father has had some college education; her mother has the equivalent of a high school education. Mina is unemployed and is currently planning to set out traveling across the country. Eventually, she would like to return to school and become a teacher.

Nikita (19) recently graduated with honors from high school, but has deferred a number of scholarships to art colleges in order to take time off to travel. She has large green eyes and an extraordinarily long green and blue mohawk. Her parents are divorced; her mother is a college teacher and her father is a civil servant. Nikita supports herself while traveling by making and selling jewelry; she also wears a good amount of bracelets, necklaces, and earrings. She is quite noticeable; when we met, she was wearing a plaid shirt and plaid pants, featuring different patterns that clashed so as to be visually deafening. Nikita plans to marry her boyfriend; although she sees herself eventually going to art school, her dream is to sail around the world in her own boat.

Rosie (17) is quite remarkable; articulate, opinionated, and intelligent, she stands out in a crowd. Her short spiky hair is purple, fading to lavender from repeated washings; she wears green lipstick and blue and black eyeliner in squiggly lines behind her glasses. Rosie has a high school education and does not plan to go on to college. She has just moved into an apartment with two roommates; as she is ideologically opposed to working, she supports herself through panhandling. Rosie's entry into the punk subculture was mediated by her political commitment to anarchism. She has broken off all contact with her parents; her mother is a homemaker and her father is a stockbroker. She was the lead singer of a band in the past, and hopes to continue in some form of artistic or musical field in the future. She describes herself as confused, nervous, a freak, and a procrastinator, adding, "I'm still young. I have to figure everything out. I can't arrange everything today. I have to do it tomorrow."

Rudie (31) grew up in New York city, where she attended art college and worked, until recently, as a stagehand on a soap opera. She is small and thin, with green eyes and a short brown/auburn mohawk shot through with gray hairs. She often wears a gray patched hooded sweatshirt, black jeans with plaid patches, and heavy black boots. She has a pierced septum, some blackwork tattoos, and a beautifully colored Mexican-style tattoo-in-progress of a flaming heart. Rudie is slow speaking but talkative and has many interesting stories about her experiences as a squatter punk. Having fallen on hard times while taking care of her very ill boyfriend, she is currently squatting and avoids thinking about the future.

Sheila (19) has shaggy blue hair and lip piercings and wears black boots, oversize black jeans, and black sweatshirts. She gets along with her mother, who collects welfare, and currently travels, living out of a friend's van. A relaxed and open person, she would like to become as social worker: "Probably I see more than most people ever see and I learn a lot from people." Although she sees her experiences as a punk as valuable for her future as a counselor, she also worries that she is not moving forward with her plans to further herself.

Sloopy (21) wears her acid-green and blue hair up in a Pebbles Flintstone–type of ponytail on top of her head. She wears a Mickey Mouse T-shirt with her black jeans and boots. Sloopy's mother is a beautician and her father works as a communications engineer; her parents are divorced, and she gets along with both of them. Open and intelligent, she recently dropped out of college and is currently traveling. "I like to hang out with my friends and I have a pretty good personality, I guess. You're nice to me, I'm nice to you," she says. She would like to settle down eventually, with a house and a job of an as-yet-undetermined nature.

Sophie (18) is shy, although friendly: "I'm shy when I don't know the person, after that I get used to them. I'm not jealous. I'm generous. I can't say no. People take advantage of me. I'm too generous. I get along really well with people." She wears her hair shaved, except for multicolored bangs, and sports a number of homemade tattoos. Sophie dropped out of school in the tenth grade; she ran away frequently and had trouble concentrating due to family problems. She lived in foster care for three years and now lives in a group home for girls; she is currently on welfare. Her parents are still together; they live outside the city and sell jewelry and antiques at flea markets. Sophie does not plan to marry or have children; until recently, she was working toward a career in modeling, but has since decided against it. She is at present without future plans, and foresees that she will wind up on welfare.

Stone (18) is small and thin, appearing to be much younger than her age. She reports that she has been living on the streets for a number of years, having left an abusive home. She describes herself as an individualist who is "usually happy": "I never let anything get to me for long. If shit happens, I deal with it then and there and leave it behind. That's me. I learned to do that, because if I didn't, I'd be dead." She has very curly blonde hair, which is styled into a wide mohawk with short sidelocks. A street punk, she wears baggy khaki shorts, a black T-shirt, and brown boots. She squats and travels. She admits that she is a loner, and that she prefers this. She would like to get off the street and hopes one day to move to Australia.

Sue (15) is very thin and delicate looking, with a long green mohawk and large combat boots. She says, "I consider myself to be intelligent, but not educated fully. And also, I'm rather small, I'm extremely defensive, and I want to argue politics. I will argue politics until the day I die. The left wing is right." Indeed open, friendly, and intelligent, she attends art school, where she is majoring in visual art; she then intends to further her education and finally to have a career in broadcast communications. Her parents are recently divorced; she lives with her mother, who works in management for the government. Her father, with whom she does not get along, owns a hair studio; both parents have some college education. When not in school, Sue works in retail. She used to be a model, but that was before she shaved her head.

Tori (21) has been on her own since the age of twelve; her parents separated prior to her birth and her mother, who works as a waitress, was a drug abuser until fairly recently. Tori is of medium height with a solid build; she usually wears black boots, black tights, a red kilt, and a T-shirt with a large grinning Cheshire cat on it. She wears her blonde hair cropped short in a Chelsea cut, with longer bangs, and her eyes are blue with flecks of gray. Tori is a thoughtful and articulate speaker and an advocate of the rights of squatters and drug users. She was married once, and gave up her child for an open adoption. She is currently enrolled in a vocational computer course and hopes to continue her activism in establishing a "[drug] users' network" in her city.

Wanda (26) says, "I just have try be me. I try to be nice to everybody and I'm friendly. I talk to people, I talk to everybody, I think. I like everybody to be happy." She has been in and out of the punk scene for ten years or so. She is divorced and has a daughter, who lives with her parents; Wanda's mother is a bookkeeper and her father a maintenance man. Wanda also lives with her parents when she is not traveling and squatting, although she does not get along with them. She has some training as a medical assistant, but is currently between jobs. She wears her dark, curly hair long on top (usually in a pony tail) and shaved along the sides and the back. She is of medium height and heavyset, with a nose ring and a missing front tooth. Wanda describes herself as friendly and nice, and objects to the violent and antisocial image of the punk subculture.

Appendix C: Interview Guide and Statement of Purpose

I have included the preliminary statement, interview guide, and statement of purpose in a style which closely replicates that which I used toward the end of my research. The guide was revised throughout the time I was in the field. Left-justified questions are main questions and the indented questions appearing below these are "probe" questions (Lofland and Lofland 1995).

Preliminary Statement

Name: Age:

Date: Time:

Place:

- I have to start by asking you: Is it OK with you if I tape this?
- Like I said, this is for a study that I'm doing for a book that I'm writing about punk girls.
- I might quote you in print, but I won't use your real name.
- Everything that you say to me will be kept in strict confidence. No one listens to this tape but me and after I transcribe it, I destroy it.
- I'm not going to ask you any questions about sex, drugs, alcohol, or anything illegal.

- I'm not going to ask you any questions that I'm not prepared to answer myself.
- I'm trying to find out what your personal experiences and your opinions are.
- If you don't want to answer a question, you don't have to.
- If you find a question to be too weird or unclear, you can ask me, "What do you mean by that?"
- If you want to suggest any questions that I haven't asked, that would be great.
- You're welcome to interrupt if you don't agree with something I've said.
- This should only take an hour or so, but if you want to stop early or go on longer, that's fine too.

Interview Guide

Are you in school?
  Yes: Where?
    What year?
    What are you studying?
  No: When did you stop?
    What were you studying?
    Do you ever plan to go back?
Are you working?
  Yes: Doing what?
    How many hours a week?
  No: Are you looking for a job?
    How are you supporting yourself?
Where do you live?
  With whom?
Where were you raised?
  When did you leave home?
What does your mom do?
  Did she go to college?
What does your dad do?
  Did he go to college?
Are they still together?
Do you get along with them?
How would you describe yourself?
  Do you identify as a punk?
How would you define *punk*?
  What is it about you that makes you a punk?

When did you become a punk?

How did you become a punk?

  When/how did you first hear about punk?

  When did you first hear punk music?

  When/how did you first meet other punks?

What first attracted you to the punk scene?

What do you like about being a punk?

  Is there anything that you don't like about being a punk?

Did anything change in your life because you became a punk?

  Yes: What changed?

How did people react when you became a punk?

  How did your parents react?

  How did your family react?

  How did friends/people at school react?

Do you feel that the punk scene has changed since you first got into it?

  Yes: In what way?

Are many/most of your friends punks?

  Are they mostly guys or mostly girls?

  Why do you think that is?

How often do you see your friends?

  What do you do when you're together?

What do you do on a typical day?

  How often do you go to shows?

  How often do you hang out with other punks?

Are you involved in a relationship with someone?

  Yes: Is your partner a punk?

How do male punks treat you?

  Like "a girl" or like "a pal"?

Do you always dress like a punk?

  Is there any circumstance where you would change/tone down your look?

Do you feel that people treat you differently than they treat other people, because you're a punk?

  Yes: In what way?

Do you think that your experiences as a female punk are very different from those of the male punks?

  Yes: In what way?

Do you ever get hassled because you're a punk? Do people ever get in your face?

  Yes: By who?

  How often does it happen?

What do you do about it?

Do you ever feel pressured to change your style?

    Yes: By who?

Have you ever gotten [sexually] harassed?

    Yes: By who?

    In what circumstances?

    How often does it happen?

    What do you do about it?

Do you think that being a punk has ever caused you any major problems?

    For example, with the police or at school?

    Yes: Like what?

What do you think you would have been like if you had never become a punk?

Do you think you'll ever stop being a punk?

Do you consider yourself to be "feminine"?

    Yes: In what way?

    No: Why not?

Are you politically active?

    Are you a member of any political group?

Would you call yourself a feminist?

    Yes: What do you mean by *feminist*?

What do you think you'll be doing in five years?

    Are you planning to have a career?

    Do you expect to get married?

    Do you ever want to have kids?

I'm pretty much out of questions. Is there anything you'd like to add? Anything that I haven't asked you about that you think I should know?

Notes:

How we met:

How the interview went:

Physical description:
    approximate height:
    approximate weight:
    eyes:
    hair:
    clothes:
    piercings/jewelry:

scars/tattoos:
makeup:
demeanor:

Statement of Purpose

First of all, thank you for allowing me to interview you. The opinions and experiences that you have shared with me today are very valuable in allowing me to write about punk girls in North America. I am doing this research and writing this book because I think that what punk girls have to say is very important and should be heard. In doing this research, and in finding out about how and why girls become punks, I am hoping to let people know more about the punk scene and about the kind of people who are punks. I am finding that there are many similarities in punk girls' experiences, and I think that it is important for people in general to know how punk girls are dealing with things like sexual harassment or issues of self-esteem. I think that what punk girls have to say about these things is unique and can be useful for other girls, as well as for people like parents and teachers, who deal with girls every day.

I think that it's also important for punk girls to be able to talk to each other and to find out what each other has to say. For this reason, I would like to make anything that I write available to you. For example, I might write some articles based on your and other girls' stories, and much of what you shared with me today will definitely be in my book. If you're interested in having copies of anything that I write about punk girls, a written copy of the interview that we did, or a copy of the book when it's done (the book will take a couple of years, though), or if you have any questions about the interview or about any part of my research, you can write to me at this address: Lauraine Leblanc, [current address], or you can call me at [telephone number].

I'd be really happy to hear from you and to send you anything I write. You don't need to send any money or anything. Then, if you want to add anything to what you already said, or comment on anything that I write, we could correspond. I would very much like to hear from you.

As I said during the interview, although I may quote you in print, I won't use your real name. I'll take the first letter of your name and make up a name for you, so if and when you read anything on this, you'll know who you are. Everything that you say to me will be kept in strict confidence. If you have any further concerns about the research itself, and you want to talk to someone other than me, you can also contact [Department Chair, address].

Again, let me say thanks for talking to me, and to let you know that I would really like to hear from you in the future. Thank you.

Notes

One "The Punk Girl Thing"

1. Throughout this text, I use the terms *girl* and *young woman* interchangeably. The issue of naming is a particularly thorny one for feminists; *girls* has long been used to refer to adult women, thereby infantilizing us. The young women I interviewed ranged in age from 14 to 37; clearly, not all of them are girls (nor, some would say, are they even properly "young"). Nevertheless, I adhere to the term "girl," offering in support of this practice the fact that this is how punk girls usually refer to themselves ("young punk women" or "punk young women" being somewhat unwieldy terms), as well as recent attempts by one faction of the punk movement, Riot Grrrls, to reclaim the term for feminist use.

   In the same vein, I refer to male punks as "guys," as this reflects the way that both male and female punks refer to male punks. Although *boys* might more adequately parallel *girls,* the term *guys* is that most often employed by punks.
2. There are significant effects of race, class, and culture on gender differences in self-esteem. Researchers from the AAUW and CACSW, as well as others (see Richman, Clark, and Brown 1985; Gibbs 1985) consistently find that black girls score higher on measures of self-esteem than do white and Latina girls. White girls have the lowest self-esteem throughout their developmental years, and Latina girls experience the most dramatic drop in self-esteem. The CACSW found that these drops in self-esteem were also muted among Québécoises teens, with young women in Québec reporting overwhelmingly positive self-assessments. Regardless of demographic distinctions, there is a significant gap between male and female adolescents' levels of self-esteem and a perceptible overall decline in girls' self-assessments. This is especially true for middle-class white girls. As the girls involved in this study were predominantly white and from lower to upper-middle class, these findings are especially pertinent.

3. One important exception is the work of Carol Gilligan's colleagues, Annie Rogers, Lyn Brown, and Mark Tappan (1994), who found in a longitudinal study that a standardized psychological test measuring ego development showed that adolescent girls regressed or remained at the same ego level over three years. Contrasting these with contemporaneously conducted in-depth interviews, they found that adolescent girls' losses in psychological tests of ego development could be interpreted as "a healthy resistance to cultural norms of femininity" (31).
4. One notable exception to this is Paul Willis's ethnographic research, reported in *Learning to Labour* (1977) and *Profane Culture* (1978). Willis does focus on style, but unlike his contemporaries at the Birmingham school, he documents his interviews with members of the subcultures he researched and centers his analysis on transcribed interviews as well as his own observations. Interview data is conspicuously absent from other Birmingham school researchers' accounts.
5. The term is Donna Haraway's (1988).
6. See chapter 2 and appendix A, "Punk Glossary," for further definition of these terms.

Two "Punk's Not Dead—It Just Smells That Way"

1. For more detailed accounts of this early punk scene, see Kozak (1988) and McNeil and McCain (1996). Most accounts place bands such as Blondie and the Talking Heads within the punk genre. It should be noted that prior to entering the recording studio, both of these bands produced power pop music that was significantly less synthesizer-laden and mainstream-oriented than their recordings suggest (Gaar 1992).
2. Belsito and Davis (1983) claim that this was in fact L.A. scenester Hellin Killer.
3. See Becker (1963:3–8) for various definitions of deviance. "Statistical deviance" defines as deviant anything that differs too much from the average; "pathological deviance," metaphorically based on a model of disease, invokes images of dysfunction and stigma, resulting in efforts to control such deviance for the good of society.

Three "I Grew Up and I Was a Punk"

1. For examples of the results of such a focus, see the work of Anne Campbell (1984) and Angela McRobbie (1991, 1994).
2. As an aside, it is interesting to note that Baron argues that males find available jobs (which would include service sector jobs) undesirable because "the pay is poor, provides little status, and is alienating," and yet assumes that young women in the service sector do not view their work that way. The implication is that females have a higher tolerance for drudgery and exploitation than do males!
3. I began each interview with a series of questions designed to explore each girl's life history. These questions covered aspects of family background, school and work experiences, initial contact with the punk subculture, factors precipitating her decision to become a punk, and her subsequent subcultural experiences (see appendix C). Because these narratives were elicited through the girls' accounts, they allow access to aspects of retrospective self-reporting and detail a temporally ordered process. As such, they are valuable in presenting the recursive or reciprocal effects of various influences and events. However, it is important to note that such narratives

are also open to retrospective bias, to the extent that individuals' recollections and representations of the past are brought into concordance with their current self-concepts (see Mason-Schrock's 1996 discussion of transsexuals' narrative constructions of "true selves" for an overview of social-psychological perspectives of narrative, as well as a fine example of such identity construction). A more philosophical account of narrative maintains that the structure of narrative "inheres in the events themselves" (Carr 1986:117); narratives do not necessarily reflect nor distort reality, but construct it. This perspective argues for the validity of narratives as a phenomenological tool, as in W.I. Thomas's oft-cited dictum that "If men [*sic*] define situations as real, they are real in their consequences." Thus, I make no truth claims about these narratives, but rather offer them as glimpses into the everyday constructed reality of these punk girls.

4. In this sense, punk families or "tribes" are like the extended kinship networks Carol Stack (1974) found among urban black communities.

5. See the works of Robert Agnew (1992), Ronald Akers (1985), Howard Becker (1963), Albert Cohen (1955), Travis Hirschi (1969), Edwin Lemert (1972), Robert Merton (1938), and Edwin Sutherland and Donald Cressey (1974) for major causal theories of deviance from a male perspective.

6. See Albert Cohen (1955). I expand on this in the following chapter.

Four "The Punk Guys Will Really Overpower What the Punk Girls Have to Say"

1. For a tangible example of this, compare the masculinities of middle-class Richie Cunningham and the (working-class) Fonz in the sitcom *Happy Days*.

2. See also the account of Rattler's behavior, with which I opened this chapter. Although I did not pursue this line of questioning, many more girls reported being raped by nonpunks, or having experienced incest—only a small part of the abuse punk girls experience comes from fellow punks. This is not to excuse male punks' abuse of punk girls, but rather to place them within the larger context of the sex offenders who prey on punk girls.

Five "I'll Slap on My Lipstick and Then Kick Their Ass"

1. Susan Brownmiller (1984) minutely describes these standards and the ways in which women seek to achieve them under the rubrics "body," "hair," "clothes," "voice," "skin," "movement," "emotion," and "ambition." See also the work of Iris Marion Young (1990) on female embodiment.

2. See Adrienne Rich (1980) on the construction of "compulsory heterosexuality" and the contradiction such a demand creates in women's lives.

Six "Oh, I Hope I Don't Catch Anything"

1. Although all of my formal interviews and the bulk of my observations focused on punk girls, this chapter reflects the ways in which most punks encounter harassment from mainstream others, except for the case of sexual harassment, which I treat separately in the following chapter. In some cases, male punks may be subject

to more harassment than are girls, or may be more often physically threatened or assaulted. These differences, however, are quantitative, rather than qualitative. Admittedly, my focus on punk girls offers a partial perspective on general punk harassment, but in my experience in the field, I found that punks of both genders are subject to the same kinds of harassment detailed in this chapter.

2. See the work of Erving Goffman (1959) for further analysis of public interactions between strangers and the uses of "access information."

3. For the purposes of this analysis, I did not include incidents of harassment that are precipitated by panhandling or other events in which punks initiated contact. The incidents reported here were described as unexpected and unprovoked.

4. The categories of exclusion, exploitation, and evaluation are based on the excellent work of Carol Brooks Gardner (1995) on the street harassment women experience.

5. The ejection of punks from public places such as parks played an important role in precipitating an uprising in Montreal during the summer of 1996, when the city rezoned a public square as a park, imposed a curfew, and attempted to eject all the punks who had either hung out or squatted there legally until the ordinance changed. The uprising enjoyed front-page newspaper coverage, which I analyze elsewhere (Leblanc, forthcoming).

6. Feagin (1991), for example, found that some of the blacks he interviewed resorted to threats of lawsuits or media attention in order to counter some forms of harassment, especially exclusionary practices

Seven   "I Bet a Steel-Capped Boot Could Shut You Up"

1. For both analyses of and strategies to combat on-campus harassment in both colleges and high schools, see AAUW Educational Foundation (1993), Benson and Thomson (1982), Crocker (1983), Dziech and Weiner (1984), Hoffman (1986), Larkin (1994), McCormack (1985), Paludi and Barickman (1991), and Stein (1993).

2. The assumption that the onus is on women to act to reduce the amount of sexual threat is made especially clear by a popular account: Reportedly, in response to a rise in stranger rapes in the early 1970s, the Israeli Parliament proposed instituting a nighttime curfew on women. Then-prime minister Golda Meir retorted that if a curfew were mandated, it was men who should be banned from the streets at night, as it was they who were committing these crimes. Women continue to protest male dominance of the streets by annually participating in numerous Take Back the Night marches, races, and activities throughout North America.

3. Indeed, it lacks a consistent label; some writers refer to it as "street hassling" (Blair 1984), others as "street remarks" (Gardner 1980, 1995; Kissling and Kramarae 1991), as "public harassment" (Gardner 1995), or as "street harassment" (Bowman 1993; di Leonardo 1981; Kissling 1991; Packer 1986). Feminist theorists and female travelers have noted that this phenomenon is not unique to North America, but occurs worldwide in urban areas (Bowman 1993; Van Gelder 1981; Wise and Stanley 1987). It is interesting to note that some cultures do, indeed, have names for this behavior without having formal prohibitions (Kissling 1991); in India, for example, it is called "Eve-teasing."

4. In fact, public sexual harassment that involves the threat of repercussions (for example, threats of sexual assault or other damage) is likely to be already subject to

statutes concerning the use of threatening language and behavior, as well as those pertaining to stalking and sexual assault.

5. For these few accounts of resistance, see Gardner (1995—especially chapter 6), and Langelan (1993).

6. This is *not* to say that punk girls' choice of apparel *causes* their harassment. The sole cause of harassment is the harasser. However, punk girls' use of bondage gear does open the door to more harassment than women in, say, nuns' habits or suits experience.

7. These last two accounts also highlight some of the racism found within the punk subculture. Tori participated in the skinhead scene, but now otherwise denounces racism. Alexea, who reported having once been a skinhead, appeared to regret that there were no longer many "Nazi punks." The punk subculture, as a whole, does not espouse racist ideology, but rather presents itself as antiracist, especially through such events as Rock Against Racism concerts. Nevertheless, the punk subculture is predominantly white, and many members dislike predominantly African-American forms of youth cultural resistance, such as rap music. Thus, although most punks are not explicitly racist, the subculture implicitly excludes people of color.

8. For an explicitly feminist account of such an avoidance strategy, see Williamson (1971).

9. I include this incident as one of sexual harassment due to the sexualized nature of the exchange. Justine confronted what she perceived as initial rudeness by using an expletive which refers to copulation, "fuck you," but with widespread usage, it has been stripped of its sexual connotation. The stranger's response, "Suck my dick," however, still retains strong sexualized connotations. For this reason, I have included this as an incidence of sexual harassment, because the conflict and power differentials between Justine and the stranger became sexualized (in an intentionally degrading manner) at the moment of his utterance. Furthermore, Justine reported this incident within the context of her discussion of "*always* being harassed by men," thereby identifying it as one such instance.

Eight   "Girls Kick Ass"

1. The original French reads *"réduire les aspects negatifs de son comportement"*; my translation.

Works Cited

Aggarwal, Arjun P. 1992. *Sexual Harassment: A Guide for Understanding and Prevention.* Toronto.: Butterworths Canada.

Agnew, Robert. 1992. "Foundation for a General Strain Theory of Crime and Delinquency." *Criminology* 30:47–87.

Akers, Ronald L. 1985. *Deviant Behavior: A Social Learning Approach.* Belmont, Calif.: Wadsworth Publishing.

Allgood-Merten, Betty, and Jean Stockard. 1991. "Sex Role Identity and Self-Esteem: A Comparison of Children and Adolescents." *Sex Roles* 25:129–139.

American Association of University Women. 1991. *Shortchanging Girls, Shortchanging America.* Washington, D.C.: Greenberg-Lake, The Analysis Group.

American Association of University Women Educational Foundation. 1992. *How Schools Shortchange Girls: The AAUW Report.* New York: Marlowe.

———. 1993. *Hostile Hallways: The AAUW Survey on Sexual Harassment in America's Schools.* New York: Harris/Scholastic Research.

Arnett, Jeffrey Jensen. 1996. *Metalheads: Heavy Metal Music and Adolescent Alienation.* Boulder, Colo.: Westview Press.

Babbie, Earl. 1989. *The Practice of Social Research,* fifth edition. Belmont, Calif.: Wadsworth Publishing.

Backhouse, Connie, and Leah Cohen. 1981. *Sexual Harassment on the Job: How to Avoid the Working Woman's Nightmare.* Englewood Cliffs, N.J.: Prentice-Hall.

Bale, Jeff, and Tim Yohannen. 1986. "The Punk Counterculture." *Utne Reader* (June/July):62.

Barreca, Regina. 1991. *They Used to Call Me Snow White . . . But I Drifted.* New York: Penguin.

Baron, Stephen W. 1989a. "The Canadian West Coast Punk Subculture: A Field Study." *Canadian Journal of Sociology/Cahiers Canadiens de Sociologie* 14:289–316.

————. 1989b. "Resistance and its Consequences: The Street Culture of Punks." *Youth and Society* 21:207–237.

Beaumont, Stephen. 1989. "Do Punks Get Bad Rap?" *Toronto Star* (November 1):A27.

Becker, Howard S. 1963. *Outsiders: Studies in the Sociology of Deviance*. New York: Free Press.

Belsito, Peter, and Bob Davis. 1983. *Hardcore California: A History of Punk and New Wave*. San Francisco: Last Gasp.

Benet, Lorenzo. 1986. "Taking Control of the Punk Who Happens to Be Your Kid." *Chicago Tribune* (March 10):C1.

Benson, Donna J., and Gregory E. Thomson. 1982. "Sexual Harassment on a University Campus: The Confluence of Authority Relations, Sexual Interest and Gender Stratification." *Social Problems* 29:236–251.

Bepko, Claudia, and Jo-Ann Krestan. 1990. *Too Good for Her Own Good*. New York: HarperCollins.

Blair, Gwenda. 1984. "Street Hassling: Putting Up With Put-Downs." *Mademoiselle* (July):118–119+.

Blakely, Mary Kay. 1982. "True or False: 'All Men Like to Girl-Watch, and Girls Don't Mind It.'" *Vogue* (January):57+.

Blazak, Randy. 1991. Status Frustration and Racism: A Case Study of Orlando Skinheads. M.A. thesis, Emory University.

————. 1995. The Suburbanization of Hate: An Ethnographic Study of the Skinhead Subculture. Ph.D. diss., Emory University.

Bohan, Janis S. 1973. "Age and Sex Differences in Self-Concept." *Adolescence* 8:379–384.

Booth, William. 1996. "'Gutter Punks': Angry, White Rebels are Homeless by Choice." *Washington Post* (February 11):A1.

Bowman, Cynthia Grant. 1993. "Street Harassment and the Informal Ghettoization of Women." *Harvard Law Review* 106:517–580.

Brake, Michael. 1980. *The Sociology of Youth Culture and Youth Subcultures: Sex and Drugs and Rock 'n' Roll?* London: Routledge and Kegan Paul.

————. 1985. *Comparative Youth Culture*. London: Routledge and Kegan Paul.

Bravo, Ellen, and Ellen Cassedy. 1992. *The 9 to 5 Guide to Combating Sexual Harassment: Candid Advice from 9 to 5, the National Association of Working Women*. New York: John Wiley & Sons.

Broeske, Pat H. 1985. "Deprivations and the Power of Punk: A Program That Says it Reclaims Kids from Their Music." *Washington Post* (November 29):C1.

Broverman, Inge K., Donald M. Broverman, Frank E. Clarkson, Paul S. Rosenkrantz, and Susan R. Vogel. 1970. "Sex Role Stereotypes and Clinical Judgements of Mental Health." *Journal of Consulting and Clinical Psychology* 34:1–7.

Brown, Lyn Mikel, and Carol Gilligan. 1992. *Meeting at the Crossroads: Women's Psychology and Girls' Development*. Cambridge, Mass.: Harvard University Press.

Brown, Mary Ellen. 1994. *Soap Opera and Women's Talk: The Pleasure of Resistance*. Thousand Oaks, Calif.: Sage Publications.

Brownmiller, Susan. 1984. *Femininity*. New York: Fawcett Colombine.

Burchill, Julie, and Tony Parsons. 1978. *"The Boy Looked at Johnny": The Obituary of Rock 'n' Roll*. Boston: Faber & Faber.

Burr, A. 1984. "The Ideologies of Despair: A Symbolic Interpretation of Punks' and Skinheads' Usage of Barbiturates." *Social Science and Medicine* 19:929–938.

Bush, Diane E., Roberta G. Simmons, Bruce Hutchinson, and Dale A. Blyth. 1977/1978. "Adolescent Perceptions of Sex-Roles in 1968 and 1975." *Public Opinion Quarterly* 41:459–474.

Campbell, Anne. 1984. *The Girls in the Gang: A Report from New York City.* New York: Basil Blackwell Publishers.

Canadian Advisory Council on the Status of Women/Conseil consultatif Canadien sur le statut de la femme. 1992. *Young Women Speak Out: 1992 Symposium Report/ La Parole aux Jeunes Filles: Compte Rendu du Colloque de 1992.* Ottawa: Canadian Advisory Council on the Status of Women/Conseil consultatif Canadien sur le statut de la femme.

Carr, David. 1986. "Narrative and the Real World: An Argument for Continuity." *History and Theory* 25:117–131.

Carter, Angela. 1992. "Ups and Downs for the Babes in Bondage." *New Statesman and Society* 5:xiv–xv.

Cashmore, Ernest. 1984. *No Future: Youth and Society.* London: Heinemann.

Chapkis, Wendy. 1986. *Beauty Secrets: Women and the Politics of Appearance.* London: Women's Press.

Chesney-Lind, Meda. 1973. "Judicial Enforcement of the Female Sex Role: The Family Court and the Female Delinquent." *Issues in Criminology* 8:51–69.

———. 1989. "Girls' Crime and Woman's Place: Toward a Feminist Model of Female Delinquency." *Crime and Delinquency* 35:5–29.

Clarke, John. 1976. "Style." In *Resistance through Rituals,* ed. S. Hall and T. Jefferson, 175–191. London: Hutchison.

Cohen, Albert K. 1955. *Delinquent Boys: The Culture of the Gang.* Glencoe, Ill.: Free Press.

Cohen, Phil. 1980. "Subcultural Conflict and Working-Class Community." In *Culture, Media, Language,* ed. S. Hall, 78–87. London: Hutchison.

Cohen, Stanley. 1972. *Folk Devils and Moral Panics.* London: Macgibbon and Kee.

Comer, James P. 1989. "What's Normal?" *Parents* (January):132.

Comité pour les droits des jeunes en centres d'accueil. 1988. *Les droits des jeunes en centres d'accueil.* Montreal: Bibliothéque CSSMM.

Conklin, Ellis E. 1985a. "Are Punks and Heavy Metal 'Stoners' Dangerous to Society?" UPI, May 15 [available: Lexis/Nexus].

———. 1985b. "Punk and Heavy Metal: Teen Rebellion or Something Darker!" UPI, May 28 [available: Lexis/Nexus].

Connolly, Cynthia, Lesley Clague, and Sharon Cheslow. 1992. *Banned in D.C.: Photos and Anecdotes from the D.C. Punk Underground (79–85).* Washington, D.C.: Sun Dog Propaganda.

Cowie, Celia, and Sue Lees. 1981. "Slags or Drags." *Feminist Review* 9:17–31.

Cox, Alex, and Abbe Wool. 1986. *Sid and Nancy.* Dir. Alex Cox; w. Alex Cox and Abbe Wool. Zenith Productions/Initial Pictures.

Crocker, Phyllis L. 1983. "An Analysis of University Definitions of Sexual Harassment." *Signs* 8:696–707.

Dancis, Bruce. 1978. "Safety Pins and Class Struggle: Punk Rock and the Left." *Socialist Review* 8:58–83.

de Beauvoir, Simone. 1989. *The Second Sex.* Translated by H. M. Parshley. New York: Alfred A. Knopf.

di Leonardo, Micaela. 1981. "Political Economy of Street Harassment." *Aegis* (summer):51–57.

Dziech, Billie Wright, and Linda Weiner. 1984. *The Lecherous Professor: Sexual Harassment on Campus.* Boston, Mass.: Beacon Press.

Eder, Donna. 1985. "The Cycle of Popularity: Interpersonal Relations among Female Adolescents." *Sociology of Education* 58:154–165.

Eicher, Joanne B., Suzanne Baizerman, and John Michelman. 1991. "Adolescent Dress, Part II: A Qualitative Study of Suburban High School Students." *Adolescence* 26:679–686.

England, Paula, and Irene Browne. 1992. "Internalization and Constraint in Women's Subordination." *Current Perspectives in Social Theory* 12:97–123.

Farley, Lyn. 1978. *Sexual Shakedown: The Sexual Harassment of Women on the Job.* New York: McGraw-Hill.

Feagin, Joe R. 1991. "The Continuing Significance of Race: Antiblack Discrimination in Public Places." *American Sociological Review* 56:101–116.

Feiring, Candice, and Michael Lewis. 1991. "The Transition from Middle Childhood to Early Adolescence: Sex Differences in the Social Network and Perceived Self-Competence." *Sex Roles* 24:489–509.

Ferrell, Jeff. 1993. *Crimes of Style: Urban Graffiti and the Politics of Criminality.* New York: Garland.

Fetterley, Judith. 1978. *The Resisting Reader: A Feminist Approach to American Fiction.* Bloomington: Indiana University Press.

Fine, Gary Alan, and Sherryl Kleinman. 1979. "Rethinking Subculture: An Interactionist Analysis." *American Journal of Sociology* 85:1–20.

Fish, Stanley. 1980. *Is There a Text in This Class? The Authority of Interpretive Communities.* Cambridge, Mass.: Harvard University Press.

Fisher, Ian. 1996. "Erin's Looking for Leg-Rub Steve." *New York Times Magazine* (Dec.8):72–77

Fox, Greer Litton. 1977. "'Nice Girl': Social Control of Women through a Value Construct." *Signs* 2:805–817.

Fox, Kathryn Joan. 1987. "Real Punks and Pretenders: The Social Organization of a Counterculture." *Journal of Contemporary Ethnography* 16:344–370.

Frith, Simon. 1978. "The Punk Bohemians." *New Society* 43:535–536.

Gaar, Gillian G. 1992. *She's a Rebel: The History of Women in Rock and Roll.* Seattle, Wash.: Seal Press.

Gaines, Donna. 1992. *Teenage Wasteland: Suburbia's Dead End Kids.* New York: HarperCollins.

Gardner, Carol Brooks. 1980. "Passing By: Street Remarks, Address Rights, and the Urban Female." *Sociological Inquiry* 50:328–356.

———. 1995. *Passing By: Gender and Public Harassment.* Berkeley: University of California Press.

Gibbs, Jewelle Taylor. 1985. "City Girls: Psychosocial Adjustment of Urban Black Adolescent Females." *Sage* 2:28–36.

Gilligan, Carol, Janie Victoria Ward, and Jill McLean Taylor, eds. 1988. *Mapping the Moral Domain.* Cambridge, Mass.: Harvard University Press.

Gilligan, Carol, Nona P. Lyons, and Trudy J. Hanmer, eds. 1989. *Making Connections: The Relational Worlds of Adolescent Girls at Emma Willard School.* Cambridge, Mass.: Harvard University Press.

Gilligan, Carol, Annie G. Rogers, and Deborah L. Tolman. 1991. *Women, Girls, and Psychotherapy: Reframing Resistance.* Binghamton, N.Y.: Haworth Press.

Giroux, Henry A. 1983. *Theory and Resistance in Education.* South Hadley, Mass.: Bergin & Garvey Publishers.

Glick, Peter, Judith A. DeMorest, and Carla A. Hotze. 1988. "Keeping Your Distance: Group Membership, Personal Space, and Requests for Small Favors." *Journal of Applied Psychology* 18:315–330.

Goffman, Erving. 1959. *The Presentation of Self in Everyday Life.* New York: Anchor Books.

Gouvernement du Québec. 1990. *Cadre de référence sur l'orientation et l'organisation des centres de réadaptation pour jeunes en difficulté d'adaptation.* Québec: Ministère de la santé et des services sociaux, Direction des communications.

Gratz, Kim L. 1995. "Gender Differences in Perceptions and Attitudes Toward Sexual Harassment." Paper presented at the Southern Sociological Society Fifty-Eighth Annual Meeting, Atlanta, Ga., April 6–9.

Grossberg, Lawrence. 1994. "The Political Status of Youth and Youth Culture." In *Adolescents and Their Music,* ed. J. S. Epstein, 25–46. New York: Garland Publishing.

Gutek, Barbara. 1985. *Sex and the Workplace: The Impact of Sexual Behavior and Harassment on Women, Men, and Organizations.* San Francisco: Jossey-Bass Publishers.

Hall, Stuart, and Tony Jefferson, eds. 1976. *Resistance through Rituals.* London: Hutchison.

Hancock, Emily. 1989. *The Girl Within.* New York: Fawcett Columbine.

Hansen, Christine Hall, and Ranald D. Hansen. 1991. "Constructing Personality and Social Reality Through Music: Individual Differences Among Fans of Punk and Heavy Metal Music." *Journal of Broadcasting and Electronic Media* 35:335–350.

Haraway, Donna. 1988. "Situated Knowledges: The Science Question in Feminism and the Privilege of Partial Perspective." *Feminist Studies* 14:575–599.

Hebdige, Dick. 1976. "The Meaning of Mod." In *Resistance through Rituals,* ed. S. Hall and T. Jefferson, 87–98. London: Hutchison.

———. 1979. *Subculture: The Meaning of Style.* London: Routledge and Kegan Paul.

Henry, Tricia. 1989. *Break All Rules! Punk Rock and the Making of a Style.* Ann Arbor, Mich.: UMI Research Press.

Hirschi, Travis. 1969. *Causes of Delinquency.* Berkeley: University of California Press.

Hoare, Philip. 1991. "Anarchy in the U.K.? Forget It: What Has Happened to the Punk Generation? Being a Girl Wasn't an Issue." *The Independent* (May 28):14.

Hochschild, Arlie, with Anne Machung. 1989. *The Second Shift.* New York: Avon Books.

Hoffman, Frances L. 1986. "Sexual Harassment in Academia: Feminist Theory and Institutional Practice." *Harvard Educational Review* 56:105–120.

Holmes, Janelle, and Eliane Leslau Silverman. 1992. *We're Here, Listen to Us! A Survey of Young Women in Canada.* Ottawa: Canadian Advisory Council on the Status of Women/Conseil consultatif Canadien sur le statut de la femme.

Holstrom, John, ed. 1996. *Punk: The Original.* New York: Trans-High.

Home, Stewart. 1995. *Cranked Up Really High: An Inside Account of Punk Rock.* Hove, U.K.: Code X.

Hudson, Barbara. 1984. "Femininity and Adolescence." In *Gender and Generation,* eds. A. McRobbie and M. Nava, 31–53. London: Macmillan Publishers.

Hurley, Bri. 1989. *Making a Scene: New York Hardcore in Photos, Lyrics, and Commentary.* Winchester, Mass.: Faber and Faber.

Jefferson, Tony. 1976. "Cultural Responses of the Teds: The Defence of Space and Status." In *Resistance through Rituals*, ed. S. Hall and T. Jefferson, 81–86. London: Hutchison.

Joe, Karen A., and Meda Chesney-Lind. 1994. "'Just Every Mother's Angel': An Analysis of Gender and Ethnic Variations in Youth Gang Membership." *Gender and Society* 9:408–431.

Jones, Dylan. 1990. *Haircults: Fifty Years of Styles and Cuts.* London: Thames and Hudson.

Kennedy, Leslie W., and Stephen W. Baron. 1993. "Routine Activities and a Subculture of Violence: A Study of Violence on the Street." *Journal of Research in Crime and Delinquency* 30:88–112.

Kissling, Elizabeth Arveda. 1991. "Street Harassment: The Language of Sexual Terrorism." *Discourse and Society* 2:451–460.

Kissling, Elizabeth Arveda, and Cheris Kramarae. 1991. "Stranger Compliments: The Interpretation of Street Remarks." *Women's Studies in Communication* 14:75–93.

Kliman, Todd. 1990. "Punk is Beautiful." *Washington Post* (December 9):WMAG24–128+.

Kogan, Marcela. 1991. "When Your Kids Go Punk." *Washington Post* (April 11):D5.

Kotarba, Joseph A., and Laura Wells. 1987. "Styles of Adolescent Participation in an All-Ages Rock 'n' Roll Nightclub: An Ethnographic Analysis." *Youth and Society* 18:398–427.

Kozak, Roman. 1988. *This Ain't No Disco: The Story of CBGB.* Boston: Faber & Faber.

Laing, David. 1985. *One Chord Wonders: Power and Meaning in Punk Rock.* Philadelphia: Open University Press.

Lamy, Philip, and Jack Levin. 1985. "Punk and Middle-Class Values: A Content Analysis." *Youth and Society* 17:157–170.

Langelan, Martha J. 1993. *Back Off! How to Confront and Stop Sexual Harassment and Harassers.* New York: Fireside.

Langellier, Kristin M., and Deanna L. Hall. 1989. "Interviewing Women: A Phenomenological Approach to Feminist Communication Research." In *Doing Research on Women's Communication*, ed. K. Carter and C. Spitzack, 193–220. Norwood, N.J.: Ablex Publishing.

Larkin, June. 1994. *Sexual Harassment: High School Girls Speak Out.* Toronto: Second Story Press.

Leaf, Bruce. 1984. "Regional News." UPI, July 12 [available: Lexis/Nexus].

Leblanc, Lauraine. Forthcoming. "Punky in the Middle: Cultural Constructions of the 1996 Montreal Summer Uprisings." In *Cultural Representations of Crime and Deviance*, ed. Jeff Ferrell and Neil Websdale. Hawthorne, N.Y.: Aldine de Gruyter.

Legault, Jean Benoit, and Mathieu Perreault. 1996. "Le Conflit Prend de l'Ampleur: Punks et Police Se Confrontent au Milieu de la Nuit à l'Ex-square Berri." *La Presse* (July 30):A1–A2.

Leger, Marie France. 1994. "Des Jeunes Punks Affirment Avoir Été Malmenés par des Agents de la STCUM" (Young punks allege maltreatment by STCUM officers). *La Presse* (June 11).

Lemert, Edwin M. 1972. *Human Deviance, Social Problems, and Social Control.* 2d ed. Englewood Cliffs, N.J.: Prentice-Hall.

Leong, Lawrence Wai-Teng. 1992. "Cultural Resistance: The Cultural Terrorism of British Male Working-Class Youth." *Current Perspectives in Social Theory* 12:29–58.

Levine, Harold G., and Steven H. Stumpf. 1983. "Statements of Fear through Cultural Symbols: Punk Rock as a Reflexive Subculture." *Youth and Society* 14:417–435.

Lewin, Miriam, and Lilli M. Tragos. 1987. "Has the Feminist Movement Influenced Adolescent Sex Role Attitudes? A Reassessment after a Quarter Century." *Sex Roles* 16:125–135.

Lewis, Lisa A. 1990. *Gender Politics and MTV: Voicing the Difference.* Philadelphia: Temple University Press.

Lewis, Randy. 1986. "Pop Beat: Handbook Weighs Heavy Metal for Parents." *Los Angeles Times* (August 22):CAL25.

Lofland, John, and Lyn H. Lofland. 1995. *Analyzing Social Settings: A Guide to Qualitative Observation and Analysis.* 3d ed. Belmont, Calif.: Wadsworth Publishing.

Lull, James. 1987. "Thrashing in the Pit: an Ethnography of San Francisco Punk Subculture." In *Natural Audiences*, ed. T. R. Lindlof, 225–252. Norwood, N.J.: Ablex Publishing.

Lydon, John, with Keith Zimmerman and Kent Zimmerman. 1994. *Rotten: No Irish, No Blacks, No Dogs.* New York: St. Martin's Press.

McCann, Nancy Dodd, and Thomas A. McGinn. 1992. *Harassed: 100 Women Define Inappropriate Behavior in the Workplace.* Homewood, Ill.: Business One Irwin.

McCormack, Arlene. 1985. "The Sexual Harassment of Students by Teachers: The Case of Students in Science." *Sex Roles* 13:21–32.

McKay, George. 1996. *Senseless Acts of Beauty: Cultures of Resistance Since the Sixties.* London: Verso.

MacKinnon, Catharine. 1979. *Sexual Harassment of Working Women.* New Haven, Conn.: Yale University Press.

McLellan, Dennis. 1985. "Spikes and Studs: Tipping the Scales Against Heavy Metal, Punk." *Los Angeles Times* (February 21):sec.5, p.1.

MacLeod, Jay. 1987/1995. *Ain't No Makin' It: Leveled Aspirations in a Low-Income Neighborhood.* Boulder, Colo.: Westview Press.

McNeil, Legs, and Gillian McCain. 1996. *Please Kill Me: The Uncensored Oral History of Punk.* New York: Grove Press.

McRobbie, Angela. 1991. *Feminism and Youth Culture.* Boston: Unwin Hyman.

———. 1994. *Postmodernism and Popular Culture.* New York: Routledge.

McRobbie, Angela, and Jenny Garber. 1976. "Girls and Subcultures." In *Resistance through Rituals*, ed. S. Hall and T. Jefferson, 209–222. London: Hutchison.

Marcus, Greil. 1989. *Lipstick Traces: A Secret History of the Twentieth Century.* Cambridge, Mass.: Harvard University Press.

Marsh, Peter. 1977. "Dole Queue Rock." *New Society* 746:112–115.

Martin, Susan Ehrlich. 1989. "Sexual Harassment: The Link Joining Gender Stratification, Sexuality, and Women's Economic Status." In *Women: A Feminist Perspective.* 4th ed., ed. J. Freeman, 57–75. Mountain View, Calif.: Mayfield Publishing.

Mason-Schrock, Douglas. 1996. "Transsexuals' Narrative Construction of the 'True Self.'" *Social Psychology Quarterly* 59:176–192.

Matlock, Glen, with Pete Silverton. 1990. *I Was a Teenage Sex Pistol.* Boston: Faber & Faber.

Mays, John Bentley. 1991. "Green-Haired Teens in Their Social Scenes." *The Toronto Globe and Mail* (April 20):C13.

Merton, Robert K. 1938. "Social Structure and Anomie." *American Sociological Review* 3:672–682.

Messerschmidt, James W. 1993. *Masculinities and Crime: Critique and Reconceptualization of Theory.* Lanham, Md.: Rowman & Littlefield Publishers.

Miller, Eleanor M. 1986. *Street Woman.* Philadelphia: Temple University Press.

Millman, Marcia. 1975. "She Did It All for Love: A Feminist View of the Sociology of Deviance." In *Another Voice,* ed. M. Millman and R. M. Kanter, 251–279. New York: Anchor Books.

Mintz, Laurie B., and Nancy E. Betz. 1985. "Sex Differences in Nature, Realism, and Correlates of Body Image." *Sex Roles* 15:185–195.

Monk, Noel E., and Jimmy Guterman. 1990. *12 Days on the Road: The Sex Pistols and America.* New York: William Morrow.

Nehring, Neil. 1993. *Flowers in the Dustbin: Culture, Anarchy, and Postwar England.* Ann Arbor: University of Michigan Press.

Nelson, Jenny L. 1989. "Phenomenology as Feminist Methodology: Explicating Interviews." In *Doing Research on Women's Communication,* ed. K. Carter and C. Spitzack, 221–241. Norwood, N.J.: Ablex Publishing.

O'Brien, Lucy. 1995. *She Bop: The Definitive Study of Women in Rock, Pop, and Soul.* New York: Penguin.

O'Hara, Craig. 1995. *The Philosophy of Punk: More Than Noise!!* San Francisco: AK Press.

Orenstein, Peggy. 1994. *SchoolGirls: Young Women, Self-Esteem, and the Confidence Gap.* New York: Doubleday.

———. 1995. "Teenage Wasteland." *Details* (April):170–173+.

Packer, Jaclyn. 1986. "Sex Differences in the Perception of Street Harassment." *Women and Therapy* 5:331–338.

Paludi, Michele A., and Richard Barickman. 1991. *Academic and Workplace Harassment: A Resource Manual.* Albany: State University of New York Press.

Pipher, Mary. 1994. *Reviving Ophelia: Saving the Selves of Adolescent Girls.* New York: Putnam and Grosset Group.

Pollitt, Katha. 1985. "Hers." *New York Times* (December12): C2.

Press, Andrea L. 1991. *Women Watching Television: Gender, Class and Generation in the American Television Experience.* Philadelphia: University of Pennsylvania Press.

Radway, Janice. 1984. *Reading the Romance: Women, Patriarchy, and Popular Literature.* Chapel Hill: University of North Carolina Press.

Rauste-von Wright, Maijaliisa. 1989. "Body Image Satisfaction in Adolescent Girls and Boys: A Longitudinal Study." *Journal of Youth and Adolescence* 18:71–83.

Reynolds, Simon, and Joy Press. 1995. *The Sex Revolts: Gender, Rebellion, and Rock 'n' Roll.* Cambridge, Mass.: Harvard University Press.

Rich, Adrienne. 1980. "Compulsory Heterosexuality and Lesbian Existence." *Signs* 5:631–660.

Richman, Charles L., M. L. Clark and Kathryn P. Brown. 1985. "General and Specific Self-Esteem in Late Adolescent Students: Race <x> Gender <x> SES Effects." *Adolescence* 20:555–566.

Riot Grrrl. 1992. "What Is Riot Grrrl?" P.O. Box 11002, Washington D.C., 20008: Riot Grrrl.

Rogers, Annie G., Lyn Mikel Brown, and Mark B. Tappan. 1994. "Interpreting Loss in Ego Development in Girls." In *Exploring Identity and Gender,* vol. 2, ed. A. Lieblich and R. Josselson, 1–33. Thousand Oaks, Calif.: Sage Publications.

Rogers, Joseph W., and M. D. Buffalo. 1975. "Fighting Back: Nine Modes of Adaptation to a Deviant Label." *Social Problems* 22:101–118.

Roman, Leslie G. 1988. "Intimacy, Labor, and Class: Ideologies of Feminine Sexuality in the Punk Slam Dance." In *Becoming Feminine,* ed. L. G. Roman, L. K. Christian-Smith, and E. Ellsworth, 143–184. London: Falmer Press.

Rosenbaum, Jill L., and Lorraine Prinsky. 1987. "Sex, Violence and Rock 'n' Roll: Youths' Perceptions of Popular Music." *Popular Music and Society* 11:79–90.

———. 1991. "The Presumption of Influence: Recent Responses to Popular Music Subcultures." *Crime and Delinquency* 37:528–535.

Rosenberg, Florence R., and Roberta G. Simmons. 1975. "Sex Differences in the Self-Concept in Adolescence." *Sex Roles* 1:147–159.

Savage, Jon. 1991. *England's Dreaming: Sex Pistols and Punk Rock.* London: Faber & Faber.

Scott, James C. 1985. *Weapons of the Weak: Everyday Forms of Peasant Resistance.* New Haven, Conn.: Yale University Press.

Simonds, Wendy. 1992. *Women and Self-Help Culture: Reading between the Lines.* New Brunswick, N.J.: Rutgers University Press.

Smith, Dorothy E. 1979. "A Sociology for Women." In *The Prism of Sex,* ed. J. Sherman and E.T. Beck, 135–187. Madison: University of Wisconsin Press.

———. 1988. "Femininity as Discourse." In *Becoming Feminine,* ed. L.G. Roman, L. K. Christian-Smith, and E. Ellsworth, 37–59. London: Falmer Press.

Smith, Leslie Shacklady. 1978. "Sexist Assumptions and Female Delinquency." In *Women, Sexuality, and Social Control,* ed. C. Smart and B. Smart, 74–88. London: Routledge and Kegan Paul.

Spain, Daphne. 1992. *Gendered Spaces.* Chapel Hill: University of North Carolina Press.

Stacey, Judith. 1988. "Can There Be a Feminist Ethnography?" *Women's Studies International Forum* 11:21–27.

Stack, Carol. 1974. *All Our Kin: Strategies for Survival in a Black Community.* New York: Harper and Row.

Stark, James. 1992. *Punk '77: An Inside Look at the San Francisco Rock 'n' Roll Scene, 1977.* San Francisco: Stark Graphix.

Stein, Nan. 1993. "No Laughing Matter: Sexual Harassment in K–12 Schools." In *Transforming a Rape Culture,* ed. E. Buchwald, P. R. Fletcher, and M. Roth, 311–331. Minneapolis, Minn.: Milkweed Editions.

Stombler, Mindy. 1994. "'Buddies' or 'Slutties': The Collective Sexual Reputation of Fraternity Little Sisters." *Gender and Society* 8:293–323.

Sutherland, Edwin H., and Donald R. Cressey. 1974. *Criminology,* 9th ed. Philadelphia: J. B. Lippincott.

Thompson, Paul. 1979. "Youth Culture and Youth Politics in Britain." *Radical America* 13:53–65.

Thrasher, Frederick M. 1927. *The Gang: A Study of 1,313 Gangs in Chicago.* Chicago: University of Chicago Press.

U.S. House of Representatives. 1980. "Hearings on Sexual Harassment in the Federal Government." Committee on the Post Office and Civil Service, Subcommittee on Investigations. Washington, D.C.: U.S. Government Printing Office.

Van Gelder, Lindsy. 1981. "The International Language of Street Hassling." *Ms.* (May):15+.

Wagner, Ellen J. 1992. *Sexual Harassment in the Workplace: How to Prevent, Investigate, and Resolve Problems in Your Organization.* New York: AMACOM Books.

Wells, Kathleen. 1980. "Gender-Role Identity and Psychological Adjustment in Adolescence." *Journal of Youth and Adolescence* 9:59–73.

West, Candace, and Don H. Zimmerman. 1987. "Doing Gender." In *The Social Construction of Gender*, ed. J. Lorber and S. A. Farrell, 13–37. Newbury Park, Calif.: Sage Publications.

Whyte, William Foote. 1943. *Street Corner Society: The Social Structure of an Italian Slum.* Chicago: University of Chicago Press.

Widdicombe, Sue, and Rob Wooffitt. 1990. "'Being' Versus 'Doing' Punk: On Achieving Authenticity as a Member." *Journal of Language and Social Psychology* 9:257–277.

Williamson, N. 1971. "The Case for Studied Ugliness." *Second Wave* 1:10–11.

Willis, Paul.1977. *Learning to Labour: How Working-Class Kids Get Working-Class Jobs.* New York: Columbia University Press.

———. 1978. *Profane Culture.* London: Routledge and Kegan Paul.

Willis, Susan. 1991. "Hardcore: Subculture American Style." *Critical Inquiry* 19:365–383.

Wilson, Deirdre. 1978. "Sexual Codes and Conduct: A Study of Teenage Girls." In *Women, Sexuality, and Social Control*, ed. C. Smart and B. Smart, 65–73. London: Routledge and Kegan Paul.

Wise, Sue, and Liz Stanley. 1987. *Georgie Porgie: Sexual Harassment in Everyday Life.* London: Pandora.

Wojcik, Daniel. 1995. *Punk and Neo-Tribal Body Art.* Jackson: University Press of Mississippi.

Wolf, Naomi. 1990. *The Beauty Myth.* New York and Toronto: Vintage Books.

Wooden, Wayne S. 1995. *Renegade Kids, Suburban Outlaws: From Youth Culture to Delinquency.* Belmont, Calif.: Wadsworth Publishing.

Woolf, Virginia. 1929. *A Room of One's Own.* London: Grafton Books.

Yardley, Jim. 1996. "Gutter Punks: They're Proud; They're Profane: And No One Knows What to Do about Them." *Atlanta Journal/Constitution* (February 18):E6.

Young, Iris Marion. 1990. *Throwing Like a Girl and Other Essays.* Bloomington: Indiana University Press.

Index

Cressey, Donald R., 101, 261n5
crime. *See* delinquency; deviance
Crocker, Phyllis L., 262n1
crusty punks, 62. *See also* gutter punks

Damned, the, 40
dances: "the pogo," 39; "slam," 51; "the
    strangle," 39; "thrash," 51; violence
    in, 39, 51
Dancis, Bruce, 39, 47
Dank, Serena, and Parents of Punkers,
    57, 96
Davis, Bob, 50, 260n2
Dead Boys, the, 35, 47
Dead Kennedys, 50, 54
de Beavoir, Simone, 11
delinquency, of punks: perceptions of,
    57–58, 170; research on, 58. *See also*
    deviance
DeMorest, Judith A., 56
"de-punking," 57–58
deviance: critical perspectives on, 168–
    169, 194; as cultivated image in
    punk, 39, 56, 58, 63, 169–170;
    female, 68, 121, 226; social construc-
    tion of, 168; social control of, 168,
    183, 194; statistical vs. pathological,
    56, 260n3; theories of, 101, 261n5
di Leonardo, Michaela, 202–203, 262n3
DIY: in grunge, 59; in music, 38–39;
    origins of, 35; in punk dress, 40, 42,
    52; in 'zines, 35, 38
do-it-yourself. *See* DIY
Dziech, Billie Wright, 262n1

eating disorders, 10, 12, 138, 139
Eder, Donna, 10
Eicher, Joanne B., 55
England, Paula, 12, 13, 138
England's Dreaming (Savage), 105
ethnography: in BCCCS research, 15–
    16, 260n4; critiques of, 20–21; as
    methodology, 20–21, 24–25; of
    resistance, 20–21. *See also* method-
    ology
Exploited, the, 48, 50, 54, 60

family: as influence on girls' becoming
    punks, 76, 82–83; punk subculture
    as, 71–72, 91–92; rejection of punk
    girls by, 95–96. *See also* parents
fans: punk girls as, 35, 38, 47, 50; role
    of, in punk, 35, 38, 47
Farley, Lyn, 200
fashion. *See* punk girls' dress style
fashion industry's co-optation of punk,
    48, 59
Feagin, Joe R., 173, 262n6
Feiring, Candace, 10
female punks. *See* punk girls
femininity: in appearance, 154; in
    behavior, 155; as discourse, 139–
    140; as game, 135–139; as ideal,
    11–12, 135–136; impact of race,
    sexuality, and class on 136; internal-
    ization and constraints of, 12, 138;
    media definitions of, 12; as norma-
    tive, 12, 136, 137–138, 139; punk
    girls' rejection of, 141–148, 160–163;
    punk girls' stereotypes of, 143–147;
    reconstructions of, 13–14, 160, 164–
    165; in relation to masculinity, 11–
    12, 136–137, 138–139; resistance to,
    13, 140. *See also* punk femininity
feminism, of punk girls, 121
feminist cultural studies, 16–17
feminist research, 20–21, 228. *See also*
    methodology
Ferrell, Jeff, 68
Fetterley, Judith, 16
field research. *See* ethnography
Fine, Gary Alan, 169
Fish, Stanley, 16
Fisher, Ian, 62, 63
flirting, 127–129
Flowers in the Dustbin (Nehring), 33
"folk devils": original formulation,
    39; punks as, 39, 56–58, 62–63, 167–
    168
foster care, punk girls' experiences of,
    80, 97, 229–230
Fox, Greer Litton, 12
Fox, Kathryn Joan, 26, 55, 86, 88, 106,
    140–141

friendship: influence of, on becoming
punk, 83–84; between punk girls,
143–148, 149; between punk girls
and punk guys, 120–121, 147–148
Frith, Simon, 42

Gaar, Gillian G., 260n1
Gaines, Donna, 68
Garber, Jenny, 67
Gardner, Carol Brooks: on public
harassment, 171, 176–177, 179,
262n4; on public sexual harassment,
202, 208, 210, 262n3, 263n5
gender, social construction of, 136–139;
and crime, 107–108; feminist
theories of, 8. *See also* femininity;
masculinity
gender roles: adolescent perceptions
of, 11–12; critique of, 139; in punk,
110–111; role of mainstream public
in maintaining, 112–114; role of
punk guys in maintaining, 111–112.
See also femininity; masculinity
gender socialization, 138, 227–228;
subjectivity in, 12–13, 227–228
Generation X, 38
Gibbs, Jewelle Taylor, 259n2
Gilligan, Carol, 10, 102, 260n3
girls: punk girls' isolation from, 147;
punk girls' rejection of, 143–147. *See
also* punk girls
Giroux, Henry A., 17–18
Glick, Peter, 56
Glitter, Gary, 44
Goffman, Erving, 170, 262n2
Go-gos, the, 50, 51
Goth: origins of, 40; subculture, 81–82
Gouvernement du Québec, 229
Gratz, Kim L., 202
Grossberg, Lawrence, 171
groupies: punk girls as, 47, 108; in
rock, 36, 47
grunge, 59
Gutek, Barbara, 202
Guterman, Jimmy, 47
gutter punks, 26, 61–63; demographics
of, 61; itinerance and, 61–62; media

depictions of, 62–63; and rebellion,
90; relationship to punk rockers, 63;
survivalism and, 62, 91

hairstyles, of punks, 38, 42; as ammunition for harassment, 180–181; role
of, in maintaining femininity, 158, 161
Hall, Deanna L., 21
Hall, Stuart, 67
Hancock, Emily, 11, 102
Hanmer, Trudy J., 10, 102
Hansen, Christine Hall, 58
Hansen, Ranald D., 58
harassment, public: definition of, 171;
as discrimination, 194–195; evaluation of, 179–183; exclusion as, 173–
176; exploitation as, 176–179;
incidence of, 172–173; punk girls'
responses to, 180, 184–193; as social
control, 194. *See also* sexual
harassment
Haraway, Donna, 260n5
hardcore, 48–59; as folk devil, 56–59; as
indicative of commitment to punk,
55–56, 61; masculinization of, 50–53,
55, 105; origins of, 48–49; in U.S.,
50–59
Harry, Debbie, 35, 36, 45, 49. *See also*
Blondie
Hebdige, Dick, 15, 107; on the origins
of punk, 36–37, 39, 64; on style, 15,
40, 63, 156, 167
Hell, Richard, 35, 37, 38, 41, 42. *See also*
Television
Henry, Tricia, 33
heterosexuality: as normative of
femininity, 127, 136; as normative in
punk scene, 125–127
Hirschi, Travis, 101, 261n5
History of Rock 'n' Roll (TV documen-
tary), 59
Hoare, Philip, 45
Hochschild, Arlie, 136
Hoffman, Frances L., 262n1
Holmes, Janelle, 9, 10
Holstrom, John, 35. *See also Punk* ('zine)
Home, Stewart, 45

homophobia, 125
Hook, Pamela. *See* Jordan
Hotze, Carla A., 56
Houston, Penelope, 49–50
Hudson, Barbara, 137
humor, punk girls' use of, 215–216
Hurley, Bri, 55
Hutchison, Bruce, 12
Hynde, Chrissie, 45

Idol, Billy, 38
interactions, between youth subcultures and mainstream culture, 168–172. *See also* harassment, public; sexual harassment, public
interpretivist sociology, 16, 18
interviews, 26–29: in feminist cultural studies, 16; as phenomenological accounts, 21; and retrospective bias, 260n3. *See also* methodology

Jefferson, Tony, 67, 107
Jett, Joan, 45
Joe, Karen A., 226
Jones, Dylan, 38, 42
Jordan, 37, 46

Kaye, Lenny, 35
Kennedy, Leslie W., 106, 111, 185
Killer, Hellin, 47, 50, 260n2
Kissling, Elizabeth Arveda, 200, 202, 203, 262n3
Kleinman, Sherryl, 169
Kliman, Todd, 54
Kogan, Marcela, 57, 176
Kotarba, Joseph A., 55
Kozak, Roman, 35, 50, 260n1
Kramarae, Cheris, 200, 203, 262n3
Krestan, Jo-Ann, 137–138

labeling perspective, 168. *See also* deviance
Laing, David, 45, 46, 47, 48, 49, 108
Lamar. *See* Killer, Hellin
Lamy, Philip, 56
Langelan, Martha J., 201, 209–210, 211,

214, 263n5
Langellier, Kristin M., 21
Larkin, June, 262n1
Leaf, Bruce, 58
Learning to Labour (Willis), 67, 260n4
Leblanc, Lauraine, 262n5
Lees, Sue, 130
Legault, Jean Benoit, 33
Leger, Marie France, 63
Lemert, Edwin M., 261n5
Leong, Lawrence Wai-Teng, 15
Letts, Don, 39
Levin, Jack, 56
Levine, Harold G., 56, 64, 89, 106, 163
Lewin, Miriam, 12
Lewis, Lisa A., 200–201
Lewis, Michael, 10
Lewis, Randy, 57
Lipstick Traces (Marcus), 33
Lofland, John, 29, 253
Lofland, Lyn H., 29, 253
Lull, James, 51, 106, 142
Lunch, Lydia, 50
Lydon, John, 38, 60. *See also* Rotten, Johnny
Lyons, Nona P., 10, 102

McCain, Gillian, 47, 60, 105, 260n1
McCann, Nancy Dodd, 200
McCormack, Arlene, 262n1
McGinn, Thomas A., 200
McKay, George, 49
MacKinnon, Catharine, 198–199
McLaren, Malcolm, 37–38, 39, 42, 44
McLellan, Dennis, 57
MacLeod, Jay, 67, 68, 107
McNeil, Legs, 35, 47, 60, 105, 260n1
McRobbie, Angela, 67, 68, 142, 164, 260n1
male domination, of punk: masculinist, 106–116; numerical, 105–106; punk girls' accommodation to, 132–133; punk girls' recognition of, 108–133. *See also* masculinity
male punks. *See* punk guys
Marcus, Greil, 33
Marley, Bob, 39

of, 33–34; London, 36–39; Los Angeles, 50; Montreal, 21, 63; New Orleans, 21–22, 61, 62–63; New York City, 34–36; North American, 54–55, 56; San Francisco, 21–22, 49–50, 61; West Coast U.S., 50–51

punk style: of bands, 40; and body modification, 41–43; and bondage gear, 37, 40; as bricolage, 40; as DIY, 40, 52; early U.K., 36–38, 40–44; gutter punk, 62, 141; hardcore punk, 52–53, 56; influence of skinheads on, 54; and jewelry, 41–42; and masculinity, 52–53, 109; meaning of, 40–42, 44; as politics, 43–44; and public harassment, 194–195; as resistance, 15, 37–38, 40–42, 44–47, 140, 160–165; role of, in creating authenticity, 86, 109. *See also* hairstyles; punk girls' dress style; style

punk subculture: abstract readings of, 33; art school origins of, 42–43; attractions of, 35; class origins of, 42–43; committing to, 55; demographics of, 26; as egalitarian, 115, 123; geographic origins of, 34; as marketing ploy, 37–38; masculinization of, 50–51, 55, 105; misogyny in, 47; phenomenology of, 34; purported death of, 34, 48; purported revival of, 59; and race, 64, 115; racism in, 64, 263n7; as reference group, 81; as reflexive, 41, 56, 63, 89, 163; softcore/hardcore split in, 55, 88; as survival network, 90–93. *See also* hardcore

queercore, 59, 125
Quincy punks, 85

race: and femininity, 136; and masculinity, 108; in punk, 64, 115; and self-esteem, 259n2
Radway, Janice, 16
Ramones, 35, 38, 49, 60
rape. *See* sexual abuse
Rastafarianism, 37, 39, 44

Rauste-von Wright, Maijaliisa, 10
reader-response theory, 16
rebellion: in punk, 64, 71, 89–90; in rock iconography, 137
reciprocity, among punks, 92–93
reggae, 39, 59, 64
Repo Man (movie), 85
resistance: conceptualizations of, 14; as discursive, 17; effects of, 140; to femininity, 13, 140, 159–165, 227–228; feminist accounts of, 16–17; humor in, 215–216; lifestyle as, 68–69, 86; as masculine, 68–69, 109, 197; as political behavior, 17–18; to public harassment, 184–193; to public sexual harassment, 207–217; reconceptualization of, 17–18; role of subjectivity in accounts of, 18; style as, 14–16, 37–38, 40–42, 44–47, 140; in subculture theory, 14–16, 140, 226. *See also* accommodation
Resistance Through Rituals. *See* Birmingham Centre for Cultural Studies
respect, of punk guys: punk girls' earning of, 120–122, 130–131; punk girls' loss of, 129–130, 132. *See also* punk guys
Reviving Ophelia (Pipher), 8, 12–13, 102
Reynolds, Simon, 36, 137
Rhodes, Zhandra, 48
Rich, Adrienne, 125, 261n2
Richman, Charles L., 259n2
Riot Grrrl, 59, 64, 132, 259n1
Rock Against Racism, 39, 44, 54, 64
Rock Against Reagan, 54
Rock Against Sexism, 44
rock music: punks' disaffection with, 35; traditional roles of women in, 36, 45
Rock 'n' Roll (TV documentary), 59
Rogers, Annie G., 102, 228, 260n3
Rogers, Joseph W., 180
Roman, Leslie G., 105, 140
Rorschach, Ivy, 36
Rosenbaum, Jill L., 58, 229

About the Author

Lauraine Leblanc was born and raised in Montréal, Québec, where she was expelled from high school for shaving her head. Undeterred, she completed degrees in modern languages at Dawson College and in philosophy at McGill University. She lived in Atlanta, Georgia, for six years, completing her doctoral work in women's studies at Emory University. She has published on the topics of media representations of deviance, women in cyberpunk fiction, and teaching research methods. She has worked as a stablehand, a jewelry maker, a bicycle courier, a bookbinder, a dog groomer, and a professor at both Emory and Oglethorpe universities in Georgia, teaching courses on gender, deviance, research methods, and youth subcultures. She spends her spare time reading children's literature, getting pierced and tattooed, drinking Guinness, memorizing poems, listening to a wide range of music, writing to her grandmother, eating pesto, and shopping for black frocks. She is often seen in the park accompanied by her well-behaved blooper dog, Lucky 7. They are both often defiantly unleashed.